Creative Keyboard Presents

12 SPIRITUALS FOR PIANO SOLO

by Gail Smith

Contents

© 2000 BY MEL BAY PUBLICATIONS, INC., PACIFIC, MO 63069.
ALL RIGHTS RESERVED. INTERNATIONAL COPYRIGHT SECURED. B.M.I. MADE AND PRINTED IN U.S.A.
No part of this publication may be reproduced in whole or in part, or stored in a retrieval system, or transmitted in any form
or by any means, electronic, mechanical, photocopy, recording, or otherwise, without written permission of the publisher.

Visit us on the Web at http://www.melbay.com — E-mail us at email@melbay.com

Foreword

Most beautiful of all American folk songs are the spirituals – Negro folk songs with religious themes. They were composed and sung by slaves in the old plantation days of the South. These spirituals gave expression to the simple faith of a people in bondage and to their longing to find the road to heaven.

The slaves were often beset by trouble, sickness and backbreaking labor. They constantly looked toward "another world." To the Negro slave, heaven was "home." He found comfort in the Bible story of Elijah. This great prophet was snatched by a whirlwind and carried to heaven in a chariot of fire drawn by horses of fire. In the Negro slaves' imagination, Elijah's fiery chariot became the "Sweet Chariot" that would carry each faithful laborer home.

One might expect to find themes of bitterness and hate, but this is entirely lacking in most of the spirituals. Instead, you find a quality of deep melancholy, patient resignation and quiet confidence that faith will be vindicated and right will prevail eventually.

The spirituals stand as one of the great classic expressions of religious emotion. These songs were first brought to national attention through the concert tours of the "Jubilee Singers" of Fisk University, Nashville, Tennessee, from 1871-1878.

Thomas Jefferson indicated that he too was impressed by the musical talents of the Negro. He wrote, "In music they are generally more gifted than the whites..."

Today the rich melodies, deep feeling, and personal tone of these songs have made them beloved throughout the world.

I hope you will enjoy playing these twelve spirituals that I have arranged.

-Gail Smith

Swing Low, Sweet Chariot

Swing Low, Sweet Chariot

Spiritual
Arr. by Gail Smith

This page has been
left blank to avoid
awkward page turns

Nobody Knows de Trouble I See

Nobody Knows de Trouble I See

Spiritual
Arr. by Gail Smith

9

This page has been
left blank to avoid
awkward page turns

My Lord, What a Mornin'

My Lord, What a Mornin'

Spiritual
Arr. by Gail Smith

13

All God's Chillun Got a Robe

Spiritual

With happy spirit

1. I got a robe, you got a robe, All o'God's Chil-lun got a
2. I got-a wings, you got-a wings, All o'God's Chil-lun got a

robe. When I get to Heab'n I'm goin' to put on my robe, I'm goin' to
wings. When I get to Heab'n I'm goin' to put on my wings, I'm goin' to

shout all ov - ah God's Heab'n, _____ Heab'n, _____ Heab'n, _____
fly all ov - ah God's Heab'n, _____ Heab'n, _____ Heab'n, _____

Ev - 'ry - bo - dy talk - in' 'bout Heab'n ain't goin' dere; Heab'n, _____
Ev - 'ry - bo - dy talk - in' 'bout Heab'n ain't goin' dere; Heab'n, _____

Heab'n, _____ I'm goin' to shout all ov - ah God's Heab'n. _____
Heab'n, _____ I'm goin' to fly all ov - ah God's Heab'n. _____

3. I got a harp, you got a harp, All o'God's Chil-lun got a

harp, When I get to Heab'n I'm goin' to take up my harp, I'm, goin' to

play all ov - ah God's Heab'n,_____ Heab'n,_____ Heab'n,_____

Ev - y - bo - dy talk - in' 'bout Heab'n ain't goin' dere, Heab'n_____ Heab'n _____ I'm goin' to

play all ov - ah God's Heab'n._____ I got shoes, you got shoes,

All o'God's Chil - lun got shoes. When I get to Heab'n I'm goin' to

put on my shoes, I'm goin' to walk all ov - ah God's Heab'n,_____ Heab'n,_____

Heab'n,_____ Ev -'y bo - dy talk in' 'bout Heab'n ain't goin' dere, Heab'n,_____

Heab'n,_____ I'm goin' to walk all ov - ah God's Heab'n _____ I'm goin' to walk all ov - ah God's

Heab'n,_____ I'm goin' to walk all ov - ah God's Heab _____ 'n, I'm goin' to

walk all ov - ah, goin' to talk all ov _____ ah, God's Heab _____ 'n.

All God's Chillun Got a Robe

Spiritual
Arr. by Gail Smith

Joshua Fit de Battle of Jerico

Josh-ua fit de bat-tle ob Jer-i-co,__ Jer-i-co,__ Jer-i-co,_____ Josh-ua fit de bat-tle ob Jer-i-co,__ An' de walls come tum-blin' down. You may talk a-bout yo' king ob Gid-e-on, You may talk a-bout yo' man ob Saul, Dere's none like good ole Josh-ua At de bat-tle ob Jer-i-co, Up to de walls, ob Jer-i-co. He marched with spear in han' "Go blow dem ram horns" Josh-u-a cried "Kase de bat-tle am in my han'." Den de lam' ram sheep horns be-gin to blow, trum-pets be-gin to soun; Josh-u-a co-man-ded de chil-len to shout, An' de walls come tum-blin' down. Dat morn-in' Josh-ua fit de bat-tle ob Jer-i-co,__ Jer-i-co,__ Jer-i-co,_____ Josh-ua fit de bat-tle ob Jer-i-co,__ An' de walls come tum-blin' down.

Joshua Fit de Battle of Jerico

Spiritual
Arr. by Gail Smith

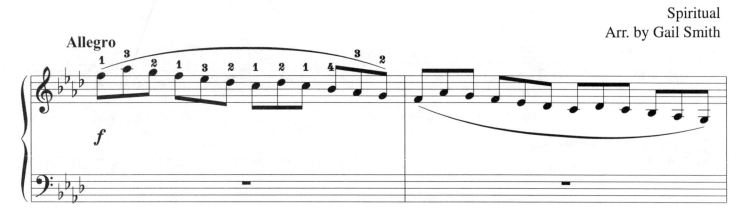

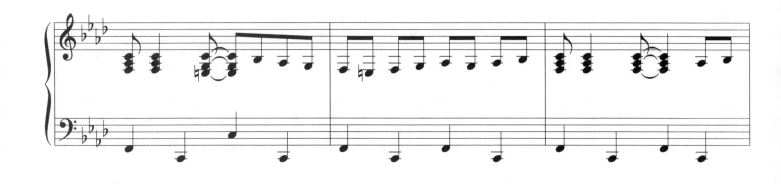

Gimme dat Ol'-Time Religion

Gimme dat ol' - time re - ligion, gimme dat ol' time re - li - gion, gimme dat ol' - time re - li - gion,____ It's good e - nough for me. Jus' gimme dat ol' - time re - li - gion, gimme dat ol' time re - li - gion, gimme dat ol' - time re - li - gion,____ It's good e - nough for me It was good for de He - brew children, it was good for de He - brew child - ren, it was good for de He - brew child - ren An it's good e - nough for me. It will

do when de world's on fi - ah, It will do when de world's on fi - ah, It will do when de world's on fi - ah An it's good e - nough for me. Oh, gimme dat

ol' - time re - li - gion, gimme dat ol' - time re - li - gion, gimme dat ol' - time re - li - gion ____ It's good e - nough for me

Gimme dat Ol'-Time Religion

Spiritual
Arr. by Gail Smith

'Zekiel Saw de Wheel

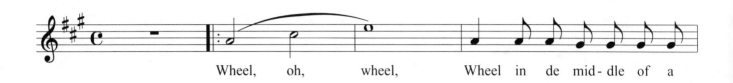

Wheel, oh, wheel, Wheel in de mid-dle of a

wheel; Wheel, oh, wheel, Wheel in de mid-dle of a wheel.

'Ze-kiel saw de wheel of time, Wheel in de mid-dle of a wheel,
'Way up yon-der on de moun-tain top, Wheel in de mid-dle of a wheel,

Ev-'ry spoke was hu-man kind, Wheel in de mid-dle of a wheel.
My Lord spoke an 'de char-iot stop, Wheel in de mid-dle of a wheel.

'Ze-kiel saw de wheel, 'Way up in de mid-dle of de air,

'Ze-kiel saw de wheel. 'Way in de mid-dle of de air. De

big wheel run by faith, Lit - tle wheel run by de grace of God;

Wheel wid - in a wheel, 'Way in de mid - dle of de air, Oh de

big wheel run by faith, Lit - tle wheel run by de grace of God;

Wheel wid - in a wheel, 'Way in de mid - dle of de air

pp

Wheel, oh, wheel, Wheel in de mid - dle of a wheel.

Wheel, oh, wheel, Wheel in de mid - dle of a wheel.

'Zekiel Saw de Wheel

Spiritual
Arr. by Gail Smith

Wade in de Water

Allegro

Wade_____ in de wa - ter, chil - dren, Wade_____ in de wa - ter, chil - dren.

Wade_____ in de wa - ter, chil - dren, God's a- gwine-ter trou - ble de wa - ter.

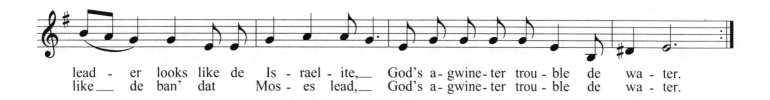

See dat host all dressed in white,____ God's a- gwine-ter trou - ble de wa - ter; De
See dat host all dressed in red,_____ God's a- gwine-ter trou - ble de wa - ter; Looks

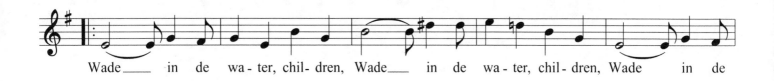

lead - er looks like de Is - rael - ite,__ God's a- gwine-ter trou - ble de wa - ter.
like__ de ban' dat Mos - es lead,__ God's a- gwine-ter trou - ble de wa - ter.

Wade_____ in de wa - ter, chil - dren, Wade__ in de wa - ter, chil - dren, Wade in de

wa - ter, chil - dren, God's a- gwine-ter trou - ble de wa - ter. 1. wa - ter. 2. water._____

Wade in de Water

Spiritual
Arr. by Gail Smith

*This page has been
left blank to avoid
awkward page turns*

Go Down Moses

Go down, Mos - es 'Way down in E - gypt land,____

Tell ole ___ Pha - raoh, To let my peo - ple go.

Go down, Mos - es, 'Way down in E - gypt land.____

Tell ole ___ Pha - raoh, To let my peo - ple go. When

Is - rael was in E - gypt's land: Let my peo - ple go, Op -
spoke the Lord," bold Mos - es said; Let my peo - ple go, If

pressed so hard they could not stand, Let my peo - ple go. "Thus go.
not I'll smite your first born dead, Let my peo - ple

Go down, Mos - es, 'Way down in E - gypt land,____

Tell ole ___ Pha - raoh, To let my peo - ple go. O

let my peo - ple go.____

Go Down Moses

Spiritual
Arr. by Gail Smith

Were You There When They Crucified My Lord?

Were You There When They Cucified My Lord?

Spiritual
Arr. by Gail Smith

Lord, I Want to Be a Christian in-a My Heart

Lord, I want to be a Chris-tian in-a my heart, in-a my
want to be more ho-ly in-a my heart, in-a my

heart, Lord, I want to be a Chris-tian in-a my heart._____
heart, Lord, I want to be more ho-ly in-a my heart._____

_____ I don't want to be like Ju-das in-a-my heart, in-a-my
_____ I just want to be like Je-sus in-a-my heart, in-a-my

heart, I don't want to be like Ju-das in-a my heart._____
heart, I just want to be like Je-sus in-a my heart._____

last time

_____ In-a my heart _____ In-a my heart,_____ Lord, I

little slower

1.

want to be a Chris-tian in-a my heart,_____ In-a my

2 *omit after last verse*   **3** *last time*

heart. _____ Lord I heart._____

41

Lord, I Want to Be a Christian in-a My Heart

Spiritual
Arr. by Gail Smith

Let Us Break Bread Together

1. Let us break bread to - geth - er on our knees,
2. Let us drink the cup to - geth - er on our knees,
3. Let us praise God to - geth - er on our knees,

Let us break bread to - geth - er on our knees;
Let us drink the cup to - geth - er on our knees;
Let us praise God to - geth - er on our knees;

When I fall on my knees, With my face to the ri - sing

sun, O Lord, have mer - cy on me.

Let Us Break Bread Together

Spiritual
Arr. by Gail Smith

FROM THE GRADUATE MANAGEMENT ADMISSION COU

D129195

THE OFFICIAL GUIDE FO

GMAT

2016

QUANTITATIVE REVIEW

The ONLY study guide focusing on the Quant section, from the creators of the GMAT® exam

Includes 25% NEW content

300 Problem Solving and Data Sufficiency questions with answer explanations

Create your own **practice sets onl** using past exam questions

Exclusive online videos with study tips and test-taking strategies

mb

THE OFFICIAL GUIDE FOR GMAT® QUANTITATIVE REVIEW 2016

For general information on our other products and services or to obtain technical support please contact our Customer Care Department within the U.S. at (877) 762-2974, outside the U.S. at (317) 572-3993 or fax (317) 572-4002.

Wiley also publishes its books in a variety of electronic formats. Some content that appears in print may not be available in electronic books. For more information about Wiley products, please visit our Web site at www.wiley.com.

ISBN 978-1-119-04259-4 (pbk); ISBN 978-1-119-04261-7 (ePDF); ISBN 978-1-119-04260-0 (ePub)

Printed in the United States of America

10 9 8 7 6 5 4 3 2 1

Updates to this book are available on the Downloads tab at this site: http://www.wiley.com/go/gmat2016updates.

Table of Contents

Visit gmat.wiley.com to access web-based supplemental features available in the print book as well. There you can access a question bank with customizable practice sets and answer explanations using 300 Problem Solving and Data Sufficiency questions and review topics like Arithmetic, Algebra, Geometry, and Word Problems. Watch exclusive videos stressing the importance of big data skills in the real world and offering insight into math skills necessary to be successful on the Quantitative section of the exam.

1.0 What Is the GMAT®?

1.0 What Is the GMAT®?

The Graduate Management Admission Test® (GMAT®) is a standardized, three-part test delivered in English. The test was designed to help admissions officers evaluate how suitable individual applicants are for their graduate business and management programs. It measures basic verbal, mathematical, and analytical writing skills that a test-taker has developed over a long period of time through education and work.

The GMAT exam does not measure a person's knowledge of specific fields of study. Graduate business and management programs enroll people from many different undergraduate and work backgrounds, so rather than test your mastery of any particular subject area, the GMAT exam will assess your acquired skills. Your GMAT score will give admissions officers a statistically reliable measure of how well you are likely to perform academically in the core curriculum of a graduate business program.

Of course, there are many other qualifications that can help people succeed in business school and in their careers—for instance, job experience, leadership ability, motivation, and interpersonal skills. The GMAT exam does not gauge these qualities. That is why your GMAT score is intended to be used as one standard admissions criterion among other, more subjective, criteria, such as admissions essays and interviews.

1.1 Why Take the GMAT® Exam?

GMAT scores are used by admissions officers in roughly 1,800 graduate business and management programs worldwide. Schools that require prospective students to submit GMAT scores in the application process are generally interested in admitting the best-qualified applicants for their programs, which means that you may find a more beneficial learning environment at schools that require GMAT scores as part of your application.

Because the GMAT exam gauges skills that are important to successful study of business and management at the graduate level, your scores will give you a good indication of how well prepared you are to succeed academically in a graduate management program; how well you do on the test may also help you choose the business schools to which you apply. Furthermore, the percentile table you receive with your scores will tell you how your performance on the test compares to the performance of other test-takers, giving you one way to gauge your competition for admission to business school.

Myth -vs- **FACT**

M – **If I don't score in the 90th percentile, I won't get into any school I choose.**

F – **Very few people get very high scores.**

Fewer than 50 of the more than 200,000 people taking the GMAT exam each year get a perfect score of 800. Thus, while you may be exceptionally capable, the odds are against your achieving a perfect score. Also, the GMAT exam is just one piece of your application packet. Admissions officers use GMAT scores in conjunction with undergraduate records, application essays, interviews, letters of recommendation, and other information when deciding whom to accept into their programs.

Schools consider many different aspects of an application before making an admissions decision, so even if you score well on the GMAT exam, you should contact the schools that interest you to learn more about them and to ask about how they use GMAT scores and other admissions criteria (such as your undergraduate grades, essays, and letters of recommendation) to evaluate candidates for admission. School admissions offices, school Web sites, and materials published by the school are the best sources for you to tap when you are doing research about where you might want to go to business school.

For more information on the GMAT exam, test registration, appropriate uses of GMAT scores, sending your scores to schools, and applying to business school, please visit our web site at mba.com.

1.2 GMAT® Exam Format

The GMAT exam consists of four separately timed sections (see the table on the next page). You start the test with two 30-minute Analytical Writing Assessment (AWA) questions that require you to type your responses using the computer keyboard. The writing section is followed by two 75-minute, multiple-choice sections: the Quantitative and Verbal sections of the test.

Myth -vs- **FACT**

M – **Getting an easier question means I answered the last one wrong.**

F – **Getting an easier question does not necessarily mean you got the previous question wrong.**

To ensure that everyone receives the same content, the test selects a specific number of questions of each type. The test may call for your next question to be a relatively hard problem-solving item involving arithmetic operations. But, if there are no more relatively difficult problem-solving items involving arithmetic, you might be given an easier item.

Most people are not skilled at estimating item difficulty, so don't worry when taking the test or waste valuable time trying to determine the difficulty of the questions you are answering.

The GMAT is a computer-adaptive test (CAT), which means that in the multiple-choice sections of the test, the computer constantly gauges how well you are doing on the test and presents you with questions that are appropriate to your ability level. These questions are drawn from a huge pool of possible test questions. So, although we talk about the GMAT as one test, the GMAT exam you take may be completely different from the test of the person sitting next to you.

Here's how it works. At the start of each GMAT multiple-choice section (Verbal and Quantitative), you will be presented with a question of moderate difficulty. The computer uses your response to that first question to determine which question to present next. If you respond correctly, the test usually will give you questions of increasing difficulty. If you respond incorrectly, the next question you see usually will be easier than the one you answered incorrectly. As you continue to respond to the questions presented, the computer will narrow your score to the number that best characterizes your ability. When you complete each section, the computer will have an accurate assessment of your ability.

Because each question is presented on the basis of your answers to all previous questions, you must answer each question as it appears. You may not skip, return to, or change your responses to previous questions. Random guessing can significantly lower your scores. If you do not know the answer to a question, you should try to eliminate as many choices as possible, then select the answer you think is best. If you answer a question incorrectly by mistake—or correctly by lucky guess—your answers to subsequent questions will lead you back to questions that are at the appropriate level of difficulty for you.

Each multiple-choice question used in the GMAT exam has been thoroughly reviewed by professional test developers. New multiple-choice questions are tested each time the test is administered. Answers to trial questions are not counted in the scoring of your test, but the trial questions are not identified and could appear anywhere in the test. Therefore, you should try to do your best on every question.

The test includes the types of questions found in this guide, but the format and presentation of the questions are different on the computer. When you take the test:

- Only one question at a time is presented on the computer screen.

- The answer choices for the multiple-choice questions will be preceded by circles, rather than by letters.

- Different question types appear in random order in the multiple-choice sections of the test.

- You must select your answer using the computer.

- You must choose an answer and confirm your choice before moving on to the next question.

- You may not go back to change answers to previous questions.

Format of the GMAT® Exam		
	Questions	Timing
Analytical Writing 　　Analysis of an Argument	1	30 min.
Integrated Reasoning 　　Multi-Source Reasoning 　　Table Analysis 　　Graphics Interpretation 　　Two-Part Analysis	12	30 min.
Optional break		
Quantitative 　　Problem Solving 　　Data Sufficiency	37	75 min.
Optional break		
Verbal 　　Reading Comprehension 　　Critical Reasoning 　　Sentence Correction	41	75 min.
	Total Time:	210 min.

1.3 What Is the Content of the Test Like?

It is important to recognize that the GMAT exam evaluates skills and abilities developed over a relatively long period of time. Although the sections contain questions that are basically verbal and mathematical, the complete test provides one method of measuring overall ability.

Keep in mind that although the questions in this guide are arranged by question type and ordered from easy to difficult, the test is organized differently. When you take the test, you may see different types of questions in any order.

1.4 Quantitative Section

The GMAT Quantitative section measures your ability to reason quantitatively, solve quantitative problems, and interpret graphic data.

Two types of multiple-choice questions are used in the Quantitative section:

- Problem Solving
- Data sufficiency

Problem solving and data sufficiency questions are intermingled throughout the Quantitative section. Both types of questions require basic knowledge of:

- Arithmetic
- Elementary algebra
- Commonly known concepts of geometry

To review the basic mathematical concepts that will be tested in the GMAT Quantitative questions, see the math review in chapter 3. For test-taking tips specific to the question types in the Quantitative section of the GMAT exam, sample questions, and answer explanations, see chapters 4 and 5.

1.5 Verbal Section

The GMAT Verbal section measures your ability to read and comprehend written material, to reason and evaluate arguments, and to correct written material to conform to standard written English. Because the Verbal section includes reading sections from several different content areas, you may be generally familiar with some of the material; however, neither the reading passages nor the questions assume detailed knowledge of the topics discussed.

Three types of multiple-choice questions are used in the Verbal section:

- Reading Comprehension
- Critical reasoning
- Sentence correction

These question types are intermingled throughout the Verbal section.

For test-taking tips specific to each question type in the Verbal section, sample questions, and answer explanations, see *The Official Guide for GMAT Review*, 2016 Edition, or *The Official Guide for GMAT Verbal Review*, 2016 Edition; both are available for purchase at www.mba.com.

1.6 What Computer Skills Will I Need?

You only need minimal computer skills to take the GMAT Computer-Adaptive Test (CAT). You will be required to type your essays on the computer keyboard using standard word-processing keystrokes. In the multiple-choice sections, you will select your responses using either your mouse or the keyboard.

To learn more about the specific skills required to take the GMAT CAT, download the free test-preparation software available at www.mba.com.

1.7 What Are the Test Centers Like?

The GMAT exam is administered at a test center providing the quiet and privacy of individual computer workstations. You will have the opportunity to take two optional breaks—one after completing the essays and another between the Quantitative and Verbal sections. An erasable notepad will be provided for your use during the test.

1.8 How Are Scores Calculated?

Your GMAT scores are determined by:

- The number of questions you answer
- Whether you answer correctly or incorrectly
- The level of difficulty and other statistical characteristics of each question

Your Verbal, Quantitative, and Total GMAT scores are determined by a complex mathematical procedure that takes into account the difficulty of the questions that were presented to you and how you answered them. When you answer the easier questions correctly, you get a chance to answer harder questions—making it possible to earn a higher score. After you have completed all the questions on the test—or when your time is up—the computer will calculate your scores. Your scores on the Verbal and Quantitative sections are combined to produce your Total score. If you have not responded to all the questions in a section (37 Quantitative questions or 41 Verbal questions), your score is adjusted, using the proportion of questions answered.

Your GMAT score includes a percentile ranking that compares your skill level with other test takers from the past three years. The percentile rank of your score shows the percentage of tests taken with scores lower than your score. Every July, percentile ranking tables are updated. Visit http://www.mba .com/percentilerankings to view the most recent percentile rankings tables.

1.9 Analytical Writing Assessment Scores

The Analytical Writing Assessment consists of two writing tasks: Analysis of an Issue and Analysis of an Argument. The responses to each of these tasks are scored on a 6-point scale, with 6 being the highest score and 1, the lowest. A score of zero (0) is given to responses that are off-topic, are in a foreign language, merely attempt to copy the topic, consist only of keystroke characters, or are blank.

The readers who evaluate the responses are college and university faculty members from various subject matter areas, including management education. These readers read holistically—that is, they respond to the overall quality of your critical thinking and writing. (For details on how readers are qualified, visit www.mba.com.) In addition, responses may be scored by an automated scoring program designed to reflect the judgment of expert readers.

Each response is given two independent ratings. If the ratings differ by more than a point, a third reader adjudicates. (Because of ongoing training and monitoring, discrepant ratings are rare.)

Your final score is the average (rounded to the nearest half point) of the four scores independently assigned to your responses—two scores for the Analysis of an Issue and two for the Analysis of an Argument. For example, if you earned scores of 6 and 5 on the Analysis of an Issue and 4 and 4 on the Analysis of an Argument, your final score would be 5: $(6 + 5 + 4 + 4) \div 4 = 4.75$, which rounds up to 5.

Your Analytical Writing Assessment scores are computed and reported separately from the multiple-choice sections of the test and have no effect on your Verbal, Quantitative, or Total scores. The schools that you have designated to receive your scores may receive your responses to the Analytical Writing Assessment with your score report. Your own copy of your score report will not include copies of your responses.

1.10 Test Development Process

The GMAT exam is developed by experts who use standardized procedures to ensure high-quality, widely appropriate test material. All questions are subjected to independent reviews and are revised or discarded as necessary. Multiple-choice questions are tested during GMAT exam administrations. Analytical Writing Assessment tasks are tried out on first-year business school students and then assessed for their fairness and reliability. For more information on test development, see www.mba.com.

2.0 How to Prepare

2.0 How to Prepare

2.1 How Can I Best Prepare to Take the Test?

We at the Graduate Management Admission Council® (GMAC®) firmly believe that the test-taking skills you can develop by using this guide—and *The Official Guide for GMAT® Review*, 2016 Edition, and *The Official Guide for GMAT® Verbal Review*, 2016 Edition, if you want additional practice—are all you need to perform your best when you take the GMAT® exam. By answering questions that have appeared on the GMAT exam before, you will gain experience with the types of questions you may see on the test when you take it. As you practice with this guide, you will develop confidence in your ability to reason through the test questions. No additional techniques or strategies are needed to do well on the standardized test if you develop a practical familiarity with the abilities it requires. Simply by practicing and understanding the concepts that are assessed on the test, you will learn what you need to know to answer the questions correctly.

2.2 What About Practice Tests?

Because a computer-adaptive test cannot be presented in paper form, we have created GMATPrep® software to help you prepare for the test. The software is available for download at no charge for those who have created a user profile on www.mba.com. It is also provided on a disk, by request, to anyone who has registered for the GMAT exam. The software includes two practice GMAT exams plus additional practice questions, information about the test, and tutorials to help you become familiar with how the GMAT exam will appear on the computer screen at the test center.

We recommend that you download the software as you start to prepare for the test. Take one practice test to familiarize yourself with the test and to get an idea of how you might score. After you have studied using this book, and as your test date approaches, take the second practice test to determine whether you need to shift your focus to other areas you need to strengthen.

Myth -vs- FACT

M – **You may need very advanced math skills to get a high GMAT score.**

F – **The math skills test on the GMAT exam are quite basic.**

The GMAT exam only requires basic quantitative analytic skills. You should review the math skills (algebra, geometry, basic arithmetic) presented both in this book (chapter 3) and in *The Official Guide for GMAT® Review*, 2016 Edition, but the required skill level is low. The difficulty of GMAT Quantitative questions stems from the logic and analysis used to solve the problems and not the underlying math skills.

2.3 Where Can I Get Additional Practice?

If you complete all the questions in this guide and think you would like additional practice, you may purchase *The Official Guide for GMAT® Review*, 2016 Edition, or *The Official Guide for GMAT® Verbal Review*, 2016 Edition, at www.mba.com.

Note: There may be some overlap between this book and the review sections of the GMATPrep® software.

2.4 General Test-Taking Suggestions

Specific test-taking strategies for individual question types are presented later in this book. The following are general suggestions to help you perform your best on the test.

1. Use your time wisely.

Although the GMAT exam stresses accuracy more than speed, it is important to use your time wisely. On average, you will have about 1¾ minutes for each verbal question and about 2 minutes for each quantitative question. Once you start the test, an onscreen clock will continuously count the time you have left. You can hide this display if you want, but it is a good idea to check the clock periodically to monitor your progress. The clock will automatically alert you when 5 minutes remain in the allotted time for the section you are working on.

2. Answer practice questions ahead of time.

After you become generally familiar with all question types, use the sample questions in this book to prepare for the actual test. It may be useful to time yourself as you answer the practice questions to get an idea of how long you will have for each question during the actual GMAT exam as well as to determine whether you are answering quickly enough to complete the test in the time allotted.

3. Read all test directions carefully.

The directions explain exactly what is required to answer each question type. If you read hastily, you may miss important instructions and lower your scores. To review directions during the test, click on the Help icon. But be aware that the time you spend reviewing directions will count against the time allotted for that section of the test.

4. Read each question carefully and thoroughly.

Before you answer a multiple-choice question, determine exactly what is being asked, then eliminate the wrong answers and select the best choice. Never skim a question or the possible answers; skimming may cause you to miss important information or nuances.

5. Do not spend too much time on any one question.

If you do not know the correct answer, or if the question is too time-consuming, try to eliminate choices you know are wrong, select the best of the remaining answer choices, and move on to the next question. Try not to worry about the impact on your score—guessing may lower your score, but not finishing the section will lower your score more.

Bear in mind that if you do not finish a section in the allotted time, you will still receive a score.

6. Confirm your answers ONLY when you are ready to move on.

Once you have selected your answer to a multiple-choice question, you will be asked to confirm it. Once you confirm your response, you cannot go back and change it. You may not skip questions, because the computer selects each question on the basis of your responses to preceding questions.

7. Plan your essay answers before you begin to write.

The best way to approach the two writing tasks that comprise the Analytical Writing Assessment is to read the directions carefully, take a few minutes to think about the question, and plan a response before you begin writing. Take care to organize your ideas and develop them fully, but leave time to reread your response and make any revisions that you think would improve it.

Myth -vs- FACT

M – It is more important to respond correctly to the test questions than it is to finish the test.

F – There is a severe penalty for not completing the GMAT exam.

If you are stumped by a question, give it your best guess and move on. If you guess incorrectly, the computer program will likely give you an easier question, which you are likely to answer correctly, and the computer will rapidly return to giving you questions matched to your ability. If you don't finish the test, your score will be reduced greatly. Failing to answer five verbal questions, for example, could reduce your score from the 91st percentile to the 77th percentile. Pacing is important.

Myth -vs- FACT

M – The first 10 questions are critical and you should invest the most time on those.

F – All questions count.

It is true that the computer-adaptive testing algorithm uses the first 10 questions to obtain an initial estimate of your ability; however, that is only an *initial* estimate. As you continue to answer questions, the algorithm self-corrects by computing an updated estimate on the basis of all the questions you have answered, and then administers items that are closely matched to this new estimate of your ability. Your final score is based on all your responses and considers the difficulty of all the questions you answered. Taking additional time on the first 10 questions will not game the system and can hurt your ability to finish the test.

3.0 Math Review

3.0 Math Review

Although this chapter provides a review of some of the mathematical concepts of arithmetic, algebra, and geometry, it is not intended to be a textbook. You should use this chapter to familiarize yourself with the kinds of topics that may be tested in the GMAT® exam. You may wish to consult an arithmetic, algebra, or geometry book for a more detailed discussion of some of the topics.

Section 3.1, "Arithmetic," includes the following topics:

1. Properties of Integers
2. Fractions
3. Decimals
4. Real Numbers
5. Ratio and Proportion
6. Percents
7. Powers and Roots of Numbers
8. Descriptive Statistics
9. Sets
10. Counting Methods
11. Discrete Probability

Section 3.2, "Algebra," does not extend beyond what is usually covered in a first-year high school algebra course. The topics included are as follows:

1. Simplifying Algebraic Expressions
2. Equations
3. Solving Linear Equations with One Unknown
4. Solving Two Linear Equations with Two Unknowns
5. Solving Equations by Factoring
6. Solving Quadratic Equations
7. Exponents
8. Inequalities
9. Absolute Value
10. Functions

Section 3.3, "Geometry," is limited primarily to measurement and intuitive geometry or spatial visualization. Extensive knowledge of theorems and the ability to construct proofs, skills that are usually developed in a formal geometry course, are not tested. The topics included in this section are the following:

1. Lines
2. Intersecting Lines and Angles
3. Perpendicular Lines
4. Parallel Lines
5. Polygons (Convex)
6. Triangles
7. Quadrilaterals
8. Circles
9. Rectangular Solids and Cylinders
10. Coordinate Geometry

Section 3.4, "Word Problems," presents examples of and solutions to the following types of word problems:

1. Rate Problems
2. Work Problems
3. Mixture Problems
4. Interest Problems
5. Discount
6. Profit
7. Sets
8. Geometry Problems
9. Measurement Problems
10. Data Interpretation

3.1 Arithmetic

1. Properties of Integers

An *integer* is any number in the set {. . . –3, –2, –1, 0, 1, 2, 3, . . .}. If x and y are integers and $x \neq 0$, then x is a *divisor* (*factor*) of y provided that $y = xn$ for some integer n. In this case, y is also said to be *divisible* by x or to be a *multiple* of x. For example, 7 is a divisor or factor of 28 since $28 = (7)(4)$, but 8 is not a divisor of 28 since there is no integer n such that $28 = 8n$.

If x and y are positive integers, there exist unique integers q and r, called the *quotient* and *remainder*, respectively, such that $y = xq + r$ and $0 \leq r < x$. For example, when 28 is divided by 8, the quotient is 3 and the remainder is 4 since $28 = (8)(3) + 4$. Note that y is divisible by x if and only if the remainder r is 0; for example, 32 has a remainder of 0 when divided by 8 because 32 is divisible by 8. Also, note that when a smaller integer is divided by a larger integer, the quotient is 0 and the remainder is the smaller integer. For example, 5 divided by 7 has the quotient 0 and the remainder 5 since $5 = (7)(0) + 5$.

Any integer that is divisible by 2 is an *even integer*; the set of even integers is {. . . –4, –2, 0, 2, 4, 6, 8, . . .}. Integers that are not divisible by 2 are *odd integers*; {. . . –3, –1, 1, 3, 5, . . .} is the set of odd integers.

If at least one factor of a product of integers is even, then the product is even; otherwise the product is odd. If two integers are both even or both odd, then their sum and their difference are even. Otherwise, their sum and their difference are odd.

A *prime* number is a positive integer that has exactly two different positive divisors, 1 and itself. For example, 2, 3, 5, 7, 11, and 13 are prime numbers, but 15 is not, since 15 has four different positive divisors, 1, 3, 5, and 15. The number 1 is not a prime number since it has only one positive divisor. Every integer greater than 1 either is prime or can be uniquely expressed as a product of prime factors. For example, $14 = (2)(7)$, $81 = (3)(3)(3)(3)$, and $484 = (2)(2)(11)(11)$.

The numbers –2, –1, 0, 1, 2, 3, 4, 5 are *consecutive integers*. Consecutive integers can be represented by n, $n + 1$, $n + 2$, $n + 3$, . . . , where n is an integer. The numbers 0, 2, 4, 6, 8 are *consecutive even integers*, and 1, 3, 5, 7, 9 are *consecutive odd integers*. Consecutive even integers can be represented by $2n$, $2n + 2$, $2n + 4$, . . . , and consecutive odd integers can be represented by $2n + 1$, $2n + 3$, $2n + 5$, . . . , where n is an integer.

Properties of the integer 1. If n is any number, then $1 \cdot n = n$, and for any number $n \neq 0$, $n \cdot \dfrac{1}{n} = 1$.

The number 1 can be expressed in many ways; for example, $\dfrac{n}{n} = 1$ for any number $n \neq 0$.

Multiplying or dividing an expression by 1, in any form, does not change the value of that expression.

Properties of the integer 0. The integer 0 is neither positive nor negative. If n is any number, then $n + 0 = n$ and $n \cdot 0 = 0$. Division by 0 is not defined.

2. Fractions

In a fraction $\frac{n}{d}$, n is the *numerator* and d is the *denominator*. The denominator of a fraction can never be 0, because division by 0 is not defined.

Two fractions are said to be *equivalent* if they represent the same number. For example, $\frac{8}{36}$ and $\frac{14}{63}$ are equivalent since they both represent the number $\frac{2}{9}$. In each case, the fraction is reduced to lowest terms by dividing both numerator and denominator by their *greatest common divisor* (gcd). The gcd of 8 and 36 is 4 and the gcd of 14 and 63 is 7.

Addition and subtraction of fractions.

Two fractions with the same denominator can be added or subtracted by performing the required operation with the numerators, leaving the denominators the same. For example, $\frac{3}{5} + \frac{4}{5} = \frac{3+4}{5} = \frac{7}{5}$ and $\frac{5}{7} - \frac{2}{7} = \frac{5-2}{7} = \frac{3}{7}$. If two fractions do not have the same denominator, express them as equivalent fractions with the same denominator. For example, to add $\frac{3}{5}$ and $\frac{4}{7}$, multiply the numerator and denominator of the first fraction by 7 and the numerator and denominator of the second fraction by 5, obtaining $\frac{21}{35}$ and $\frac{20}{35}$, respectively; $\frac{21}{35} + \frac{20}{35} = \frac{41}{35}$.

For the new denominator, choosing the *least common multiple* (lcm) of the denominators usually lessens the work. For $\frac{2}{3} + \frac{1}{6}$, the lcm of 3 and 6 is 6 (not $3 \times 6 = 18$), so

$$\frac{2}{3} + \frac{1}{6} = \frac{2}{3} \times \frac{2}{2} + \frac{1}{6} = \frac{4}{6} + \frac{1}{6} = \frac{5}{6}.$$

Multiplication and division of fractions.

To multiply two fractions, simply multiply the two numerators and multiply the two denominators.

For example, $\frac{2}{3} \times \frac{4}{7} = \frac{2 \times 4}{3 \times 7} = \frac{8}{21}$.

To divide by a fraction, invert the divisor (that is, find its *reciprocal*) and multiply. For example,

$\frac{2}{3} \div \frac{4}{7} = \frac{2}{3} \times \frac{7}{4} = \frac{14}{12} = \frac{7}{6}$.

In the problem above, the reciprocal of $\frac{4}{7}$ is $\frac{7}{4}$. In general, the reciprocal of a fraction $\frac{n}{d}$ is $\frac{d}{n}$, where n and d are not zero.

Mixed numbers.

A number that consists of a whole number and a fraction, for example, $7\frac{2}{3}$, is a mixed number:

$7\frac{2}{3}$ means $7 + \frac{2}{3}$.

To change a mixed number into a fraction, multiply the whole number by the denominator of the fraction and add this number to the numerator of the fraction; then put the result over the

denominator of the fraction. For example, $7\frac{2}{3} = \dfrac{(3 \times 7) + 2}{3} = \dfrac{23}{3}$.

3. Decimals

In the decimal system, the position of the period or *decimal point* determines the place value of the digits. For example, the digits in the number 7,654.321 have the following place values:

Thousands	Hundreds	Tens	Ones or units	Tenths	Hundredths	Thousandths
7 ,	6	5	4 .	3	2	1

Some examples of decimals follow.

$$0.321 = \frac{3}{10} + \frac{2}{100} + \frac{1}{1,000} = \frac{321}{1,000}$$

$$0.0321 = \frac{0}{10} + \frac{3}{100} + \frac{2}{1,000} + \frac{1}{10,000} = \frac{321}{10,000}$$

$$1.56 = 1 + \frac{5}{10} + \frac{6}{100} = \frac{156}{100}$$

Sometimes decimals are expressed as the product of a number with only one digit to the left of the decimal point and a power of 10. This is called *scientific notation*. For example, 231 can be written as 2.31×10^{2} and 0.0231 can be written as 2.31×10^{-2}. When a number is expressed in scientific notation, the exponent of the 10 indicates the number of places that the decimal point is to be moved in the number that is to be multiplied by a power of 10 in order to obtain the product. The decimal point is moved to the right if the exponent is positive and to the left if the exponent is negative. For example, 2.013×10^{4} is equal to 20,130 and 1.91×10^{-4} is equal to 0.000191.

Addition and subtraction of decimals.

To add or subtract two decimals, the decimal points of both numbers should be lined up. If one of the numbers has fewer digits to the right of the decimal point than the other, zeros may be inserted to the right of the last digit. For example, to add 17.6512 and 653.27, set up the numbers in a column and add:

$$
\begin{array}{r}
17.6512 \\
+\ 653.2700 \\
\hline
670.9212
\end{array}
$$

Likewise for 653.27 minus 17.6512:

$$
\begin{array}{r}
653.2700 \\
-\ 17.6512 \\
\hline
635.6188
\end{array}
$$

Multiplication of decimals.

To multiply decimals, multiply the numbers as if they were whole numbers and then insert the decimal point in the product so that the number of digits to the right of the decimal point is equal to the sum of the numbers of digits to the right of the decimal points in the numbers being multiplied. For example:

$$
\begin{array}{r}
2.09 \quad \left(2 \text{ digits to the right}\right)\\
\times\ 1.3 \quad \left(1 \text{ digit to the right}\right)\\
\hline
627 \\
2090 \\
\hline
2.717 \quad \left(2+1 = 3 \text{ digits to the right}\right)
\end{array}
$$

Division of decimals.

To divide a number (the dividend) by a decimal (the divisor), move the decimal point of the divisor to the right until the divisor is a whole number. Then move the decimal point of the dividend the same number of places to the right, and divide as you would by a whole number. The decimal point in the quotient will be directly above the decimal point in the new dividend. For example, to divide 698.12 by 12.4:

$$
12.4\overline{)698.12}
$$

will be replaced by:

$$
124\overline{)6981.2}
$$

and the division would proceed as follows:

$$
\begin{array}{r}
56.3 \\
124\overline{)6981.2} \\
\underline{620} \\
781 \\
\underline{744} \\
372 \\
\underline{372} \\
0
\end{array}
$$

4. Real Numbers

All *real* numbers correspond to points on the number line and all points on the number line correspond to real numbers. All real numbers except zero are either positive or negative.

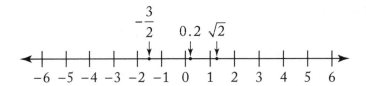

On a number line, numbers corresponding to points to the left of zero are negative and numbers corresponding to points to the right of zero are positive. For any two numbers on the number line, the number to the left is less than the number to the right; for example,

$$-4 < -3 < -\frac{3}{2} < -1, \text{ and } 1 < \sqrt{2} < 2.$$

To say that the number n is between 1 and 4 on the number line means that $n > 1$ and $n < 4$, that is, $1 < n < 4$. If n is "between 1 and 4, inclusive," then $1 \le n \le 4$.

The distance between a number and zero on the number line is called the *absolute value* of the number. Thus 3 and -3 have the same absolute value, 3, since they are both three units from zero. The absolute value of 3 is denoted $|3|$. Examples of absolute values of numbers are

$$|-5| = |5| = 5, \quad \left|-\frac{7}{2}\right| = \frac{7}{2}, \text{ and } |0| = 0.$$

Note that the absolute value of any nonzero number is positive.

Here are some properties of real numbers that are used frequently. If x, y, and z are real numbers, then

(1) $x + y = y + x$ and $xy = yx$.
 For example, $8 + 3 = 3 + 8 = 11$, and $(17)(5) = (5)(17) = 85$.

(2) $(x + y) + z = x + (y + z)$ and $(xy)z = x(yz)$.
 For example, $(7 + 5) + 2 = 7 + (5 + 2) = 7 + (7) = 14$, and $(5\sqrt{3})(\sqrt{3}) = (5)(\sqrt{3}\sqrt{3}) = (5)(3) = 15$.

(3) $xy + xz = x(y + z)$.
 For example, $718(36) + 718(64) = 718(36 + 64) = 718(100) = 71,800$.

(4) If x and y are both positive, then $x + y$ and xy are positive.

(5) If x and y are both negative, then $x + y$ is negative and xy is positive.

(6) If x is positive and y is negative, then xy is negative.

(7) If $xy = 0$, then $x = 0$ or $y = 0$. For example, $3y = 0$ implies $y = 0$.

(8) $|x + y| \le |x| + |y|$. For example, if $x = 10$ and $y = 2$, then $|x + y| = |12| = 12 = |x| + |y|$; and if $x = 10$ and $y = -2$, then $|x + y| = |8| = 8 < 12 = |x| + |y|$.

5. Ratio and Proportion

The *ratio* of the number a to the number b $\left(b \neq 0\right)$ is $\frac{a}{b}$.

A ratio may be expressed or represented in several ways. For example, the ratio of 2 to 3 can be written as 2 to 3, 2:3, or $\frac{2}{3}$. The order of the terms of a ratio is important. For example, the ratio of the number of months with exactly 30 days to the number with exactly 31 days is $\frac{4}{7}$, not $\frac{7}{4}$.

A *proportion* is a statement that two ratios are equal; for example, $\frac{2}{3} = \frac{8}{12}$ is a proportion. One way to solve a proportion involving an unknown is to cross multiply, obtaining a new equality. For example, to solve for n in the proportion $\frac{2}{3} = \frac{n}{12}$, cross multiply, obtaining $24 = 3n$; then divide both sides by 3, to get $n = 8$.

6. Percents

Percent means *per hundred* or *number out of 100*. A percent can be represented as a fraction with a denominator of 100, or as a decimal. For example:

$$37\% = \frac{37}{100} = 0.37.$$

To find a certain percent of a number, multiply the number by the percent expressed as a decimal or fraction. For example:

$$20\% \text{ of } 90 = 0.2 \times 90 = 18$$

$$\text{or}$$

$$20\% \text{ of } 90 = \frac{20}{100} \times 90 = \frac{1}{5} \times 90 = 18.$$

Percents greater than 100%.

Percents greater than 100% are represented by numbers greater than 1. For example:

$$300\% = \frac{300}{100} = 3$$

$$250\% \text{ of } 80 = 2.5 \times 80 = 200.$$

Percents less than 1%.

The percent 0.5% means $\frac{1}{2}$ of 1 percent. For example, 0.5% of 12 is equal to $0.005 \times 12 = 0.06$.

Percent change.

Often a problem will ask for the percent increase or decrease from one quantity to another quantity. For example, "If the price of an item increases from \$24 to \$30, what is the percent increase in price?" To find the percent increase, first find the amount of the increase; then divide this increase by the original amount, and express this quotient as a percent. In the example above, the percent increase would be found in the following way: the amount of the increase is $\left(30 - 24\right) = 6$. Therefore, the percent increase is $\frac{6}{24} = 0.25 = 25\%$.

Likewise, to find the percent decrease (for example, the price of an item is reduced from $30 to $24), first find the amount of the decrease; then divide this decrease by the original amount, and express this quotient as a percent. In the example above, the amount of decrease is $(30 - 24) = 6$.

Therefore, the percent decrease is $\frac{6}{30} = 0.20 = 20\%$.

Note that the percent increase from 24 to 30 is not the same as the percent decrease from 30 to 24.

In the following example, the increase is greater than 100 percent: If the cost of a certain house in 1983 was 300 percent of its cost in 1970, by what percent did the cost increase?

If n is the cost in 1970, then the percent increase is equal to $\frac{3n - n}{n} = \frac{2n}{n} = 2$, or 200%.

7. Powers and Roots of Numbers

When a number k is to be used n times as a factor in a product, it can be expressed as k^n, which means the nth power of k. For example, $2^2 = 2 \times 2 = 4$ and $2^3 = 2 \times 2 \times 2 = 8$ are powers of 2.

Squaring a number that is greater than 1, or raising it to a higher power, results in a larger number; squaring a number between 0 and 1 results in a smaller number. For example:

$$3^2 = 9 \qquad (9 > 3)$$

$$\left(\frac{1}{3}\right)^2 = \frac{1}{9} \qquad \left(\frac{1}{9} < \frac{1}{3}\right)$$

$$(0.1)^2 = 0.01 \quad (0.01 < 0.1)$$

A *square root* of a number n is a number that, when squared, is equal to n. The square root of a negative number is not a real number. Every positive number n has two square roots, one positive and the other negative, but $\sqrt{n}$ denotes the positive number whose square is n. For example, $\sqrt{9}$ denotes 3. The two square roots of 9 are $\sqrt{9} = 3$ and $-\sqrt{9} = -3$.

Every real number r has exactly one real *cube root*, which is the number s such that $s^3 = r$. The real cube root of r is denoted by $\sqrt[3]{r}$. Since $2^3 = 8$, $\sqrt[3]{8} = 2$. Similarly, $\sqrt[3]{-8} = -2$, because $(-2)^3 = -8$.

8. Descriptive Statistics

A list of numbers, or numerical data, can be described by various statistical measures. One of the most common of these measures is the *average*, or *(arithmetic) mean*, which locates a type of "center" for the data. The average of n numbers is defined as the sum of the n numbers divided by n. For

example, the average of 6, 4, 7, 10, and 4 is $\frac{6 + 4 + 7 + 10 + 4}{5} = \frac{31}{5} = 6.2$.

The *median* is another type of center for a list of numbers. To calculate the median of n numbers, first order the numbers from least to greatest; if n is odd, the median is defined as the middle number, whereas if n is even, the median is defined as the average of the two middle numbers. In the example above, the numbers, in order, are 4, 4, 6, 7, 10, and the median is 6, the middle number.

For the numbers 4, 6, 6, 8, 9, 12, the median is $\dfrac{6+8}{2} = 7$. Note that the mean of these numbers is 7.5.

The median of a set of data can be less than, equal to, or greater than the mean. Note that for a large set of data (for example, the salaries of 800 company employees), it is often true that about half of the data is less than the median and about half of the data is greater than the median; but this is not always the case, as the following data show.

3, 5, 7, 7, 7, 7, 7, 7, 8, 9, 9, 9, 9, 10, 10

Here the median is 7, but only $\dfrac{2}{15}$ of the data is less than the median.

The *mode* of a list of numbers is the number that occurs most frequently in the list. For example, the mode of 1, 3, 6, 4, 3, 5 is 3. A list of numbers may have more than one mode. For example, the list 1, 2, 3, 3, 3, 5, 7, 10, 10, 10, 20 has two modes, 3 and 10.

The degree to which numerical data are spread out or dispersed can be measured in many ways. The simplest measure of dispersion is the *range*, which is defined as the greatest value in the numerical data minus the least value. For example, the range of 11, 10, 5, 13, 21 is $21 - 5 = 16$. Note how the range depends on only two values in the data.

One of the most common measures of dispersion is the *standard deviation*. Generally speaking, the more the data are spread away from the mean, the greater the standard deviation. The standard deviation of n numbers can be calculated as follows: (1) find the arithmetic mean, (2) find the differences between the mean and each of the n numbers, (3) square each of the differences, (4) find the average of the squared differences, and (5) take the nonnegative square root of this average. Shown below is this calculation for the data 0, 7, 8, 10, 10, which have arithmetic mean 7.

x	$x - 7$	$(x - 7)^2$
0	−7	49
7	0	0
8	1	1
10	3	9
10	3	9
	Total	68

Standard deviation $\sqrt{\dfrac{68}{5}} \approx 3.7$

Notice that the standard deviation depends on every data value, although it depends most on values that are farthest from the mean. This is why a distribution with data grouped closely around the mean will have a smaller standard deviation than will data spread far from the mean. To illustrate this, compare the data 6, 6, 6.5, 7.5, 9, which also have mean 7. Note that the numbers in the second set of data seem to be grouped more closely around the mean of 7 than the numbers in the first set. This is reflected in the standard deviation, which is less for the second set (approximately 1.1) than for the first set (approximately 3.7).

There are many ways to display numerical data that show how the data are distributed. One simple way is with a *frequency distribution*, which is useful for data that have values occurring with varying frequencies. For example, the 20 numbers

$$
\begin{array}{cccccccccc}
-4 & 0 & 0 & -3 & -2 & -1 & -1 & 0 & -1 & -4 \\
-1 & -5 & 0 & -2 & 0 & -5 & -2 & 0 & 0 & -1
\end{array}
$$

are displayed on the next page in a frequency distribution by listing each different value x and the frequency f with which x occurs.

Data Value x	Frequency f
–5	2
–4	2
–3	1
–2	3
–1	5
0	7
Total	20

From the frequency distribution, one can readily compute descriptive statistics:

Mean: $= \dfrac{(-5)(2)+(-4)(2)+(-3)(1)+(-2)(3)+(-1)(5)+(0)(7)}{20} = -1.6$

Median: –1 (the average of the 10th and 11th numbers)
Mode: 0 (the number that occurs most frequently)
Range: $0-(-5) = 5$

Standard deviation: $\sqrt{\dfrac{(-5+1.6)^2(2)+(-4+1.6)^2(2)+\ldots+(0+1.6)^2(7)}{20}} \approx 1.7$

9. Sets

In mathematics a *set* is a collection of numbers or other objects. The objects are called the *elements* of the set. If S is a set having a finite number of elements, then the number of elements is denoted by $|S|$. Such a set is often defined by listing its elements; for example, $S = \{-5,\ 0,\ 1\}$ is a set with $|S| = 3$. The order in which the elements are listed in a set does not matter; thus $\{-5,\ 0,\ 1\} = \{0,\ 1,\ -5\}$.

If all the elements of a set S are also elements of a set T, then S is a *subset* of T; for example, $S = \{-5,\ 0,\ 1\}$ is a subset of $T = \{-5,\ 0,\ 1,\ 4,\ 10\}$.

For any two sets A and B, the *union* of A and B is the set of all elements that are in A *or* in B *or* in both. The *intersection* of A and B is the set of all elements that are both in A *and* in B. The union is denoted by $A \cup B$ and the intersection is denoted by $A \cap B$. As an example, if $A = \{3,\ 4\}$ and $B = \{4,\ 5,\ 6\}$, then $A \cup B = \{3,\ 4,\ 5,\ 6\}$ and $A \cap B = \{4\}$. Two sets that have no elements in common are said to be *disjoint* or *mutually exclusive*.

The relationship between sets is often illustrated with a *Venn diagram* in which sets are represented by regions in a plane. For two sets S and T that are not disjoint and neither is a subset of the other, the intersection $S \cap T$ is represented by the shaded region of the diagram below.

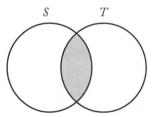

This diagram illustrates a fact about any two finite sets S and T: the number of elements in their union equals the sum of their individual numbers of elements minus the number of elements in their intersection (because the latter are counted twice in the sum); more concisely,

$$|S \cup T| = |S| + |T| - |S \cap T|.$$

This counting method is called the general addition rule for two sets. As a special case, if S and T are disjoint, then

$$|S \cup T| = |S| + |T|$$

since $|S \cap T| = 0$.

10. Counting Methods

There are some useful methods for counting objects and sets of objects without actually listing the elements to be counted. The following principle of multiplication is fundamental to these methods.

If an object is to be chosen from a set of m objects and a second object is to be chosen from a different set of n objects, then there are mn ways of choosing both objects simultaneously.

As an example, suppose the objects are items on a menu. If a meal consists of one entree and one dessert and there are 5 entrees and 3 desserts on the menu, then there are $5 \times 3 = 15$ different meals that can be ordered from the menu. As another example, each time a coin is flipped, there are two possible outcomes, heads and tails. If an experiment consists of 8 consecutive coin flips, then the experiment has 2^8 possible outcomes, where each of these outcomes is a list of heads and tails in some order.

A symbol that is often used with the multiplication principle is the *factorial*. If n is an integer greater than 1, then n factorial, denoted by the symbol $n!$, is defined as the product of all the integers from 1 to n. Therefore,

$$2! = (1)(2) = 2,$$
$$3! = (1)(2)(3) = 6,$$
$$4! = (1)(2)(3)(4) = 24, \text{ etc.}$$

Also, by definition, $0! = 1! = 1$.

The factorial is useful for counting the number of ways that a set of objects can be ordered. If a set of n objects is to be ordered from 1st to nth, then there are n choices for the 1st object, $n-1$ choices for the 2nd object, $n-2$ choices for the 3rd object, and so on, until there is only 1 choice for the nth object. Thus, by the multiplication principle, the number of ways of ordering the n objects is

$$n(n-1)(n-2) \cdots (3)(2)(1) = n!.$$

For example, the number of ways of ordering the letters A, B, and C is 3!, or 6:

ABC, ACB, BAC, BCA, CAB, and CBA.

These orderings are called the *permutations* of the letters A, B, and C.

A permutation can be thought of as a selection process in which objects are selected one by one in a certain order. If the order of selection is not relevant and only k objects are to be selected from a larger set of n objects, a different counting method is employed.

Specifically, consider a set of n objects from which a complete selection of k objects is to be made without regard to order, where $0 \leq k \leq n$. Then the number of possible complete selections of k objects is called the number of *combinations* of n objects taken k at a time and is denoted by $\binom{n}{k}$.

The value of $\binom{n}{k}$ is given by $\binom{n}{k} = \dfrac{n!}{k!(n-k)!}$.

Note that $\binom{n}{k}$ is the number of k-element subsets of a set with n elements. For example, if $S = \{A, B, C, D, E\}$, then the number of 2-element subsets of S, or the number of combinations of 5 letters taken 2 at a time, is $\binom{5}{2} = \dfrac{5!}{2!3!} = \dfrac{120}{(2)(6)} = 10$.

The subsets are {A, B}, {A, C}, {A, D}, {A, E}, {B, C}, {B, D}, {B, E}, {C, D}, {C, E}, and {D, E}.

Note that $\binom{5}{2} = 10 = \binom{5}{3}$ because every 2-element subset chosen from a set of 5 elements corresponds to a unique 3-element subset consisting of the elements *not* chosen. In general, $\binom{n}{k} = \binom{n}{n-k}$.

11. Discrete Probability

Many of the ideas discussed in the preceding three topics are important to the study of discrete probability. Discrete probability is concerned with *experiments* that have a finite number of *outcomes*. Given such an experiment, an *event* is a particular set of outcomes. For example, rolling a number cube with faces numbered 1 to 6 (similar to a 6-sided die) is an experiment with 6 possible outcomes: 1, 2, 3, 4, 5, or 6. One event in this experiment is that the outcome is 4, denoted {4}; another event is that the outcome is an odd number: {1, 3, 5}.

The probability that an event E occurs, denoted by $P(E)$, is a number between 0 and 1, inclusive. If E has no outcomes, then E is *impossible* and $P(E) = 0$; if E is the set of all possible outcomes of the experiment, then E is *certain* to occur and $P(E) = 1$. Otherwise, E is possible but uncertain, and $0 < P(E) < 1$. If F is a subset of E, then $P(F) \leq P(E)$. In the example above, if the probability of each of the 6 outcomes is the same, then the probability of each outcome is $\dfrac{1}{6}$, and the outcomes are said to be *equally likely*. For experiments in which all the individual outcomes are equally likely, the probability of an event E is

$$P(E) = \frac{\text{The number of outcomes in } E}{\text{The total number of possible outcomes}}.$$

In the example, the probability that the outcome is an odd number is

$$P(\{1, 3, 5\}) = \frac{|\{1, 3, 5\}|}{6} = \frac{3}{6} = \frac{1}{2}.$$

Given an experiment with events E and F, the following events are defined:
"*not E*" is the set of outcomes that are not outcomes in E;
"*E or F*" is the set of outcomes in E or F or both, that is, $E \cup F$;
"*E and F*" is the set of outcomes in both E and F, that is, $E \cap F$.

The probability that E does not occur is $P(\text{not } E) = 1 - P(E)$. The probability that "$E$ or F" occurs is $P(E \text{ or } F) = P(E) + P(F) - P(E \text{ and } F)$, using the general addition rule at the end of section 3.1.9 ("Sets"). For the number cube, if E is the event that the outcome is an odd number, $\{1, 3, 5\}$, and F is the event that the outcome is a prime number, $\{2, 3, 5\}$, then $P(E \text{ and } F) = P(\{3, 5\}) = \frac{2}{6} = \frac{1}{3}$ and so $P(E \text{ or } F) = P(E) + P(F) - P(E \text{ and } F) = \frac{3}{6} + \frac{3}{6} - \frac{2}{6} = \frac{4}{6} = \frac{2}{3}$.

Note that the event "E or F" is $E \cup F = \{1, 2, 3, 5\}$, and hence $P(E \text{ or } F) = \frac{|\{1, 2, 3, 5\}|}{6} = \frac{4}{6} = \frac{2}{3}$.

If the event "E and F" is impossible (that is, $E \cap F$ has no outcomes), then E and F are said to be *mutually exclusive* events, and $P(E \text{ and } F) = 0$. Then the general addition rule is reduced to $P(E \text{ or } F) = P(E) + P(F)$.

This is the special addition rule for the probability of two mutually exclusive events.

Two events A and B are said to be *independent* if the occurrence of either event does not alter the probability that the other event occurs. For one roll of the number cube, let $A = \{2, 4, 6\}$ and let $B = \{5, 6\}$. Then the probability that A occurs is $P(A) = \frac{|A|}{6} = \frac{3}{6} = \frac{1}{2}$, while, *presuming B occurs*, the probability that A occurs is

$$\frac{|A \cap B|}{|B|} = \frac{|\{6\}|}{|\{5, 6\}|} = \frac{1}{2}.$$

Similarly, the probability that B occurs is $P(B) = \frac{|B|}{6} = \frac{2}{6} = \frac{1}{3}$, while, *presuming A occurs*, the probability that B occurs is

$$\frac{|B \cap A|}{|A|} = \frac{|\{6\}|}{|\{2, 4, 6\}|} = \frac{1}{3}.$$

Thus, the occurrence of either event does not affect the probability that the other event occurs. Therefore, A and B are independent.

The following multiplication rule holds for any independent events E and F: $P(E \text{ and } F) = P(E)P(F)$.

For the independent events A and B above, $P(A \text{ and } B) = P(A)P(B) = \left(\frac{1}{2}\right)\left(\frac{1}{3}\right) = \left(\frac{1}{6}\right)$.

Note that the event "A and B" is $A \cap B = \{6\}$, and hence $P(A \text{ and } B) = P(\{6\}) = \frac{1}{6}$. It follows from the general addition rule and the multiplication rule above that if E and F are independent, then

$$P(E \text{ or } F) = P(E) + P(F) - P(E)P(F).$$

For a final example of some of these rules, consider an experiment with events A, B, and C for which $P(A) = 0.23$, $P(B) = 0.40$, and $P(C) = 0.85$. Also, suppose that events A and B are mutually exclusive and events B and C are independent. Then

$$P(A \text{ or } B) = P(A) + P(B) \quad \left(\text{since } A \text{ or } B \text{ are mutually exclusive}\right)$$
$$= 0.23 + 0.40$$
$$= 0.63$$
$$P(B \text{ or } C) = P(B) + P(C) - P(B)P(C) \quad \left(\text{by independence}\right)$$
$$= 0.40 + 0.85 - \left(0.40\right)\left(0.85\right)$$
$$= 0.91$$

Note that $P(A$ or $C)$ and $P(A$ and $C)$ cannot be determined using the information given. But it can be determined that A and C are *not* mutually exclusive since $P(A) + P(C) = 1.08$, which is greater than 1, and therefore cannot equal $P(A$ or $C)$; from this it follows that $P(A \text{ and } C) \geq 0.08$. One can also deduce that $P(A \text{ and } C) \leq P(A) = 0.23$, since $A \cap C$ is a subset of A, and that $P(A \text{ or } C) \geq P(C) = 0.85$ since C is a subset of $A \cup C$. Thus, one can conclude that $0.85 \leq P(A \text{ or } C) \leq 1$ and $0.08 \leq P(A \text{ and } C) \leq 0.23$.

3.2 Algebra

Algebra is based on the operations of arithmetic and on the concept of an *unknown quantity*, or *variable*. Letters such as x or n are used to represent unknown quantities. For example, suppose Pam has 5 more pencils than Fred. If F represents the number of pencils that Fred has, then the number of pencils that Pam has is $F + 5$. As another example, if Jim's present salary S is increased by 7%, then his new salary is $1.07S$. A combination of letters and arithmetic operations, such as

$F + 5$, $\dfrac{3x^2}{2x - 5}$, and $19x^2 - 6x + 3$, is called an *algebraic expression*.

The expression $19x^2 - 6x + 3$ consists of the *terms* $19x^2$, $-6x$, and 3, where 19 is the *coefficient* of x^2, -6 is the coefficient of x^1, and 3 is a *constant term* (or coefficient of $x^0 = 1$). Such an expression is called a *second degree* (or *quadratic*) *polynomial* in x since the highest power of x is 2. The expression $F + 5$ is a *first degree* (or *linear*) *polynomial* in F since the highest power of F is 1. The expression $\dfrac{3x^2}{2x - 5}$ is not a polynomial because it is not a sum of terms that are each powers of x multiplied by coefficients.

1. Simplifying Algebraic Expressions

Often when working with algebraic expressions, it is necessary to simplify them by factoring or combining *like* terms. For example, the expression $6x + 5x$ is equivalent to $\left(6 + 5\right)x$, or $11x$. In the expression $9x - 3y$, 3 is a factor common to both terms: $9x - 3y = 3\left(3x - y\right)$. In the expression $5x^2 + 6y$, there are no like terms and no common factors.

If there are common factors in the numerator and denominator of an expression, they can be divided out, provided that they are not equal to zero.

For example, if $x \neq 3$, then $\dfrac{x - 3}{x - 3}$ is equal to 1; therefore,

$$\frac{3xy - 9y}{x - 3} = \frac{3y(x - 3)}{x - 3}$$
$$= (3y)(1)$$
$$= 3y$$

To multiply two algebraic expressions, each term of one expression is multiplied by each term of the other expression. For example:

$$(3x - 4)(9y + x) = 3x(9y + x) - 4(9y + x)$$
$$= (3x)(9y) + (3x)(x) + (-4)(9y) + (-4)(x)$$
$$= 27xy + 3x^2 - 36y - 4x$$

An algebraic expression can be evaluated by substituting values of the unknowns in the expression. For example, if $x = 3$ and $y = -2$, then $3xy - x^2 + y$ can be evaluated as

$$3(3)(-2) - (3)^2 + (-2) = -18 - 9 - 2 = -29$$

2. Equations

A major focus of algebra is to solve equations involving algebraic expressions. Some examples of such equations are

$$5x - 2 = 9 - x \quad (\text{a linear equation with one unknown})$$
$$3x + 1 = y - 2 \quad (\text{a linear equation with two unknowns})$$
$$5x^2 + 3x - 2 = 7x \quad (\text{a quadratic equation with one unknown})$$
$$\frac{x(x - 3)(x^2 + 5)}{x - 4} = 0 \quad (\text{an equation that is factored on one side with 0 on the other})$$

The *solutions* of an equation with one or more unknowns are those values that make the equation true, or "satisfy the equation," when they are substituted for the unknowns of the equation. An equation may have no solution or one or more solutions. If two or more equations are to be solved together, the solutions must satisfy all the equations simultaneously.

Two equations having the same solution(s) are *equivalent equations*. For example, the equations

$$2 + x = 3$$
$$4 + 2x = 6$$

each have the unique solution $x = 1$. Note that the second equation is the first equation multiplied by 2. Similarly, the equations

$$3x - y = 6$$
$$6x - 2y = 12$$

have the same solutions, although in this case each equation has infinitely many solutions. If any value is assigned to x, then $3x - 6$ is a corresponding value for y that will satisfy both equations; for example, $x = 2$ and $y = 0$ is a solution to both equations, as is $x = 5$ and $y = 9$.

3. Solving Linear Equations with One Unknown

To solve a linear equation with one unknown (that is, to find the value of the unknown that satisfies the equation), the unknown should be isolated on one side of the equation. This can be done by performing the same mathematical operations on both sides of the equation. Remember that if the same number is added to or subtracted from both sides of the equation, this does not change the equality; likewise, multiplying or dividing both sides by the same nonzero number does not change the equality. For example, to solve the equation $\dfrac{5x-6}{3} = 4$ for x, the variable x can be isolated using the following steps:

$$5x - 6 = 12 \quad \left(\text{multiplying by } 3\right)$$
$$5x = 18 \quad \left(\text{adding } 6\right)$$
$$x = \frac{18}{5} \quad \left(\text{dividing by } 5\right)$$

The solution, $\dfrac{18}{5}$, can be checked by substituting it for x in the original equation to determine whether it satisfies that equation:

$$\frac{5\left(\dfrac{18}{5}\right) - 6}{3} = \frac{18 - 6}{3} = \frac{12}{3} = 4$$

Therefore, $x = \dfrac{18}{5}$ is the solution.

4. Solving Two Linear Equations with Two Unknowns

For two linear equations with two unknowns, if the equations are equivalent, then there are infinitely many solutions to the equations, as illustrated at the end of section 3.2.2 ("Equations"). If the equations are not equivalent, then they have either one unique solution or no solution. The latter case is illustrated by the two equations:

$$3x + 4y = 17$$
$$6x + 8y = 35$$

Note that $3x + 4y = 17$ implies $6x + 8y = 34$, which contradicts the second equation. Thus, no values of x and y can simultaneously satisfy both equations.

There are several methods of solving two linear equations with two unknowns. With any method, if a contradiction is reached, then the equations have no solution; if a trivial equation such as $0 = 0$ is reached, then the equations are equivalent and have infinitely many solutions. Otherwise, a unique solution can be found.

One way to solve for the two unknowns is to express one of the unknowns in terms of the other using one of the equations, and then substitute the expression into the remaining equation to obtain an equation with one unknown. This equation can be solved and the value of the unknown substituted into either of the original equations to find the value of the other unknown. For example, the following two equations can be solved for x and y.

$$\left(1\right)\ 3x + 2y = 11$$
$$\left(2\right)\quad x - y = 2$$

In equation (2), $x = 2 + y$. Substitute $2 + y$ in equation (1) for x:

$$3\left(2 + y\right) + 2y = 11$$
$$6 + 3y + 2y = 11$$
$$6 + 5y = 11$$
$$5y = 5$$
$$y = 1$$

If $y = 1$, then $x - 1 = 2$ and $x = 2 + 1 = 3$.

There is another way to solve for x and y by eliminating one of the unknowns. This can be done by making the coefficients of one of the unknowns the same (disregarding the sign) in both equations and either adding the equations or subtracting one equation from the other. For example, to solve the equations

$$\left(1\right)\ 6x + 5y = 29$$
$$\left(2\right)\ 4x - 3y = -6$$

by this method, multiply equation (1) by 3 and equation (2) by 5 to get

$$18x + 15y = 87$$
$$20x - 15y = -30$$

Adding the two equations eliminates y, yielding $38x = 57$, or $x = \dfrac{3}{2}$. Finally, substituting $\dfrac{3}{2}$ for x in one of the equations gives $y = 4$. These answers can be checked by substituting both values into both of the original equations.

5. Solving Equations by Factoring

Some equations can be solved by factoring. To do this, first add or subtract expressions to bring all the expressions to one side of the equation, with 0 on the other side. Then try to factor the nonzero side into a product of expressions. If this is possible, then using property (7) in section 3.1.4 ("Real Numbers") each of the factors can be set equal to 0, yielding several simpler equations that possibly can be solved. The solutions of the simpler equations will be solutions of the factored equation. As an example, consider the equation $x^3 - 2x^2 + x = -5\left(x - 1\right)^2$:

$$x^3 - 2x^2 + x + 5\left(x - 1\right)^2 = 0$$
$$x\left(x^2 - 2x + 1\right) + 5\left(x - 1\right)^2 = 0$$
$$x\left(x - 1\right)^2 + 5\left(x - 1\right)^2 = 0$$
$$\left(x + 5\right)\left(x - 1\right)^2 = 0$$
$$x + 5 = 0 \text{ or } \left(x - 1\right)^2 = 0$$
$$x = -5 \text{ or } x = 1.$$

For another example, consider $\dfrac{x(x-3)(x^2+5)}{x-4} = 0$. A fraction equals 0 if and only if its numerator equals 0. Thus, $x(x-3)(x^2+5) = 0$:

$$x = 0 \text{ or } x - 3 = 0 \text{ or } x^2 + 5 = 0$$
$$x = 0 \text{ or } x = 3 \text{ or } x^2 + 5 = 0.$$

But $x^2 + 5 = 0$ has no real solution because $x^2 + 5 > 0$ for every real number. Thus, the solutions are 0 and 3.

The solutions of an equation are also called the *roots* of the equation. These roots can be checked by substituting them into the original equation to determine whether they satisfy the equation.

6. Solving Quadratic Equations

The standard form for a *quadratic equation* is

$$ax^2 + bx + c = 0,$$

where a, b, and c are real numbers and $a \neq 0$; for example:

$$x^2 + 6x + 5 = 0$$
$$3x^2 - 2x = 0, \text{ and}$$
$$x^2 + 4 = 0$$

Some quadratic equations can easily be solved by factoring. For example:

$$(1) \qquad x^2 + 6x + 5 = 0$$
$$(x+5)(x+1) = 0$$
$$x + 5 = 0 \text{ or } x + 1 = 0$$
$$x = -5 \text{ or } x = -1$$

$$(2) \qquad 3x^2 - 3 = 8x$$
$$3x^2 - 8x - 3 = 0$$
$$(3x+1)(x-3) = 0$$
$$3x + 1 = 0 \text{ or } x - 3 = 0$$
$$x = -\frac{1}{3} \text{ or } x = 3$$

A quadratic equation has at most two real roots and may have just one or even no real root. For example, the equation $x^2 - 6x + 9 = 0$ can be expressed as $(x-3)^2 = 0$, or $(x-3)(x-3) = 0$; thus the only root is 3. The equation $x^2 + 4 = 0$ has no real root; since the square of any real number is greater than or equal to zero, $x^2 + 4$ must be greater than zero.

An expression of the form $a^2 - b^2$ can be factored as $(a-b)(a+b)$.

For example, the quadratic equation $9x^2 - 25 = 0$ can be solved as follows.

$$(3x-5)(3x+5) = 0$$
$$3x - 5 = 0 \text{ or } 3x + 5 = 0$$
$$x = \frac{5}{3} \text{ or } x = -\frac{5}{3}$$

If a quadratic expression is not easily factored, then its roots can always be found using the *quadratic formula*: If $ax^2 + bx + c = 0 \left(a \neq 0 \right)$, then the roots are

$$x = \frac{-b + \sqrt{b^2 - 4ac}}{2a} \text{ and } x = \frac{-b - \sqrt{b^2 - 4ac}}{2a}$$

These are two distinct real numbers unless $b^2 - 4ac \leq 0$. If $b^2 - 4ac = 0$, then these two expressions for x are equal to $-\dfrac{b}{2a}$, and the equation has only one root. If $b^2 - 4ac < 0$, then $\sqrt{b^2 - 4ac}$ is not a real number and the equation has no real roots.

7. Exponents

A positive integer exponent of a number or a variable indicates a product, and the positive integer is the number of times that the number or variable is a factor in the product. For example, x^5 means $(x)(x)(x)(x)(x)$; that is, x is a factor in the product 5 times.

Some rules about exponents follow.

Let x and y be any positive numbers, and let r and s be any positive integers.

(1) $\left(x^r \right)\left(x^s \right) = x^{(r + s)}$; for example, $\left(2^2 \right)\left(2^3 \right) = 2^{(2 + 3)} = 2^5 = 32$.

(2) $\dfrac{x^r}{x^s} = x^{(r - s)}$; for example, $\dfrac{4^5}{4^2} = 4^{5 - 2} = 4^3 = 64$.

(3) $\left(x^r \right)\left(y^r \right) = \left(xy \right)^r$; for example, $\left(3^3 \right)\left(4^3 \right) = 12^3 = 1{,}728$.

(4) $\left(\dfrac{x}{y} \right)^r = \dfrac{x^r}{y^r}$; for example, $\left(\dfrac{2}{3} \right)^3 = \dfrac{2^3}{3^3} = \dfrac{8}{27}$.

(5) $\left(x^r \right)^s = x^{rs} = \left(x^s \right)^r$; for example, $\left(x^3 \right)^4 = x^{12} = \left(x^4 \right)^3$.

(6) $x^{-r} = \dfrac{1}{x^r}$; for example, $3^{-2} = \dfrac{1}{3^2} = \dfrac{1}{9}$.

(7) $x^0 = 1$; for example, $6^0 = 1$.

(8) $x^{\frac{r}{s}} = \left(x^{\frac{1}{s}} \right)^r = \left(x^r \right)^{\frac{1}{s}} = \sqrt[s]{x^r}$; for example, $8^{\frac{2}{3}} = \left(8^{\frac{1}{3}} \right)^2 = \left(8^2 \right)^{\frac{1}{3}} = \sqrt[3]{8^2} = \sqrt[3]{64} = 4$

and $9^{\frac{1}{2}} = \sqrt{9} = 3$.

It can be shown that rules 1–6 also apply when r and s are not integers and are not positive, that is, when r and s are any real numbers.

8. Inequalities

An *inequality* is a statement that uses one of the following symbols:

$\neq$ not equal to

$>$ greater than

$\geq$ greater than or equal to

$<$ less than

$\leq$ less than or equal to

Some examples of inequalities are $5x - 3 < 9$, $6x \geq y$, and $\frac{1}{2} < \frac{3}{4}$. Solving a linear inequality with one unknown is similar to solving an equation; the unknown is isolated on one side of the inequality. As in solving an equation, the same number can be added to or subtracted from both sides of the inequality, or both sides of an inequality can be multiplied or divided by a positive number without changing the truth of the inequality. However, multiplying or dividing an inequality by a negative number reverses the order of the inequality. For example, $6 > 2$, but $(-1)(6) < (-1)(2)$.

To solve the inequality $3x - 2 > 5$ for x, isolate x by using the following steps:

$$3x - 2 > 5$$
$$3x > 7 \quad \left(\text{adding 2 to both sides}\right)$$
$$x > \frac{7}{3} \quad \left(\text{dividing both sides by 3}\right)$$

To solve the inequality $\frac{5x - 1}{-2} < 3$ for x, isolate x by using the following steps:

$$\frac{5x - 1}{-2} < 3$$
$$5x - 1 > -6 \quad \left(\text{multiplying both sides by } -2\right)$$
$$5x > -5 \quad \left(\text{adding 1 to both sides}\right)$$
$$x > -1 \quad \left(\text{dividing both sides by 5}\right)$$

9. Absolute Value

The absolute value of x, denoted $|x|$, is defined to be x if $x \geq 0$ and $-x$ if $x < 0$. Note that $\sqrt{x^2}$ denotes the nonnegative square root of x^2, and so $\sqrt{x^2} = |x|$.

10. Functions

An algebraic expression in one variable can be used to define a *function* of that variable. A function is denoted by a letter such as f or g along with the variable in the expression. For example, the expression $x^3 - 5x^2 + 2$ defines a function f that can be denoted by

$$f(x) = x^3 - 5x^2 + 2.$$

The expression $\frac{2z + 7}{\sqrt{z + 1}}$ defines a function g that can be denoted by

$$g(z) = \frac{2z + 7}{\sqrt{z + 1}}.$$

The symbols "$f(x)$" or "$g(z)$" do not represent products; each is merely the symbol for an expression, and is read "f of x" or "g of z."

Function notation provides a short way of writing the result of substituting a value for a variable. If $x = 1$ is substituted in the first expression, the result can be written $f(1) = -2$, and $f(1)$ is called the "value of f at $x = 1$." Similarly, if $z = 0$ is substituted in the second expression, then the value of g at $z = 0$ is $g(0) = 7$.

Once a function $f(x)$ is defined, it is useful to think of the variable x as an input and $f(x)$ as the corresponding output. In any function there can be no more than one output for any given input. However, more than one input can give the same output; for example, if $h(x) = |x + 3|$, then $h(-4) = 1 = h(-2)$.

The set of all allowable inputs for a function is called the *domain* of the function. For f and g defined above, the domain of f is the set of all real numbers and the domain of g is the set of all numbers greater than -1. The domain of any function can be arbitrarily specified, as in the function defined by "$h(x) = 9x - 5$ for $0 \leq x \leq 10$." Without such a restriction, the domain is assumed to be all values of x that result in a real number when substituted into the function.

The domain of a function can consist of only the positive integers and possibly 0. For example,

$$a(n) = n^2 + \frac{n}{5} \text{ for } n = 0, 1, 2, 3, \dots.$$

Such a function is called a *sequence* and $a(n)$ is denoted by a_n. The value of the sequence a_n at $n = 3$ is $a_3 = 3^2 + \frac{3}{5} = 9.60$. As another example, consider the sequence defined by $b_n = (-1)^n (n!)$ for $n = 1, 2, 3, \dots$. A sequence like this is often indicated by listing its values in the order $b_1, b_2, b_3, \dots, b_n, \dots$ as follows:

$-1, 2, -6, \dots, (-1)^n(n!), \dots$, and $(-1)^n(n!)$ is called the nth term of the sequence.

3.3 Geometry

1. Lines

In geometry, the word "line" refers to a straight line that extends without end in both directions.

$$\underset{\bullet}{\overset{P}{\quad}} \qquad \underset{\bullet}{\overset{Q}{\quad}} \ell$$

The line above can be referred to as line PQ or line ℓ. The part of the line from P to Q is called a *line segment*. P and Q are the *endpoints* of the segment. The notation $\overline{PQ}$ is used to denote line segment PQ and PQ is used to denote the length of the segment.

2. Intersecting Lines and Angles

If two lines intersect, the opposite angles are called *vertical angles* and have the same measure. In the figure

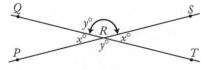

$\angle PRQ$ and $\angle SRT$ are vertical angles and $\angle QRS$ and $\angle PRT$ are vertical angles. Also, $x + y = 180°$ since PRS is a straight line.

3. Perpendicular Lines

An angle that has a measure of $90°$ is a *right angle*. If two lines intersect at right angles, the lines are *perpendicular*. For example:

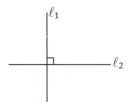

ℓ_1 and ℓ_2 above are perpendicular, denoted by $\ell_1 \perp \ell_2$. A right angle symbol in an angle of intersection indicates that the lines are perpendicular.

4. Parallel Lines

If two lines that are in the same plane do not intersect, the two lines are *parallel*. In the figure

lines ℓ_1 and ℓ_2 are parallel, denoted by $\ell_1 \parallel \ell_2$. If two parallel lines are intersected by a third line, as shown below, then the angle measures are related as indicated, where $x + y = 180°$.

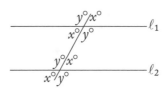

5. Polygons (Convex)

A *polygon* is a closed plane figure formed by three or more line segments, called the *sides* of the polygon. Each side intersects exactly two other sides at their endpoints. The points of intersection of the sides are *vertices*. The term "polygon" will be used to mean a convex polygon, that is, a polygon in which each interior angle has a measure of less than $180°$.

The following figures are polygons:

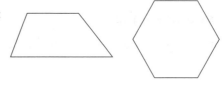

The following figures are not polygons:

A polygon with three sides is a *triangle*; with four sides, a *quadrilateral*; with five sides, a *pentagon*; and with six sides, a *hexagon*.

The sum of the interior angle measures of a triangle is $180°$. In general, the sum of the interior angle measures of a polygon with n sides is equal to $(n-2)180°$. For example, this sum for a pentagon is $(5-2)180° = (3)180° = 540°$.

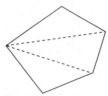

Note that a pentagon can be partitioned into three triangles and therefore the sum of the angle measures can be found by adding the sum of the angle measures of three triangles.

The *perimeter* of a polygon is the sum of the lengths of its sides.

The commonly used phrase "area of a triangle" (or any other plane figure) is used to mean the area of the region enclosed by that figure.

6. Triangles

There are several special types of triangles with important properties. But one property that all triangles share is that the sum of the lengths of any two of the sides is greater than the length of the third side, as illustrated below.

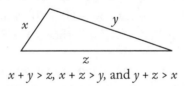

$$x + y > z, \ x + z > y, \text{ and } y + z > x$$

An *equilateral* triangle has all sides of equal length. All angles of an equilateral triangle have equal measure. An *isosceles* triangle has at least two sides of the same length. If two sides of a triangle have the same length, then the two angles opposite those sides have the same measure. Conversely, if two angles of a triangle have the same measure, then the sides opposite those angles have the same length. In isosceles triangle *PQR* below, $x = y$ since $PQ = QR$.

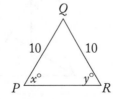

A triangle that has a right angle is a *right* triangle. In a right triangle, the side opposite the right angle is the *hypotenuse*, and the other two sides are the *legs*. An important theorem concerning right triangles is the *Pythagorean theorem*, which states: In a right triangle, the square of the length of the hypotenuse is equal to the sum of the squares of the lengths of the legs.

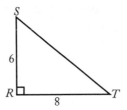

In the figure above, ΔRST is a right triangle, so $\left(RS\right)^2 + \left(RT\right)^2 = \left(ST\right)^2$. Here, $RS = 6$ and $RT = 8$, so $ST = 10$, since $6^2 + 8^2 = 36 + 64 = 100 = \left(ST\right)^2$ and $ST = \sqrt{100}$. Any triangle in which the lengths of the sides are in the ratio 3:4:5 is a right triangle. In general, if a, b, and c are the lengths of the sides of a triangle and $a^2 + b^2 = c^2$, then the triangle is a right triangle.

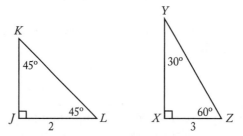

In $45°-45°-90°$ triangles, the lengths of the sides are in the ratio $1:1:\sqrt{2}$. For example, in ΔJKL, if $JL = 2$, then $JK = 2$ and $KL = 2\sqrt{2}$. In $30°-60°-90°$ triangles, the lengths of the sides are in the ratio $1:\sqrt{3}:2$. For example, in ΔXYZ, if $XZ = 3$, then $XY = 3\sqrt{3}$ and $YZ = 6$.

The *altitude* of a triangle is the segment drawn from a vertex perpendicular to the side opposite that vertex. Relative to that vertex and altitude, the opposite side is called the *base*.

The area of a triangle is equal to:

$$\frac{\left(\text{the length of the altitude}\right) \times \left(\text{the length of the base}\right)}{2}$$

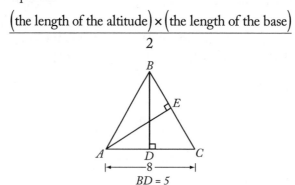

In ΔABC, $\overline{BD}$ is the altitude to base $\overline{AC}$ and $\overline{AE}$ is the altitude to base $\overline{BC}$. The area of ΔABC is equal to

$$\frac{BD \times AC}{2} = \frac{5 \times 8}{2} = 20.$$

The area is also equal to $\dfrac{AE \times BC}{2}$. If $\triangle ABC$ above is isosceles and $AB = BC$, then altitude $\overline{BD}$ bisects the base; that is, $AD = DC = 4$. Similarly, any altitude of an equilateral triangle bisects the side to which it is drawn.

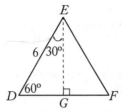

In equilateral triangle DEF, if $DE = 6$, then $DG = 3$ and $EG = 3\sqrt{3}$. The area of $\triangle DEF$ is equal to $\dfrac{3\sqrt{3} \times 6}{2} = 9\sqrt{3}$.

7. Quadrilaterals

A polygon with four sides is a *quadrilateral*. A quadrilateral in which both pairs of opposite sides are parallel is a *parallelogram*. The opposite sides of a parallelogram also have equal length.

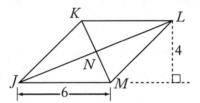

In parallelogram $JKLM$, $\overline{JK} \parallel \overline{LM}$ and $JK = LM$; $\overline{KL} \parallel \overline{JM}$ and $KL = JM$.

The diagonals of a parallelogram bisect each other (that is, $KN = NM$ and $JN = NL$).

The area of a parallelogram is equal to

$$\left(\text{the length of the altitude}\right) \times \left(\text{the length of the base}\right).$$

The area of $JKLM$ is equal to $4 \times 6 = 24$.

A parallelogram with right angles is a *rectangle*, and a rectangle with all sides of equal length is a *square*.

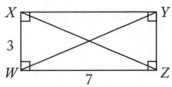

The perimeter of $WXYZ = 2\left(3\right) + 2\left(7\right) = 20$ and the area of $WXYZ$ is equal to $3 \times 7 = 21$.

The diagonals of a rectangle are equal; therefore $WY = XZ = \sqrt{9 + 49} = \sqrt{58}$.

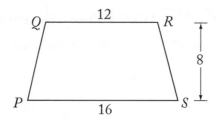

A quadrilateral with two sides that are parallel, as shown above, is a *trapezoid*. The area of trapezoid *PQRS* may be calculated as follows:

$$\frac{1}{2}\left(\text{the sum of the lengths of the bases}\right)\left(\text{the height}\right) = \frac{1}{2}\left(QR + PS\right)\left(8\right) = \frac{1}{2}\left(28 \times 8\right) = 112.$$

8. Circles

A *circle* is a set of points in a plane that are all located the same distance from a fixed point (the *center* of the circle).

A *chord* of a circle is a line segment that has its endpoints on the circle. A chord that passes through the center of the circle is a *diameter* of the circle. A *radius* of a circle is a segment from the center of the circle to a point on the circle. The words "diameter" and "radius" are also used to refer to the lengths of these segments.

The *circumference* of a circle is the distance around the circle. If r is the radius of the circle, then the circumference is equal to $2\pi r$, where π is approximately $\frac{22}{7}$ or 3.14. The *area* of a circle of radius r is equal to πr^2.

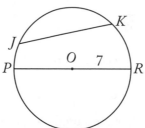

In the circle above, O is the center of the circle and $\overline{JK}$ and $\overline{PR}$ are chords. $\overline{PR}$ is a diameter and $\overline{OR}$ is a radius. If $OR = 7$, then the circumference of the circle is $2\pi\left(7\right) = 14\pi$ and the area of the circle is $\pi\left(7\right)^2 = 49\pi$.

The number of degrees of arc in a circle (or the number of degrees in a complete revolution) is 360.

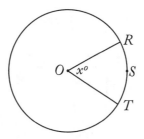

In the circle with center O above, the length of arc RST is $\dfrac{x}{360}$ of the circumference of the circle; for example, if $x = 60$, then arc RST has length $\dfrac{1}{6}$ of the circumference of the circle.

A line that has exactly one point in common with a circle is said to be *tangent* to the circle, and that common point is called the *point of tangency*. A radius or diameter with an endpoint at the point of tangency is perpendicular to the tangent line, and, conversely, a line that is perpendicular to a radius or diameter at one of its endpoints is tangent to the circle at that endpoint.

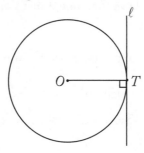

The line ℓ above is tangent to the circle and radius $\overline{OT}$ is perpendicular to ℓ.

If each vertex of a polygon lies on a circle, then the polygon is *inscribed* in the circle and the circle is *circumscribed* about the polygon. If each side of a polygon is tangent to a circle, then the polygon is *circumscribed* about the circle and the circle is *inscribed* in the polygon.

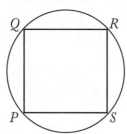 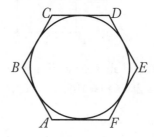

In the figure above, quadrilateral $PQRS$ is inscribed in a circle and hexagon $ABCDEF$ is circumscribed about a circle.

If a triangle is inscribed in a circle so that one of its sides is a diameter of the circle, then the triangle is a right triangle.

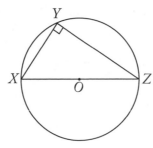

In the circle above, $\overline{XZ}$ is a diameter and the measure of $\angle XYZ$ is $90°$.

9. Rectangular Solids and Cylinders

A *rectangular solid* is a three-dimensional figure formed by 6 rectangular surfaces, as shown below. Each rectangular surface is a *face*. Each solid or dotted line segment is an *edge*, and each point at which the edges meet is a *vertex*. A rectangular solid has 6 faces, 12 edges, and 8 vertices. Opposite faces are parallel rectangles that have the same dimensions. A rectangular solid in which all edges are of equal length is a *cube*.

The *surface area* of a rectangular solid is equal to the sum of the areas of all the faces. The *volume* is equal to

$$(\text{length}) \times (\text{width}) \times (\text{height});$$

in other words, $(\text{area of base}) \times (\text{height})$.

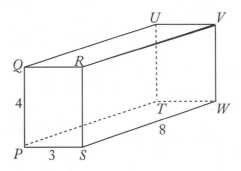

In the rectangular solid above, the dimensions are 3, 4, and 8. The surface area is equal to $2(3 \times 4) + 2(3 \times 8) + 2(4 \times 8) = 136$. The volume is equal to $3 \times 4 \times 8 = 96$.

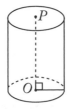

The figure above is a right circular *cylinder*. The two bases are circles of the same size with centers O and P, respectively, and altitude (height) $\overline{OP}$ is perpendicular to the bases. The surface area of a right circular cylinder with a base of radius r and height h is equal to $2(\pi r^2) + 2\pi rh$ (the sum of the areas of the two bases plus the area of the curved surface).

The volume of a cylinder is equal to $\pi r^2 h$, that is,

$$(\text{area of base}) \times (\text{height}).$$

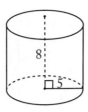

In the cylinder above, the surface area is equal to

$$2(25\pi) + 2\pi(5)(8) = 130\pi,$$

and the volume is equal to

$$25\pi(8) = 200\pi.$$

10. Coordinate Geometry

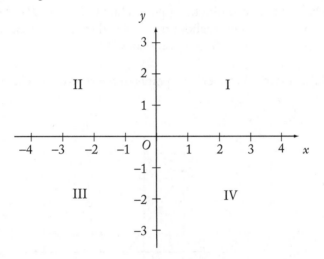

The figure above shows the (rectangular) *coordinate plane*. The horizontal line is called the *x-axis* and the perpendicular vertical line is called the *y-axis*. The point at which these two axes intersect, designated *O*, is called the *origin*. The axes divide the plane into four quadrants, I, II, III, and IV, as shown.

Each point in the plane has an *x-coordinate* and a *y-coordinate*. A point is identified by an ordered pair (x,y) of numbers in which the x-coordinate is the first number and the y-coordinate is the second number.

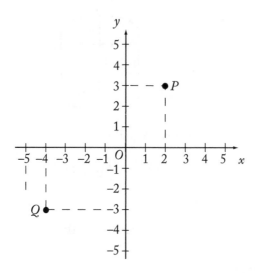

In the graph above, the (x,y) coordinates of point P are $(2,3)$ since P is 2 units to the right of the y-axis (that is, $x = 2$) and 3 units above the x-axis (that is, $y = 3$). Similarly, the (x,y) coordinates of point Q are $(-4,-3)$. The origin O has coordinates $(0,0)$.

One way to find the distance between two points in the coordinate plane is to use the Pythagorean theorem.

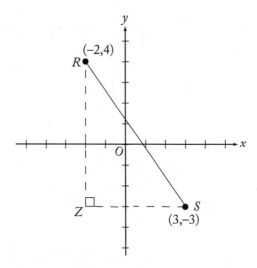

To find the distance between points R and S using the Pythagorean theorem, draw the triangle as shown. Note that Z has (x,y) coordinates $(-2,-3)$, $RZ = 7$, and $ZS = 5$. Therefore, the distance between R and S is equal to

$$\sqrt{7^2 + 5^2} = \sqrt{74}.$$

For a line in the coordinate plane, the coordinates of each point on the line satisfy a linear equation of the form $y = mx + b$ (or the form $x = a$ if the line is vertical). For example, each point on the line on the next page satisfies the equation $y = -\frac{1}{2}x + 1$. One can verify this for the points $(-2,2)$, $(2,0)$, and $(0,1)$ by substituting the respective coordinates for x and y in the equation.

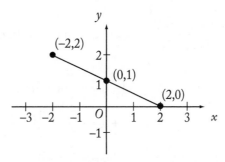

In the equation $y = mx + b$ of a line, the coefficient m is the *slope* of the line and the constant term b is the *y-intercept* of the line. For any two points on the line, the slope is defined to be the ratio of the difference in the y-coordinates to the difference in the x-coordinates. Using $(-2,2)$ and $(2,0)$ above, the slope is

$$\frac{\text{The difference in the } y\text{-coordinates}}{\text{The difference in the } x\text{-coordinates}} = \frac{0-2}{2-(-2)} = \frac{-2}{4} = -\frac{1}{2}.$$

The y-intercept is the y-coordinate of the point at which the line intersects the y-axis. For the line above, the y-intercept is 1, and this is the resulting value of y when x is set equal to 0 in the equation $y = -\frac{1}{2}x + 1$. The *x-intercept* is the x-coordinate of the point at which the line intersects the x-axis. The x-intercept can be found by setting $y = 0$ and solving for x. For the line $y = -\frac{1}{2}x + 1$, this gives

$$-\frac{1}{2}x + 1 = 0$$

$$-\frac{1}{2}x = -1$$

$$x = 2.$$

Thus, the x-intercept is 2.

Given any two points (x_1,y_1) and (x_2,y_2) with $x_1 \neq x_2$, the equation of the line passing through these points can be found by applying the definition of slope. Since the slope is $m = \dfrac{y_2 - y_1}{x_2 - x_1}$, then using a point known to be on the line, say (x_1,y_1), any point (x,y) on the line must satisfy $\dfrac{y - y_1}{x - x_1} = m$, or $y - y_1 = m(x - x_1)$. (Using (x_2,y_2) as the known point would yield an equivalent equation.) For example, consider the points $(-2,4)$ and $(3,-3)$ on the line below.

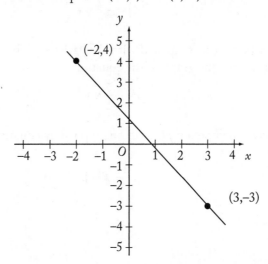

The slope of this line is $\dfrac{-3-4}{3-(-2)} = \dfrac{-7}{5}$, so an equation of this line can be found using the point $(3,-3)$ as follows:

$$y-(-3) = -\frac{7}{5}(x-3)$$

$$y+3 = -\frac{7}{5}x + \frac{21}{5}$$

$$y = -\frac{7}{5}x + \frac{6}{5}$$

The y-intercept is $\dfrac{6}{5}$. The *x-intercept* can be found as follows:

$$0 = -\frac{7}{5}x + \frac{6}{5}$$

$$\frac{7}{5}x = \frac{6}{5}$$

$$x = \frac{6}{7}$$

Both of these intercepts can be seen on the graph.

If the slope of a line is negative, the line slants downward from left to right; if the slope is positive, the line slants upward. If the slope is 0, the line is horizontal; the equation of such a line is of the form $y = b$ since $m = 0$. For a vertical line, slope is not defined, and the equation is of the form $x = a$, where a is the x-intercept.

There is a connection between graphs of lines in the coordinate plane and solutions of two linear equations with two unknowns. If two linear equations with unknowns x and y have a unique solution, then the graphs of the equations are two lines that intersect in one point, which is the solution. If the equations are equivalent, then they represent the same line with infinitely many points or solutions. If the equations have no solution, then they represent parallel lines, which do not intersect.

There is also a connection between functions (see section 3.2.10) and the coordinate plane. If a function is graphed in the coordinate plane, the function can be understood in different and useful ways. Consider the function defined by

$$f(x) = -\frac{7}{5}x + \frac{6}{5}.$$

If the value of the function, $f(x)$, is equated with the variable y, then the graph of the function in the xy-coordinate plane is simply the graph of the equation

$$y = -\frac{7}{5}x + \frac{6}{5}$$

shown above. Similarly, any function $f(x)$ can be graphed by equating y with the value of the function:

$$y = f(x).$$

So for any x in the domain of the function f, the point with coordinates $(x, f(x))$ is on the graph of f, and the graph consists entirely of these points.

As another example, consider a quadratic polynomial function defined by $f(x) = x^2 - 1$. One can plot several points $(x, f(x))$ on the graph to understand the connection between a function and its graph:

x	$f(x)$
−2	3
−1	0
0	−1
1	0
2	3

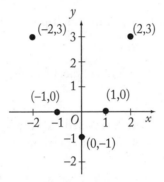

If all the points were graphed for $-2 \le x \le 2$, then the graph would appear as follows.

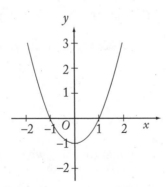

The graph of a quadratic function is called a *parabola* and always has the shape of the curve above, although it may be upside down or have a greater or lesser width. Note that the roots of the equation $f(x) = x^2 - 1 = 0$ are $x = 1$ and $x = -1$; these coincide with the x-intercepts since x-intercepts are found by setting $y = 0$ and solving for x. Also, the y-intercept is $f(0) = -1$ because this is the value of y corresponding to $x = 0$. For any function f, the x-intercepts are the solutions of the equation $f(x) = 0$ and the y-intercept is the value $f(0)$.

3.4 Word Problems

Many of the principles discussed in this chapter are used to solve word problems. The following discussion of word problems illustrates some of the techniques and concepts used in solving such problems.

1. Rate Problems

The distance that an object travels is equal to the product of the average speed at which it travels and the amount of time it takes to travel that distance, that is,

$$\text{Rate} \times \text{Time} = \text{Distance}.$$

Example 1: If a car travels at an average speed of 70 kilometers per hour for 4 hours, how many kilometers does it travel?

Solution: Since rate × time = distance, simply multiply 70 km/hour × 4 hours. Thus, the car travels 280 kilometers in 4 hours.

To determine the average rate at which an object travels, divide the total distance traveled by the total amount of traveling time.

Example 2: On a 400-mile trip, Car X traveled half the distance at 40 miles per hour (mph) and the other half at 50 mph. What was the average speed of Car X ?

Solution: First it is necessary to determine the amount of traveling time. During the first 200 miles, the car traveled at 40 mph; therefore, it took $\dfrac{200}{40} = 5$ hours to travel the first 200 miles. During the second 200 miles, the car traveled at 50 mph; therefore, it took $\dfrac{200}{50} = 4$ hours to travel the second 200 miles. Thus, the average speed of Car X was $\dfrac{400}{9} = 44\dfrac{4}{9}$ mph. Note that the average speed is *not* $\dfrac{40+50}{2} = 45$.

Some rate problems can be solved by using ratios.

Example 3: If 5 shirts cost \$44, then, at this rate, what is the cost of 8 shirts?

Solution: If c is the cost of the 8 shirts, then $\dfrac{5}{44} = \dfrac{8}{c}$. Cross multiplication results in the equation

$$5c = 8 \times 44 = 352$$

$$c = \frac{352}{5} = 70.40$$

The 8 shirts cost \$70.40.

2. Work Problems

In a work problem, the rates at which certain persons or machines work alone are usually given, and it is necessary to compute the rate at which they work together (or vice versa).

The basic formula for solving work problems is $\frac{1}{r} + \frac{1}{s} = \frac{1}{h}$, where r and s are, for example, the number of hours it takes Rae and Sam, respectively, to complete a job when working alone, and h is the number of hours it takes Rae and Sam to do the job when working together. The reasoning is that in 1 hour Rae does $\frac{1}{r}$ of the job, Sam does $\frac{1}{s}$ of the job, and Rae and Sam together do $\frac{1}{h}$ of the job.

Example 1: If Machine X can produce 1,000 bolts in 4 hours and Machine Y can produce 1,000 bolts in 5 hours, in how many hours can Machines X and Y, working together at these constant rates, produce 1,000 bolts?

Solution:

$$\frac{1}{4} + \frac{1}{5} = \frac{1}{h}$$
$$\frac{5}{20} + \frac{4}{20} = \frac{1}{h}$$
$$\frac{9}{20} = \frac{1}{h}$$
$$9h = 20$$
$$h = \frac{20}{9} = 2\frac{2}{9}$$

Working together, Machines X and Y can produce 1,000 bolts in $2\frac{2}{9}$ hours.

Example 2: If Art and Rita can do a job in 4 hours when working together at their respective constant rates and Art can do the job alone in 6 hours, in how many hours can Rita do the job alone?

Solution:

$$\frac{1}{6} + \frac{1}{R} = \frac{1}{4}$$
$$\frac{R+6}{6R} = \frac{1}{4}$$
$$4R + 24 = 6R$$
$$24 = 2R$$
$$12 = R$$

Working alone, Rita can do the job in 12 hours.

3. Mixture Problems

In mixture problems, substances with different characteristics are combined, and it is necessary to determine the characteristics of the resulting mixture.

Example 1: If 6 pounds of nuts that cost $1.20 per pound are mixed with 2 pounds of nuts that cost $1.60 per pound, what is the cost per pound of the mixture?

Solution: The total cost of the 8 pounds of nuts is

$$6($1.20) + 2($1.60) = $10.40.$$

The cost per pound is $\dfrac{$10.40}{8} = $1.30.$

Example 2: How many liters of a solution that is 15 percent salt must be added to 5 liters of a solution that is 8 percent salt so that the resulting solution is 10 percent salt?

Solution: Let n represent the number of liters of the 15% solution. The amount of salt in the 15% solution [0.15n] plus the amount of salt in the 8% solution [(0.08)(5)] must be equal to the amount of salt in the 10% mixture $\left[0.10(n+5)\right]$. Therefore,

$$0.15n + 0.08(5) = 0.10(n+5)$$
$$15n + 40 = 10n + 50$$
$$5n = 10$$
$$n = 2 \text{ liters}$$

Two liters of the 15% salt solution must be added to the 8% solution to obtain the 10% solution.

4. Interest Problems

Interest can be computed in two basic ways. With simple annual interest, the interest is computed on the principal only and is equal to $(\text{principal}) \times (\text{interest rate}) \times (\text{time})$. If interest is compounded, then interest is computed on the principal as well as on any interest already earned.

Example 1: If $8,000 is invested at 6 percent simple annual interest, how much interest is earned after 3 months?

Solution: Since the annual interest rate is 6%, the interest for 1 year is

$$(0.06)($8,000) = $480.$$

The interest earned in 3 months is $\dfrac{3}{12}($480) = $120.$

Example 2: If $10,000 is invested at 10 percent annual interest, compounded semiannually, what is the balance after 1 year?

Solution: The balance after the first 6 months would be

$$10,000 + (10,000)(0.05) = $10,500.$$

The balance after one year would be $10,500 + (10,500)(0.05) = $11,025.$

Note that the interest rate for each 6-month period is 5%, which is half of the 10% annual rate. The balance after one year can also be expressed as

$$10{,}000\left(1+\frac{0.10}{2}\right)^{2} \text{ dollars.}$$

5. Discount

If a price is discounted by n percent, then the price becomes $\left(100-n\right)$ percent of the original price.

Example 1: A certain customer paid $24 for a dress. If that price represented a 25 percent discount on the original price of the dress, what was the original price of the dress?

Solution: If p is the original price of the dress, then $0.75p$ is the discounted price and $0.75\,p = \$24$, or $p = \$32$. The original price of the dress was $32.

Example 2: The price of an item is discounted by 20 percent and then this reduced price is discounted by an additional 30 percent. These two discounts are equal to an overall discount of what percent?

Solution: If p is the original price of the item, then $0.8p$ is the price after the first discount. The price after the second discount is $\left(0.7\right)\left(0.8\right)p = 0.56\,p$. This represents an overall discount of 44 percent $\left(100\% - 56\%\right)$.

6. Profit

Gross profit is equal to revenues minus expenses, or selling price minus cost.

Example: A certain appliance costs a merchant $30. At what price should the merchant sell the appliance in order to make a gross profit of 50 percent of the cost of the appliance?

Solution: If s is the selling price of the appliance, then $s - 30 = \left(0.5\right)\left(30\right)$, or $s = \$45$. The merchant should sell the appliance for $45.

7. Sets

If S is the set of numbers 1, 2, 3, and 4, you can write $S = \left\{1,\ 2,\ 3,\ 4\right\}$. Sets can also be represented by Venn diagrams. That is, the relationship among the members of sets can be represented by circles.

Example 1: Each of 25 people is enrolled in history, mathematics, or both. If 20 are enrolled in history and 18 are enrolled in mathematics, how many are enrolled in both history and mathematics?

Solution: The 25 people can be divided into three sets: those who study history only, those who study mathematics only, and those who study history and mathematics. Thus a Venn diagram may be drawn as follows, where n is the number of people enrolled in both courses, $20 - n$ is the number enrolled in history only, and $18 - n$ is the number enrolled in mathematics only.

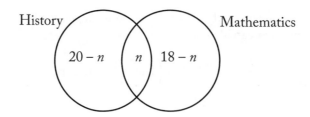

Since there is a total of 25 people, $(20-n)+n+(18-n)=25$, or $n=13$. Thirteen people are enrolled in both history and mathematics. Note that $20+18-13=25$, which is the general addition rule for two sets (see section 3.1.9).

Example 2: In a certain production lot, 40 percent of the toys are red and the remaining toys are green. Half of the toys are small and half are large. If 10 percent of the toys are red and small, and 40 toys are green and large, how many of the toys are red and large.

Solution: For this kind of problem, it is helpful to organize the information in a table:

	Red	Green	Total
Small	10%		50%
Large			50%
Total	40%	60%	100%

The numbers in the table are the percentages given. The following percentages can be computed on the basis of what is given:

	Red	Green	Total
Small	10%	40%	50%
Large	30%	20%	50%
Total	40%	60%	100%

Since 20% of the number of toys (n) are green and large, $0.20n=40$ (40 toys are green and large), or $n=200$. Therefore, 30% of the 200 toys, or $(0.3)(200)=60$, are red and large.

8. Geometry Problems

The following is an example of a word problem involving geometry.
Example:

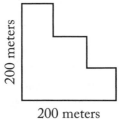

The figure above shows an aerial view of a piece of land. If all angles shown are right angles, what is the perimeter of the piece of land?

Solution: For reference, label the figure as

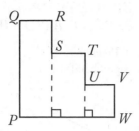

If all the angles are right angles, then $QR + ST + UV = PW$, and $RS + TU + VW = PQ$. Hence, the perimeter of the land is $2PW + 2PQ = 2 \times 200 + 2 \times 200 = 800$ meters.

9. Measurement Problems

Some questions on the GMAT involve metric units of measure, whereas others involve English units of measure. However, except for units of time, if a question requires conversion from one unit of measure to another, the relationship between those units will be given.

Example: A train travels at a constant rate of 25 meters per second. How many kilometers does it travel in 5 minutes? $\left(1 \text{ kilometer} = 1{,}000 \text{ meters}\right)$

Solution: In 1 minute the train travels $\left(25\right)\left(60\right) = 1{,}500$ meters, so in 5 minutes it travels 7,500 meters. Since 1 kilometer = 1,000 meters, it follows that 7,500 meters equals $\dfrac{7{,}500}{1{,}000}$, or 7.5 kilometers.

10. Data Interpretation

Occasionally a question or set of questions will be based on data provided in a table or graph. Some examples of tables and graphs are given below.

Example 1:

Population by Age Group (in thousands)	
Age	Population
17 years and under	63,376
18–44 years	86,738
45–64 years	43,845
65 years and over	24,054

How many people are 44 years old or younger?

Solution: The figures in the table are given in thousands. The answer in thousands can be obtained by adding 63,376 thousand and 86,738 thousand. The result is 150,114 thousand, which is 150,114,000.

Example 2:

AVERAGE TEMPERATURE AND
PRECIPITATION IN CITY X

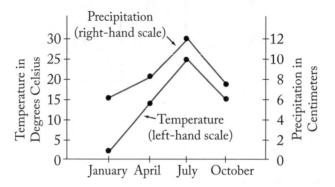

What are the average temperature and precipitation in City X during April?

Solution: Note that the scale on the left applies to the temperature line graph and the one on the right applies to the precipitation line graph. According to the graph, during April the average temperature is approximately $14°$ Celsius and the average precipitation is approximately 8 centimeters.

Example 3:

DISTRIBUTION OF AL'S WEEKLY NET SALARY

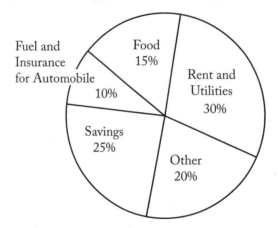

Al's weekly net salary is $350. To how many of the categories listed was at least $80 of Al's weekly net salary allocated?

Solution: In the circle graph, the relative sizes of the sectors are proportional to their corresponding values and the sum of the percents given is 100%. Note that $\frac{80}{350}$ is approximately 23%, so at least $80 was allocated to each of 2 categories—Rent and Utilities, and Savings—since their allocations are each greater than 23%.

4.0 Problem Solving

4.0 Problem Solving

The Quantitative section of the GMAT® exam uses problem solving and data sufficiency questions to gauge your skill level. This chapter focuses on problem solving questions. Remember that quantitative questions require knowledge of the following:

- Arithmetic

- Elementary algebra

- Commonly known concepts of geometry

Problem solving questions are designed to test your basic mathematical skills and understanding of elementary mathematical concepts, as well as your ability to reason quantitatively, solve quantitative problems, and interpret graphic data. The mathematics knowledge required to answer the questions is no more advanced than what is generally taught in secondary school (or high school) mathematics classes.

In these questions, you are asked to solve each problem and select the best of the five answer choices given. Begin by reading the question thoroughly to determine exactly what information is given and to make sure you understand what is being asked. Scan the answer choices to understand your options. If the problem seems simple, take a few moments to see whether you can determine the answer. Then check your answer against the choices provided.

If you do not see your answer among the choices, or if the problem is complicated, take a closer look at the answer choices and think again about what the problem is asking. See whether you can eliminate some of the answer choices and narrow down your options. If you are still unable to narrow the answer down to a single choice, reread the question. Keep in mind that the answer will be based solely on the information provided in the question—don't allow your own experience and assumptions to interfere with your ability to find the correct answer to the question.

If you find yourself stuck on a question or unable to select the single correct answer, keep in mind that you have about two minutes to answer each quantitative question. You may run out of time if you take too long to answer any one question, so you may simply need to pick the answer that seems to make the most sense. Although guessing is generally not the best way to achieve a high GMAT score, making an educated guess is a good strategy for answering questions you are unsure of. Even if your answer to a particular question is incorrect, your answers to other questions will allow the test to accurately gauge your ability level.

The following pages include test-taking strategies, directions that will apply to questions of this type, sample questions, an answer key, and explanations for all the problems. These explanations present problem solving strategies that could be helpful in answering the questions.

4.1 Test-Taking Strategies

1. **Pace yourself.**

   Consult the on-screen timer periodically. Work as carefully as possible, but do not spend valuable time checking answers or pondering problems that you find difficult.

2. **Use the erasable notepad provided.**

   Working a problem out may help you avoid errors in solving the problem. If diagrams or figures are not presented, it may help if you draw your own.

3. **Read each question carefully to determine what is being asked.**

   For word problems, take one step at a time, reading each sentence carefully and translating the information into equations or other useful mathematical representations.

4. **Scan the answer choices before attempting to answer a question.**

   Scanning the answers can prevent you from putting answers in a form that is not given (e.g., finding the answer in decimal form, such as 0.25, when the choices are given in fractional form, such as $\frac{1}{4}$). Also, if the question requires approximations, a shortcut could serve well (e.g., you may be able to approximate 48 percent of a number by using half).

5. **Don't waste time trying to solve a problem that is too difficult for you.**

   Make your best guess and move on to the next question.

4.2 The Directions

These directions are very similar to those you will see for problem solving questions when you take the GMAT exam. If you read them carefully and understand them clearly before sitting for the GMAT exam, you will not need to spend too much time reviewing them once the test begins.

Solve the problem and indicate the best of the answer choices given.

Numbers: All numbers used are real numbers.

Figures: A figure accompanying a problem solving question is intended to provide information useful in solving the problem. Figures are drawn as accurately as possible. Exceptions will be clearly noted. Lines shown as straight are straight, and lines that appear jagged are also straight. The positions of points, angles, regions, etc., exist in the order shown, and angle measures are greater than zero. All figures lie in a plane unless otherwise indicated.

4.3 Sample Questions

Solve the problem and indicate the best of the answer choices given.

<u>Numbers:</u> All numbers used are real numbers.

<u>Figures:</u>   A figure accompanying a problem solving question is intended to provide information useful in solving the problem. Figures are drawn as accurately as possible. Exceptions will be clearly noted. Lines shown as straight are straight, and lines that appear jagged are also straight. The positions of points, angles, regions, etc., exist in the order shown, and angle measures are greater than zero. All figures lie in a plane unless otherwise indicated.

1. Points A, B, C, and D, in that order, lie on a line. If $AB = 3$ cm, $AC = 4$ cm, and $BD = 6$ cm, what is CD, in centimeters?

   (A) 1
   (B) 2
   (C) 3
   (D) 4
   (E) 5

2. What is the value of $x^2yz - xyz^2$, if $x = -2$, $y = 1$, and $z = 3$?

   (A) 20
   (B) 24
   (C) 30
   (D) 32
   (E) 48

3. If $x > y$ and $y > z$, which of the following represents the greatest number?

   (A) $x - z$
   (B) $x - y$
   (C) $y - x$
   (D) $z - y$
   (E) $z - x$

4. To order certain plants from a catalog, it costs $3.00 per plant, plus a 5 percent sales tax, plus $6.95 for shipping and handling regardless of the number of plants ordered. If Company C ordered these plants from the catalog at the total cost of $69.95, how many plants did Company C order?

   (A) 22
   (B) 21
   (C) 20
   (D) 19
   (E) 18

5. Company C produces toy trucks at a cost of $5.00 each for the first 100 trucks and $3.50 for each additional truck. If 500 toy trucks were produced by Company C and sold for $10.00 each, what was Company C's gross profit?

   (A) $2,250
   (B) $2,500
   (C) $3,100
   (D) $3,250
   (E) $3,500

6. A group of store managers must assemble 280 displays for an upcoming sale. If they assemble 25 percent of the displays during the first hour and 40 percent of the remaining displays during the second hour, how many of the displays will not have been assembled by the end of the second hour?

   (A) 70
   (B) 98
   (C) 126
   (D) 168
   (E) 182

7. Of the following, which is least?

   (A) $\dfrac{0.03}{0.00071}$

   (B) $\dfrac{0.03}{0.0071}$

   (C) $\dfrac{0.03}{0.071}$

   (D) $\dfrac{0.03}{0.71}$

   (E) $\dfrac{0.03}{7.1}$

8. The maximum recommended pulse rate R, when exercising, for a person who is x years of age is given by the equation $R = 176 - 0.8x$. What is the age, in years, of a person whose maximum recommended pulse rate when exercising is 140 ?

   (A) 40
   (B) 45
   (C) 50
   (D) 55
   (E) 60

9. There are five sales agents in a certain real estate office. One month Andy sold twice as many properties as Ellen, Bob sold 3 more than Ellen, Cary sold twice as many as Bob, and Dora sold as many as Bob and Ellen together. Who sold the most properties that month?

   (A) Andy
   (B) Bob
   (C) Cary
   (D) Dora
   (E) Ellen

10. Which of the following represent positive numbers?

    I. $-3 - (-5)$
    II. $(-3)(-5)$
    III. $-5 - (-3)$

    (A) I only
    (B) II only
    (C) III only
    (D) I and II
    (E) II and III

11. If $\frac{x}{4}$ is 2 more than $\frac{x}{8}$, then $x =$

    (A) 4
    (B) 8
    (C) 16
    (D) 32
    (E) 64

12. If Mario was 32 years old 8 years ago, how old was he x years ago?

    (A) $x - 40$
    (B) $x - 24$
    (C) $40 - x$
    (D) $24 - x$
    (E) $24 + x$

13. The toll T, in dollars, for a truck using a certain bridge is given by the formula $T = 1.50 + 0.50(x - 2)$, where x is the number of axles on the truck. What is the toll for an 18-wheel truck that has 2 wheels on its front axle and 4 wheels on each of its other axles?

    (A) $2.50
    (B) $3.00
    (C) $3.50
    (D) $4.00
    (E) $5.00

14. If $\left(b - 3\right)\left(4 + \dfrac{2}{b}\right) = 0$ and $b \neq 3$, then $b =$

    (A) -8
    (B) -2
    (C) $-\dfrac{1}{2}$
    (D) $\dfrac{1}{2}$
    (E) 2

15. For what value of x between -4 and 4, inclusive, is the value of $x^2 - 10x + 16$ the greatest?

    (A) -4
    (B) -2
    (C) 0
    (D) 2
    (E) 4

16. The number $2 - 0.5$ is how many times the number $1 - 0.5$?

    (A) 2
    (B) 2.5
    (C) 3
    (D) 3.5
    (E) 4

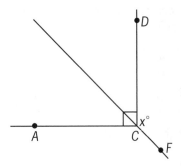

17. In the figure above, if *F* is a point on the line that bisects angle *ACD* and the measure of angle *DCF* is *x*°, which of the following is true of *x* ?

    (A) $90 \le x < 100$
    (B) $100 \le x < 110$
    (C) $110 \le x < 120$
    (D) $120 \le x < 130$
    (E) $130 \le x < 140$

18. In which of the following pairs are the two numbers reciprocals of each other?

    I. 3 and $\dfrac{1}{3}$

    II. $\dfrac{1}{17}$ and $\dfrac{-1}{17}$

    III. $\sqrt{3}$ and $\dfrac{\sqrt{3}}{3}$

    (A)   I only
    (B)   II only
    (C)   I and II
    (D)   I and III
    (E)   II and III

19. A rope 20.6 meters long is cut into two pieces. If the length of one piece of rope is 2.8 meters shorter than the length of the other, what is the length, in meters, of the longer piece of rope?

    (A)   7.5
    (B)   8.9
    (C)   9.9
    (D)   10.3
    (E)   11.7

20. What is the perimeter, in meters, of a rectangular garden 6 meters wide that has the same area as a rectangular playground 16 meters long and 12 meters wide?

    (A)   48
    (B)   56
    (C)   60
    (D)   76
    (E)   192

21. Of the total amount that Jill spent on a shopping trip, excluding taxes, she spent 50 percent on clothing, 20 percent on food, and 30 percent on other items. If Jill paid a 4 percent tax on the clothing, no tax on the food, and an 8 percent tax on all other items, then the total tax that she paid was what percent of the total amount that she spent, excluding taxes?

    (A)   2.8%
    (B)   3.6%
    (C)   4.4%
    (D)   5.2%
    (E)   6.0%

22. At the opening of a trading day at a certain stock exchange, the price per share of stock K was $8. If the price per share of stock K was $9 at the closing of the day, what was the percent increase in the price per share of stock K for that day?

    (A)   1.4%
    (B)   5.9%
    (C)   11.1%
    (D)   12.5%
    (E)   23.6%

23. The price of a certain television set is discounted by 10 percent, and the reduced price is then discounted by 10 percent. This series of successive discounts is equivalent to a single discount of

    (A)   20%
    (B)   19%
    (C)   18%
    (D)   11%
    (E)   10%

24. The number of rooms at Hotel G is 10 less than twice the number of rooms at Hotel H. If the total number of rooms at Hotel G and Hotel H is 425, what is the number of rooms at Hotel G ?

    (A)   140
    (B)   180
    (C)   200
    (D)   240
    (E)   280

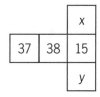

25. In the figure above, the sum of the three numbers in the horizontal row equals the product of the three numbers in the vertical column. What is the value of xy ?

    (A)   6
    (B)   15
    (C)   35
    (D)   75
    (E)   90

26. $\left(1+\sqrt{5}\right)\left(1-\sqrt{5}\right) =$

    (A) -4
    (B) 2
    (C) 6
    (D) $-4-2\sqrt{5}$
    (E) $6-2\sqrt{5}$

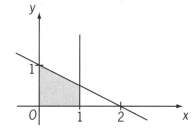

27. In the rectangular coordinate system above, the shaded region is bounded by straight lines. Which of the following is NOT an equation of one of the boundary lines?

    (A) $x = 0$
    (B) $y = 0$
    (C) $x = 1$
    (D) $x - y = 0$
    (E) $x + 2y = 2$

28. A certain population of bacteria doubles every 10 minutes. If the number of bacteria in the population initially was 10^4, what was the number in the population 1 hour later?

    (A) $2(10^4)$
    (B) $6(10^4)$
    (C) $(2^6)(10^4)$
    (D) $(10^6)(10^4)$
    (E) $(10^4)^6$

29. If the perimeter of a rectangular garden plot is 34 feet and its area is 60 square feet, what is the length of each of the longer sides?

    (A)   5 ft
    (B)   6 ft
    (C)   10 ft
    (D)   12 ft
    (E)   15 ft

30. In a poll of 66,000 physicians, only 20 percent responded; of these, 10 percent disclosed their preference for pain reliever X. How many of the physicians who responded did not disclose a preference for pain reliever X ?

    (A)   1,320
    (B)   5,280
    (C)   6,600
    (D)   10,560
    (E)   11,880

31. $\dfrac{3}{100} + \dfrac{5}{1,000} + \dfrac{7}{100,000} =$

    (A)   0.357
    (B)   0.3507
    (C)   0.35007
    (D)   0.0357
    (E)   0.03507

32. Which of the following fractions is equal to the decimal 0.0625 ?

    (A) $\dfrac{5}{8}$

    (B) $\dfrac{3}{8}$

    (C) $\dfrac{1}{16}$

    (D) $\dfrac{1}{18}$

    (E) $\dfrac{3}{80}$

33. If r and s are positive integers such that $(2^r)(4^s) = 16$, then $2r + s =$

   (A)   2
   (B)   3
   (C)   4
   (D)   5
   (E)   6

34. If positive integers x and y are not both odd, which of the following must be even?

   (A) xy
   (B) $x + y$
   (C) $x - y$
   (D) $x + y - 1$
   (E) $2(x + y) - 1$

35. The annual budget of a certain college is to be shown on a circle graph. If the size of each sector of the graph is to be proportional to the amount of the budget it represents, how many degrees of the circle should be used to represent an item that is 15 percent of the budget?

   (A) $15°$
   (B) $36°$
   (C) $54°$
   (D) $90°$
   (E) $150°$

36. During a two-week period, the price of an ounce of silver increased by 25 percent by the end of the first week and then decreased by 20 percent of this new price by the end of the second week. If the price of silver was x dollars per ounce at the beginning of the two-week period, what was the price, in dollars per ounce, by the end of the period?

   (A) $0.8x$
   (B) $0.95x$
   (C) x
   (D) $1.05x$
   (E) $1.25x$

37. In a certain pond, 50 fish were caught, tagged, and returned to the pond. A few days later, 50 fish were caught again, of which 2 were found to have been tagged. If the percent of tagged fish in the second catch approximates the percent of tagged fish in the pond, what is the approximate number of fish in the pond?

   (A)   400
   (B)   625
   (C)   1,250
   (D)   2,500
   (E)   10,000

38. $\sqrt{16 + 16} =$

   (A) $4\sqrt{2}$
   (B) $8\sqrt{2}$
   (C) $16\sqrt{2}$
   (D)   8
   (E)   16

39. The organizers of a fair projected a 25 percent increase in attendance this year over that of last year, but attendance this year actually decreased by 20 percent. What percent of the projected attendance was the actual attendance?

   (A)   45%
   (B)   56%
   (C)   64%
   (D)   75%
   (E)   80%

40. What is the ratio of $\frac{3}{4}$ to the product $4\left(\frac{3}{4}\right)$?

   (A) $\frac{1}{4}$

   (B) $\frac{1}{3}$

   (C) $\frac{4}{9}$

   (D) $\frac{9}{4}$

   (E)   4

41. If $3 - x = 2x - 3$, then $4x =$

(A) -24
(B) -8
(C) 0
(D) 8
(E) 24

$$2x + 2y = -4$$
$$4x + y = 1$$

42. In the system of equations above, what is the value of x ?

(A) -3
(B) -1
(C) $\dfrac{2}{5}$
(D) 1
(E) $1\dfrac{3}{4}$

43. If $x > 3{,}000$, then the value of $\dfrac{x}{2x+1}$ is closest to

(A) $\dfrac{1}{6}$
(B) $\dfrac{1}{3}$
(C) $\dfrac{10}{21}$
(D) $\dfrac{1}{2}$
(E) $\dfrac{3}{2}$

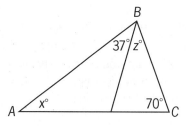

44. In $\triangle ABC$ above, what is x in terms of z ?

(A) $z + 73$
(B) $z - 73$
(C) $70 - z$
(D) $z - 70$
(E) $73 - z$

45. What is the maximum number of $1\dfrac{1}{4}$ foot pieces of wire that can be cut from a wire that is 24 feet long?

(A) 11
(B) 18
(C) 19
(D) 20
(E) 30

$$\frac{61.24 \times (0.998)^2}{\sqrt{403}}$$

46. The expression above is approximately equal to

(A) 1
(B) 3
(C) 4
(D) 5
(E) 6

47. If the numbers $\dfrac{17}{24}$, $\dfrac{1}{2}$, $\dfrac{3}{8}$, $\dfrac{3}{4}$, and $\dfrac{9}{16}$ were ordered from greatest to least, the middle number of the resulting sequence would be

(A) $\dfrac{17}{24}$
(B) $\dfrac{1}{2}$
(C) $\dfrac{3}{8}$
(D) $\dfrac{3}{4}$
(E) $\dfrac{9}{16}$

48. Last week Jack worked 70 hours and earned $1,260. If he earned his regular hourly wage for the first 40 hours worked, $1\frac{1}{2}$ times his regular hourly wage for the next 20 hours worked, and 2 times his regular hourly wage for the remaining 10 hours worked, what was his regular hourly wage?

(A) $7.00
(B) $14.00
(C) $18.00
(D) $22.00
(E) $31.50

49. Last year if 97 percent of the revenues of a company came from domestic sources and the remaining revenues, totaling $450,000, came from foreign sources, what was the total of the company's revenues?

(A) $1,350,000
(B) $1,500,000
(C) $4,500,000
(D) $15,000,000
(E) $150,000,000

50. $\dfrac{2+2\sqrt{6}}{2} =$

(A) $\sqrt{6}$
(B) $2\sqrt{6}$
(C) $1+\sqrt{6}$
(D) $1+2\sqrt{6}$
(E) $2+\sqrt{6}$

51. A certain fishing boat is chartered by 6 people who are to contribute equally to the total charter cost of $480. If each person contributes equally to a $150 down payment, how much of the charter cost will each person still owe?

(A) $80
(B) $66
(C) $55
(D) $50
(E) $45

52. Craig sells major appliances. For each appliance he sells, Craig receives a commission of $50 plus 10 percent of the selling price. During one particular week Craig sold 6 appliances for selling prices totaling $3,620. What was the total of Craig's commissions for that week?

(A) $412
(B) $526
(C) $585
(D) $605
(E) $662

53. What number when multiplied by $\frac{4}{7}$ yields $\frac{6}{7}$ as the result?

(A) $\dfrac{2}{7}$

(B) $\dfrac{3}{3}$

(C) $\dfrac{3}{2}$

(D) $\dfrac{24}{7}$

(E) $\dfrac{7}{2}$

54. If 3 pounds of dried apricots that cost x dollars per pound are mixed with 2 pounds of prunes that cost y dollars per pound, what is the cost, in dollars, per pound of the mixture?

(A) $\dfrac{3x+2y}{5}$

(B) $\dfrac{3x+2y}{x+y}$

(C) $\dfrac{3x+2y}{xy}$

(D) $5(3x+2y)$

(E) $3x+2y$

55. Which of the following must be equal to zero for all real numbers x ?

    I. $-\dfrac{1}{x}$

    II. $x+\left(-x\right)$

    III. x^0

    (A) I only
    (B) II only
    (C) I and III only
    (D) II and III only
    (E) I, II, and III

	City A	City B	City C	City D	City E	City F
City A						
City B						
City C						
City D						
City E						
City F						

56. In the table above, what is the least number of table entries that are needed to show the mileage between each city and each of the other five cities?

    (A) 15
    (B) 21
    (C) 25
    (D) 30
    (E) 36

57. If $\left(t-8\right)$ is a factor of $t^2 - kt - 48$, then $k =$

    (A) -6
    (B) -2
    (C) 2
    (D) 6
    (E) 14

58. $\dfrac{31}{125} =$

    (A) 0.248
    (B) 0.252
    (C) 0.284
    (D) 0.312
    (E) 0.320

59. Members of a social club met to address 280 newsletters. If they addressed $\dfrac{1}{4}$ of the newsletters during the first hour and $\dfrac{2}{5}$ of the remaining newsletters during the second hour, how many newsletters did they address during the second hour?

    (A) 28
    (B) 42
    (C) 63
    (D) 84
    (E) 112

60. $\dfrac{1}{3-\dfrac{1}{3-\dfrac{1}{3-1}}} =$

    (A) $\dfrac{7}{23}$

    (B) $\dfrac{5}{13}$

    (C) $\dfrac{2}{3}$

    (D) $\dfrac{23}{7}$

    (E) $\dfrac{13}{5}$

61. After 4,000 gallons of water were added to a large water tank that was already filled to $\dfrac{3}{4}$ of its capacity, the tank was then at $\dfrac{4}{5}$ of its capacity. How many gallons of water does the tank hold when filled to capacity?

    (A) 5,000
    (B) 6,200
    (C) 20,000
    (D) 40,000
    (E) 80,000

62. The sum of three integers is 40. The largest integer is 3 times the middle integer, and the smallest integer is 23 less than the largest integer. What is the product of the three integers?

    (A) 1,104
    (B) 972
    (C) 672
    (D) 294
    (E) 192

63. Five machines at a certain factory operate at the same constant rate. If four of these machines, operating simultaneously, take 30 hours to fill a certain production order, how many <u>fewer</u> hours does it take all five machines, operating simultaneously, to fill the same production order?

    (A) 3
    (B) 5
    (C) 6
    (D) 16
    (E) 24

64. If Mel saved more than $10 by purchasing a sweater at a 15 percent discount, what is the smallest amount the original price of the sweater could be, to the nearest dollar?

    (A) 45
    (B) 67
    (C) 75
    (D) 83
    (E) 150

65. If $d = 2.0453$ and d^* is the decimal obtained by rounding d to the nearest hundredth, what is the value of $d^* - d$?

    (A) -0.0053
    (B) -0.0003
    (C) 0.0007
    (D) 0.0047
    (E) 0.0153

66. At a monthly meeting, $\frac{2}{5}$ of the attendees were males and $\frac{7}{8}$ of the male attendees arrived on time. If $\frac{9}{10}$ of the female attendees arrived on time, what fraction of the attendees at the monthly meeting did <u>not</u> arrive on time?

    (A) $\frac{11}{100}$

    (B) $\frac{3}{25}$

    (C) $\frac{7}{50}$

    (D) $\frac{3}{20}$

    (E) $\frac{4}{25}$

67. The sequence a_1, a_2, a_3, a_4, a_5 is such that $a_n = a_{n-1} + 5$ for $2 \leq n \leq 5$. If $a_5 = 31$, what is the value of a_1 ?

    (A) 1
    (B) 6
    (C) 11
    (D) 16
    (E) 21

68. A certain bridge is 4,024 feet long. Approximately how many minutes does it take to cross this bridge at a constant speed of 20 miles per hour? (1 mile = 5,280 feet)

    (A) 1
    (B) 2
    (C) 4
    (D) 6
    (E) 7

69. If $S = \{0, 4, 5, 2, 11, 8\}$, how much greater than the median of the numbers in S is the mean of the numbers in S ?

    (A) 0.5
    (B) 1.0
    (C) 1.5
    (D) 2.0
    (E) 2.5

70. A total of 5 liters of gasoline is to be poured into two empty containers with capacities of 2 liters and 6 liters, respectively, such that both containers will be filled to the same percent of their respective capacities. What amount of gasoline, in liters, must be poured into the 6-liter container?

    (A) $4\frac{1}{2}$

    (B) 4

    (C) $3\frac{3}{4}$

    (D) 3

    (E) $1\frac{1}{4}$

71. When positive integer n is divided by 5, the remainder is 1. When n is divided by 7, the remainder is 3. What is the smallest positive integer k such that $k + n$ is a multiple of 35 ?

    (A)   3
    (B)   4
    (C)   12
    (D)   32
    (E)   35

72. List S consists of 10 consecutive odd integers, and list T consists of 5 consecutive even integers. If the least integer in S is 7 more than the least integer in T, how much greater is the average (arithmetic mean) of the integers in S than the average of the integers in T ?

    (A)   2
    (B)   7
    (C)   8
    (D)   12
    (E)   22

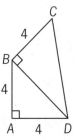

73. In the figure above, what is the area of triangular region BCD ?

    (A) $4\sqrt{2}$
    (B)   8
    (C) $8\sqrt{2}$
    (D)   16
    (E) $16\sqrt{2}$

74. Of the goose eggs laid at a certain pond, $\frac{2}{3}$ hatched, and $\frac{3}{4}$ of the geese that hatched from those eggs survived the first month. Of the geese that survived the first month, $\frac{3}{5}$ did <u>not</u> survive the first year. If 120 geese survived the first year and if no more than one goose hatched from each egg, how many goose eggs were laid at the pond?

    (A)   280
    (B)   400
    (C)   540
    (D)   600
    (E)   840

75. If $x^2 - 2x - 15 = 0$ and $x > 0$, which of the following must be equal to 0 ?

    I. $x^2 - 6x + 9$
    II. $x^2 - 7x + 10$
    III. $x^2 - 10x + 25$

    (A)   I only
    (B)   II only
    (C)   III only
    (D)   II and III only
    (E)   I, II, and III

76. If a square region has area n, what is the length of the diagonal of the square in terms of n ?

    (A) $\sqrt{2n}$
    (B) $\sqrt{n}$
    (C) $2\sqrt{n}$
    (D) $2n$
    (E) $2n^2$

77. The "prime sum" of an integer n greater than 1 is the sum of all the prime factors of n, including repetitions. For example, the prime sum of 12 is 7, since $12 = 2 \times 2 \times 3$ and $2 + 2 + 3 = 7$. For which of the following integers is the prime sum greater than 35 ?

    (A)   440
    (B)   512
    (C)   620
    (D)   700
    (E)   750

78. At a garage sale, all of the prices of the items sold were different. If the price of a radio sold at the garage sale was both the 15th highest price and the 20th lowest price among the prices of the items sold, how many items were sold at the garage sale?

    (A) 33
    (B) 34
    (C) 35
    (D) 36
    (E) 37

79. For all positive integers m and v, the expression $m \ominus v$ represents the remainder when m is divided by v. What is the value of $((98 \ominus 33) \ominus 17) - (98 \ominus (33 \ominus 17))$?

    (A) −10
    (B) −2
    (C) 8
    (D) 13
    (E) 17

80. In a certain sequence, each term after the first term is one-half the previous term. If the tenth term of the sequence is between 0.0001 and 0.001, then the twelfth term of the sequence is between

    (A) 0.0025 and 0.025
    (B) 0.00025 and 0.0025
    (C) 0.000025 and 0.00025
    (D) 0.0000025 and 0.000025
    (E) 0.00000025 and 0.0000025

81. Ada and Paul received their scores on three tests. On the first test, Ada's score was 10 points higher than Paul's score. On the second test, Ada's score was 4 points higher than Paul's score. If Paul's average (arithmetic mean) score on the three tests was 3 points higher than Ada's average score on the three tests, then Paul's score on the third test was how many points higher than Ada's score?

    (A) 9
    (B) 14
    (C) 17
    (D) 23
    (E) 25

82. The price of a certain stock increased by 0.25 of 1 percent on a certain day. By what fraction did the price of the stock increase that day?

    (A) $\dfrac{1}{2,500}$

    (B) $\dfrac{1}{400}$

    (C) $\dfrac{1}{40}$

    (D) $\dfrac{1}{25}$

    (E) $\dfrac{1}{4}$

83. Three business partners, Q, R, and S, agree to divide their total profit for a certain year in the ratios 2:5:8, respectively. If Q's share was $4,000, what was the total profit of the business partners for the year?

    (A) $26,000
    (B) $30,000
    (C) $52,000
    (D) $60,000
    (E) $300,000

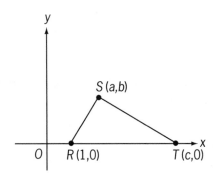

84. In the rectangular coordinate system above, the area of $\triangle RST$ is

    (A) $\dfrac{bc}{2}$

    (B) $\dfrac{b(c-1)}{2}$

    (C) $\dfrac{c(b-1)}{2}$

    (D) $\dfrac{a(c-1)}{2}$

    (E) $\dfrac{c(a-1)}{2}$

85. What is the largest integer n such that $\frac{1}{2^n} > 0.01$?

    (A) 5
    (B) 6
    (C) 7
    (D) 10
    (E) 51

86. The average (arithmetic mean) length per film for a group of 21 films is t minutes. If a film that runs for 66 minutes is removed from the group and replaced by one that runs for 52 minutes, what is the average length per film, in minutes, for the new group of films, in terms of t ?

    (A) $t + \frac{2}{3}$

    (B) $t - \frac{2}{3}$

    (C) $21t + 14$

    (D) $t + \frac{3}{2}$

    (E) $t - \frac{3}{2}$

87. If $x = -|w|$, which of the following must be true?

    (A) $x = -w$
    (B) $x = w$
    (C) $x^2 = w$
    (D) $x^2 = w^2$
    (E) $x^3 = w^3$

88. Which of the following lines in the xy-plane does <u>not</u> contain any point with integers as both coordinates?

    (A) $y = x$

    (B) $y = x + \frac{1}{2}$

    (C) $y = x + 5$

    (D) $y = \frac{1}{2}x$

    (E) $y = \frac{1}{2}x + 5$

89. One inlet pipe fills an empty tank in 5 hours. A second inlet pipe fills the same tank in 3 hours. If both pipes are used together, how long will it take to fill $\frac{2}{3}$ of the tank?

    (A) $\frac{8}{15}$ hr

    (B) $\frac{3}{4}$ hr

    (C) $\frac{5}{4}$ hr

    (D) $\frac{15}{8}$ hr

    (E) $\frac{8}{3}$ hr

90. $\left(\frac{1}{5}\right)^2 - \left(\frac{1}{5}\right)\left(\frac{1}{4}\right) =$

    (A) $-\frac{1}{20}$

    (B) $-\frac{1}{100}$

    (C) $\frac{1}{100}$

    (D) $\frac{1}{20}$

    (E) $\frac{1}{5}$

91. If the length and width of a rectangular garden plot were each increased by 20 percent, what would be the percent increase in the area of the plot?

    (A) 20%
    (B) 24%
    (C) 36%
    (D) 40%
    (E) 44%

92. The population of a bacteria culture doubles every 2 minutes. Approximately how many minutes will it take for the population to grow from 1,000 to 500,000 bacteria?

    (A) 10
    (B) 12
    (C) 14
    (D) 16
    (E) 18

93. For a light that has an intensity of 60 candles at its source, the intensity in candles, S, of the light at a point d feet from the source is given by the formula $S = \dfrac{60k}{d^2}$, where k is a constant. If the intensity of the light is 30 candles at a distance of 2 feet from the source, what is the intensity of the light at a distance of 20 feet from the source?

(A) $\dfrac{3}{10}$ candle

(B) $\dfrac{1}{2}$ candle

(C)   1 candle

(D)   2 candles

(E)   3 candles

$$\begin{array}{r} AB \\ +\ \ BA \\ \hline AAC \end{array}$$

94. In the correctly worked addition problem shown, where the sum of the two-digit positive integers AB and BA is the three-digit integer AAC, and A, B, and C are different digits, what is the units digit of the integer AAC?

(A)   9

(B)   6

(C)   3

(D)   2

(E)   0

$$3r \le 4s + 5$$

$$|s| \le 5$$

95. Given the inequalities above, which of the following CANNOT be the value of r?

(A)   −20

(B)   −5

(C)   0

(D)   5

(E)   20

96. A positive integer is divisible by 9 if and only if the sum of its digits is divisible by 9. If n is a positive integer, for which of the following values of k is $25 \times 10^n + k \times 10^{2n}$ divisible by 9?

(A)   9

(B)   16

(C)   23

(D)   35

(E)   47

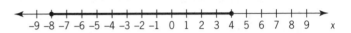

97. On the number line, the shaded interval is the graph of which of the following inequalities?

(A) $|x| \le 4$

(B) $|x| \le 8$

(C) $|x - 2| \le 4$

(D) $|x - 2| \le 6$

(E) $|x + 2| \le 6$

98. Of all the students in a certain dormitory, $\dfrac{1}{2}$ are first-year students and the rest are second-year students. If $\dfrac{4}{5}$ of the first-year students have <u>not</u> declared a major and if the fraction of second-year students who have declared a major is 3 times the fraction of first-year students who have declared a major, what fraction of all the students in the dormitory are second-year students who have <u>not</u> declared a major?

A. $\dfrac{1}{15}$

B. $\dfrac{1}{5}$

C. $\dfrac{4}{15}$

D. $\dfrac{1}{3}$

E. $\dfrac{2}{5}$

99. If the average (arithmetic mean) of x, y, and z is $7x$ and $x \neq 0$, what is the ratio of x to the sum of y and z?

   (A)   1:21
   (B)   1:20
   (C)   1:6
   (D)   6:1
   (E)   20:1

100. $\dfrac{(-1.5)(1.2)-(4.5)(0.4)}{30} =$

   (A)   −1.2
   (B)   −0.12
   (C)   0
   (D)   0.12
   (E)   1.2

101. René earns \$8.50 per hour on days other than Sundays and twice that rate on Sundays. Last week she worked a total of 40 hours, including 8 hours on Sunday. What were her earnings for the week?

   (A)   \$272
   (B)   \$340
   (C)   \$398
   (D)   \$408
   (E)   \$476

102. In a shipment of 120 machine parts, 5 percent were defective. In a shipment of 80 machine parts, 10 percent were defective. For the two shipments combined, what percent of the machine parts were defective?

   (A)   6.5%
   (B)   7.0%
   (C)   7.5%
   (D)   8.0%
   (E)   8.5%

103. If $8^{2x+3} = 2^{3x+6}$, then $x =$

   (A)   −3
   (B)   −1
   (C)   0
   (D)   1
   (E)   3

104. Of the following, the closest approximation to $\sqrt{\dfrac{5.98(601.5)}{15.79}}$ is

   (A)   5
   (B)   15
   (C)   20
   (D)   25
   (E)   225

105. Which of the following CANNOT be the greatest common divisor of two positive integers x and y?

   (A)   1
   (B) x
   (C) y
   (D) $x - y$
   (E) $x + y$

106. Last year Carlos saved 10 percent of his annual earnings. This year he earned 5 percent more than last year and he saved 12 percent of his annual earnings. The amount saved this year was what percent of the amount saved last year?

   (A)   122%
   (B)   124%
   (C)   126%
   (D)   128%
   (E)   130%

107. A corporation that had \$115.19 billion in profits for the year paid out \$230.10 million in employee benefits. Approximately what percent of the profits were the employee benefits? (Note: 1 billion $= 10^9$)

   (A)   50%
   (B)   20%
   (C)   5%
   (D)   2%
   (E)   0.2%

108. In the coordinate plane, line k passes through the origin and has slope 2. If points $(3,y)$ and $(x,4)$ are on line k, then $x + y =$

   (A)   3.5
   (B)   7
   (C)   8
   (D)   10
   (E)   14

109. If a, b, and c are constants, $a > b > c$, and $x^3 - x = (x-a)(x-b)(x-c)$ for all numbers x, what is the value of b ?

    (A) -3
    (B) -1
    (C) 0
    (D) 1
    (E) 3

110. On the number line, if $r < s$, if p is halfway between r and s, and if t is halfway between p and r, then $\dfrac{s-t}{t-r} =$

    (A) $\dfrac{1}{4}$

    (B) $\dfrac{1}{3}$

    (C) $\dfrac{4}{3}$

    (D) 3

    (E) 4

111. Company K's earnings were $12 million last year. If this year's earnings are projected to be 150 percent greater than last year's earnings, what are Company K's projected earnings this year?

    (A) $13.5 million
    (B) $15 million
    (C) $18 million
    (D) $27 million
    (E) $30 million

112. If $\dfrac{3}{x} = 2$ and $\dfrac{y}{4} = 3$, then $\dfrac{3+y}{x+4} =$

    (A) $\dfrac{10}{9}$

    (B) $\dfrac{3}{2}$

    (C) $\dfrac{20}{11}$

    (D) $\dfrac{30}{11}$

    (E) 5

113. $17^3 + 17^4 =$

    (A) 17^7
    (B) $17^3(18)$
    (C) $17^6(18)$
    (D) $2(17^3) + 17$
    (E) $2(17^3) - 17$

114. A certain clock marks every hour by striking a number of times equal to the hour, and the time required for a stroke is exactly equal to the time interval between strokes. At 6:00 the time lapse between the beginning of the first stroke and the end of the last stroke is 22 seconds. At 12:00, how many seconds elapse between the beginning of the first stroke and the end of the last stroke?

    (A) 72
    (B) 50
    (C) 48
    (D) 46
    (E) 44

115. What is the greatest number of identical bouquets that can be made out of 21 white and 91 red tulips if no flowers are to be left out? (Two bouquets are identical whenever the number of red tulips in the two bouquets is equal and the number of white tulips in the two bouquets is equal.)

    (A) 3
    (B) 4
    (C) 5
    (D) 6
    (E) 7

116. In the xy-plane, the points (c,d), $(c,-d)$, and $(-c,-d)$ are three vertices of a certain square. If $c < 0$ and $d > 0$, which of the following points is in the same quadrant as the fourth vertex of the square?

    (A) $(-5,-3)$
    (B) $(-5,3)$
    (C) $(5,-3)$
    (D) $(3,-5)$
    (E) $(3,5)$

117. For all numbers s and t, the operation $*$ is defined by $s*t = (s-1)(t+1)$. If $(-2)*x = -12$, then $x =$

    (A) 2
    (B) 3
    (C) 5
    (D) 6
    (E) 11

118. Salesperson A's compensation for any week is $360 plus 6 percent of the portion of A's total sales above $1,000 for that week. Salesperson B's compensation for any week is 8 percent of B's total sales for that week. For what amount of total weekly sales would both salespeople earn the same compensation?

    (A) $21,000

    (B) $18,000

    (C) $15,000

    (D) $4,500

    (E) $4,000

119. If $\dfrac{3}{10^4} = x\%$, then $x =$

    (A) 0.3
    (B) 0.03
    (C) 0.003
    (D) 0.0003
    (E) 0.00003

120. If a basketball team scores an average (arithmetic mean) of x points per game for n games and then scores y points in its next game, what is the team's average score for the $n+1$ games?

    (A) $\dfrac{nx+y}{n+1}$

    (B) $x + \dfrac{y}{n+1}$

    (C) $x + \dfrac{y}{n}$

    (D) $\dfrac{n(x+y)}{n+1}$

    (E) $\dfrac{x+ny}{n+1}$

121. If $xy > 0$ and $yz < 0$, which of the following must be negative?

    (A) xyz
    (B) xyz^2
    (C) xy^2z
    (D) xy^2z^2
    (E) $x^2y^2z^2$

122. At a certain pizzeria, $\dfrac{1}{8}$ of the pizzas sold in one week were mushroom and $\dfrac{1}{3}$ of the remaining pizzas sold were pepperoni. If n of the pizzas sold were pepperoni, how many were mushroom?

    (A) $\dfrac{3}{8}n$

    (B) $\dfrac{3}{7}n$

    (C) $\dfrac{7}{16}n$

    (D) $\dfrac{7}{8}n$

    (E) $3n$

123. Two trains, X and Y, started simultaneously from opposite ends of a 100-mile route and traveled toward each other on parallel tracks. Train X, traveling at a constant rate, completed the 100-mile trip in 5 hours; Train Y, traveling at a constant rate, completed the 100-mile trip in 3 hours. How many miles had Train X traveled when it met Train Y ?

    (A) 37.5
    (B) 40.0
    (C) 60.0
    (D) 62.5
    (E) 77.5

124. What is the value of $2x^2 - 2.4x - 1.7$ for $x = 0.7$?

    (A) -0.72
    (B) -1.42
    (C) -1.98
    (D) -2.40
    (E) -2.89

125. What is the remainder when 3^{24} is divided by 5 ?

    (A) 0
    (B) 1
    (C) 2
    (D) 3
    (E) 4

126. If the volume of a ball is 32,490 cubic millimeters, what is the volume of the ball in cubic centimeters? (1 millimeter = 0.1 centimeter)

    (A) 0.3249
    (B) 3.249
    (C) 32.49
    (D) 324.9
    (E) 3,249

127. David used part of $100,000 to purchase a house. Of the remaining portion, he invested $\frac{1}{3}$ of it at 4 percent simple annual interest and $\frac{2}{3}$ of it at 6 percent simple annual interest. If after a year the income from the two investments totaled $320, what was the purchase price of the house?

    (A) $96,000
    (B) $94,000
    (C) $88,000
    (D) $75,000
    (E) $40,000

128. The cost to rent a small bus for a trip is x dollars, which is to be shared equally among the people taking the trip. If 10 people take the trip rather than 16, how many more dollars, in terms of x, will it cost per person?

    (A) $\frac{x}{6}$

    (B) $\frac{x}{10}$

    (C) $\frac{x}{16}$

    (D) $\frac{3x}{40}$

    (E) $\frac{3x}{80}$

129. If x is an integer and $y = 3x + 2$, which of the following CANNOT be a divisor of y ?

    (A) 4
    (B) 5
    (C) 6
    (D) 7
    (E) 8

130. A certain electronic component is sold in boxes of 54 for $16.20 and in boxes of 27 for $13.20. A customer who needed only 54 components for a project had to buy 2 boxes of 27 because boxes of 54 were unavailable. Approximately how much more did the customer pay for each component due to the unavailability of the larger boxes?

    (A) $0.33
    (B) $0.19
    (C) $0.11
    (D) $0.06
    (E) $0.03

131. As a salesperson, Phyllis can choose one of two methods of annual payment: either an annual salary of $35,000 with no commission or an annual salary of $10,000 plus a 20 percent commission on her total annual sales. What must her total annual sales be to give her the same annual pay with either method?

    (A) $100,000
    (B) $120,000
    (C) $125,000
    (D) $130,000
    (E) $132,000

132. Last year Department Store X had a sales total for December that was 4 times the average (arithmetic mean) of the monthly sales totals for January through November. The sales total for December was what fraction of the sales total for the year?

    (A) $\frac{1}{4}$

    (B) $\frac{4}{15}$

    (C) $\frac{1}{3}$

    (D) $\frac{4}{11}$

    (E) $\frac{4}{5}$

133. Working alone, Printers X, Y, and Z can do a certain printing job, consisting of a large number of pages, in 12, 15, and 18 hours, respectively. What is the ratio of the time it takes Printer X to do the job, working alone at its rate, to the time it takes Printers Y and Z to do the job, working together at their individual rates?

(A) $\dfrac{4}{11}$

(B) $\dfrac{1}{2}$

(C) $\dfrac{15}{22}$

(D) $\dfrac{22}{15}$

(E) $\dfrac{11}{4}$

134. In the sequence x_0, x_1, x_2, ..., x_n, each term from x_1 to x_k is 3 greater than the previous term, and each term from x_{k+1} to x_n is 3 less than the previous term, where n and k are positive integers and $k < n$. If $x_0 = x_n = 0$ and if $x_k = 15$, what is the value of n?

(A)   5
(B)   6
(C)   9
(D)   10
(E)   15

135. If $x \neq 2$, then $\dfrac{3x^2(x-2)-x+2}{x-2} =$

(A) $3x^2 - x + 2$
(B) $3x^2 + 1$
(C) $3x^2$
(D) $3x^2 - 1$
(E) $3x^2 - 2$

Note: Not drawn to scale.

136. In the figure shown above, line segment QR has length 12, and rectangle $MPQT$ is a square. If the area of rectangular region $MPRS$ is 540, what is the area of rectangular region $TQRS$?

(A)   144
(B)   216
(C)   324
(D)   360
(E)   396

137. A train travels from New York City to Chicago, a distance of approximately 840 miles, at an average rate of 60 miles per hour and arrives in Chicago at 6:00 in the evening, Chicago time. At what hour in the morning, New York City time, did the train depart for Chicago? (Note: Chicago time is one hour earlier than New York City time.)

(A)   4:00
(B)   5:00
(C)   6:00
(D)   7:00
(E)   8:00

138. Last year Manfred received 26 paychecks. Each of his first 6 paychecks was $750; each of his remaining paychecks was $30 more than each of his first 6 paychecks. To the nearest dollar, what was the average (arithmetic mean) amount of his paychecks for the year?

(A) $752
(B) $755
(C) $765
(D) $773
(E) $775

139. Machines A and B always operate independently and at their respective constant rates. When working alone, Machine A can fill a production lot in 5 hours, and Machine B can fill the same lot in x hours. When the two machines operate simultaneously to fill the production lot, it takes them 2 hours to complete the job. What is the value of x ?

    (A) $3\frac{1}{3}$

    (B) 3

    (C) $2\frac{1}{2}$

    (D) $2\frac{1}{3}$

    (E) $1\frac{1}{2}$

140. A driver completed the first 20 miles of a 40-mile trip at an average speed of 50 miles per hour. At what average speed must the driver complete the remaining 20 miles to achieve an average speed of 60 miles per hour for the entire 40-mile trip? (Assume that the driver did not make any stops during the 40-mile trip.)

    (A) 65 mph
    (B) 68 mph
    (C) 70 mph
    (D) 75 mph
    (E) 80 mph

141. The figure shown above consists of three identical circles that are tangent to each other. If the area of the shaded region is $64\sqrt{3} - 32\pi$, what is the radius of each circle?

    (A) 4
    (B) 8
    (C) 16
    (D) 24
    (E) 32

142. A positive integer n is a perfect number provided that the sum of all the positive factors of n, including 1 and n, is equal to $2n$. What is the sum of the reciprocals of all the positive factors of the perfect number 28 ?

    (A) $\frac{1}{4}$

    (B) $\frac{56}{27}$

    (C) 2
    (D) 3
    (E) 4

143. The infinite sequence $a_1, a_2, \ldots, a_n, \ldots$ is such that $a_1 = 2$, $a_2 = -3$, $a_3 = 5$, $a_4 = -1$, and $a_n = a_{n-4}$ for $n > 4$. What is the sum of the first 97 terms of the sequence?

    (A) 72
    (B) 74
    (C) 75
    (D) 78
    (E) 80

144. The sequence $a_1, a_2, \ldots, a_n, \ldots$ is such that $a_n = 2a_{n-1} - x$ for all positive integers $n \geq 2$ and for a certain number x. If $a_5 = 99$ and $a_3 = 27$, what is the value of x ?

    (A) 3
    (B) 9
    (C) 18
    (D) 36
    (E) 45

145. A window is in the shape of a regular hexagon with each side of length 80 centimeters. If a diagonal through the center of the hexagon is w centimeters long, then $w =$

    (A) 80
    (B) 120
    (C) 150
    (D) 160
    (E) 240

146. On a certain transatlantic crossing, 20 percent of a ship's passengers held round-trip tickets and also took their cars aboard the ship. If 60 percent of the passengers with round-trip tickets did <u>not</u> take their cars aboard the ship, what percent of the ship's passengers held round-trip tickets?

(A) $33\frac{1}{3}\%$

(B) 40%
(C) 50%
(D) 60%
(E) $66\frac{2}{3}\%$

147. If x and k are integers and $\left(12^{x}\right)\left(4^{2x+1}\right)=\left(2^{k}\right)\left(3^{2}\right)$, what is the value of k ?

(A) 5
(B) 7
(C) 10
(D) 12
(E) 14

148. For every even positive integer m, $f(m)$ represents the product of all even integers from 2 to m, inclusive. For example, $f(12)=2\times4\times6\times8\times10\times12$. What is the greatest prime factor of $f(24)$?

(A) 23
(B) 19
(C) 17
(D) 13
(E) 11

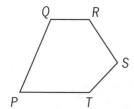

Note: Not drawn to scale.

149. In pentagon $PQRST$, $PQ=3$, $QR=2$, $RS=4$, and $ST=5$. Which of the lengths 5, 10, and 15 could be the value of PT ?

(A) 5 only
(B) 15 only
(C) 5 and 10 only
(D) 10 and 15 only
(E) 5, 10, and 15

$$3, k, 2, 8, m, 3$$

150. The arithmetic mean of the list of numbers above is 4. If k and m are integers and $k \neq m$, what is the median of the list?

(A) 2
(B) 2.5
(C) 3
(D) 3.5
(E) 4

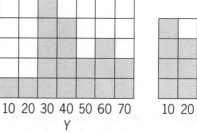

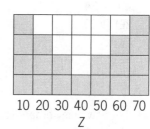

151. If the variables, X, Y, and Z take on only the values 10, 20, 30, 40, 50, 60, or 70 with frequencies indicated by the shaded regions above, for which of the frequency distributions is the mean equal to the median?

(A) X only
(B) Y only
(C) Z only
(D) X and Y
(E) X and Z

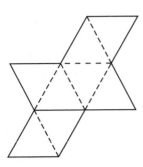

152. When the figure above is cut along the solid lines, folded along the dashed lines, and taped along the solid lines, the result is a model of a geometric solid. This geometric solid consists of 2 pyramids, each with a square base that they share. What is the sum of the number of edges and the number of faces of this geometric solid?

    (A) 10
    (B) 18
    (C) 20
    (D) 24
    (E) 25

$$2x + y = 12$$
$$|y| \leq 12$$

153. For how many ordered pairs (x,y) that are solutions of the system above are x and y both integers?

    (A)   7
    (B) 10
    (C) 12
    (D) 13
    (E) 14

154. The points R, T, and U lie on a circle that has radius 4. If the length of arc RTU is $\frac{4\pi}{3}$, what is the length of line segment RU?

    (A) $\frac{4}{3}$

    (B) $\frac{8}{3}$

    (C) 3
    (D) 4
    (E) 6

155. A certain university will select 1 of 7 candidates eligible to fill a position in the mathematics department and 2 of 10 candidates eligible to fill 2 identical positions in the computer science department. If none of the candidates is eligible for a position in both departments, how many different sets of 3 candidates are there to fill the 3 positions?

    (A)   42
    (B)   70
    (C) 140
    (D) 165
    (E) 315

156. A survey of employers found that during 1993 employment costs rose 3.5 percent, where employment costs consist of salary costs and fringe-benefit costs. If salary costs rose 3 percent and fringe-benefit costs rose 5.5 percent during 1993, then fringe-benefit costs represented what percent of employment costs at the beginning of 1993?

    (A) 16.5%
    (B) 20%
    (C) 35%
    (D) 55%
    (E) 65%

157. The subsets of the set {w, x, y} are {w}, {x}, {y}, {w, x}, {w, y}, {x, y}, {w, x, y}, and { } (the empty subset). How many subsets of the set {w, x, y, z} contain w ?

   (A)   Four
   (B)   Five
   (C)   Seven
   (D)   Eight
   (E)   Sixteen

158. There are 10 books on a shelf, of which 4 are paperbacks and 6 are hardbacks. How many possible selections of 5 books from the shelf contain at least one paperback and at least one hardback?

   (A)   75
   (B)   120
   (C)   210
   (D)   246
   (E)   252

159. If x is to be chosen at random from the set {1, 2, 3, 4} and y is to be chosen at random from the set {5, 6, 7}, what is the probability that xy will be even?

   (A) $\dfrac{1}{6}$

   (B) $\dfrac{1}{3}$

   (C) $\dfrac{1}{2}$

   (D) $\dfrac{2}{3}$

   (E) $\dfrac{5}{6}$

160. The function f is defined for each positive three-digit integer n by $f(n) = 2^x\, 3^y\, 5^z$, where x, y, and z are the hundreds, tens, and units digits of n, respectively. If m and v are three-digit positive integers such that $f(m) = 9f(v)$, then $m - v =$

   (A)   8
   (B)   9
   (C)   18
   (D)   20
   (E)   80

161. If $10^{50} - 74$ is written as an integer in base 10 notation, what is the sum of the digits in that integer?

   (A)   424
   (B)   433
   (C)   440
   (D)   449
   (E)   467

162. A certain company that sells only cars and trucks reported that revenues from car sales in 1997 were down 11 percent from 1996 and revenues from truck sales in 1997 were up 7 percent from 1996. If total revenues from car sales and truck sales in 1997 were up 1 percent from 1996, what is the ratio of revenue from car sales in 1996 to revenue from truck sales in 1996 ?

   (A)   1:2
   (B)   4:5
   (C)   1:1
   (D)   3:2
   (E)   5:3

163. If $4 < \dfrac{7-x}{3}$, which of the following must be true?

   I. $5 < x$
   II. $|x + 3| > 2$
   III. $-(x + 5)$ is positive.

   (A)   II only
   (B)   III only
   (C)   I and II only
   (D)   II and III only
   (E)   I, II, and III

164. A certain right triangle has sides of length x, y, and z, where $x < y < z$. If the area of this triangular region is 1, which of the following indicates all of the possible values of y ?

   (A) $y > \sqrt{2}$

   (B) $\dfrac{\sqrt{3}}{2} < y < \sqrt{2}$

   (C) $\dfrac{\sqrt{2}}{3} < y < \dfrac{\sqrt{3}}{2}$

   (D) $\dfrac{\sqrt{3}}{4} < y < \dfrac{\sqrt{2}}{3}$

   (E) $y < \dfrac{\sqrt{3}}{4}$

165. A set of numbers has the property that for any number t in the set, $t + 2$ is in the set. If -1 is in the set, which of the following must also be in the set?

    I. -3
    II. 1
    III. 5

    (A) I only
    (B) II only
    (C) I and II only
    (D) II and III only
    (E) I, II, and III

166. A couple decides to have 4 children. If they succeed in having 4 children and each child is equally likely to be a boy or a girl, what is the probability that they will have exactly 2 girls and 2 boys?

    (A) $\dfrac{3}{8}$

    (B) $\dfrac{1}{4}$

    (C) $\dfrac{3}{16}$

    (D) $\dfrac{1}{8}$

    (E) $\dfrac{1}{16}$

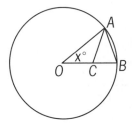

167. In the figure above, point O is the center of the circle and $OC = AC = AB$. What is the value of x ?

    (A) 40
    (B) 36
    (C) 34
    (D) 32
    (E) 30

168. When 10 is divided by the positive integer n, the remainder is $n - 4$. Which of the following could be the value of n ?

    (A) 3
    (B) 4
    (C) 7
    (D) 8
    (E) 12

169. An airline passenger is planning a trip that involves three connecting flights that leave from Airports A, B, and C, respectively. The first flight leaves Airport A every hour, beginning at 8:00 a.m., and arrives at Airport B $2\frac{1}{2}$ hours later. The second flight leaves Airport B every 20 minutes, beginning at 8:00 a.m., and arrives at Airport C $1\frac{1}{6}$ hours later. The third flight leaves Airport C every hour, beginning at 8:45 a.m. What is the least total amount of time the passenger must spend between flights if all flights keep to their schedules?

    (A) 25 min
    (B) 1 hr 5 min
    (C) 1 hr 15 min
    (D) 2 hr 20 min
    (E) 3 hr 40 min

170. If n is a positive integer and n^2 is divisible by 72, then the largest positive integer that must divide n is

    (A) 6
    (B) 12
    (C) 24
    (D) 36
    (E) 48

171. If n is a positive integer and $k + 2 = 3^n$, which of the following could NOT be a value of k ?

    (A) 1
    (B) 4
    (C) 7
    (D) 25
    (E) 79

172. A certain grocery purchased x pounds of produce for p dollars per pound. If y pounds of the produce had to be discarded due to spoilage and the grocery sold the rest for s dollars per pound, which of the following represents the gross profit on the sale of the produce?

(A) $(x-y)s - xp$

(B) $(x-y)p - ys$

(C) $(s-p)y - xp$

(D) $xp - ys$

(E) $(x-y)(s-p)$

173. If x, y, and z are positive integers such that x is a factor of y, and x is a multiple of z, which of the following is NOT necessarily an integer?

(A) $\dfrac{x+z}{z}$

(B) $\dfrac{y+z}{x}$

(C) $\dfrac{x+y}{z}$

(D) $\dfrac{xy}{z}$

(E) $\dfrac{yz}{x}$

174. Running at their respective constant rates, Machine X takes 2 days longer to produce w widgets than Machine Y. At these rates, if the two machines together produce $\dfrac{5}{4}w$ widgets in 3 days, how many days would it take Machine X alone to produce $2w$ widgets?

(A) 4

(B) 6

(C) 8

(D) 10

(E) 12

175. A square wooden plaque has a square brass inlay in the center, leaving a wooden strip of uniform width around the brass square. If the ratio of the brass area to the wooden area is 25 to 39, which of the following could be the width, in inches, of the wooden strip?

I.   1

II.   3

III.   4

(A) I only

(B) II only

(C) I and II only

(D) I and III only

(E) I, II, and III

176. $\dfrac{2\frac{3}{5} - 1\frac{2}{3}}{\frac{2}{3} - \frac{3}{5}} =$

(A) 16

(B) 14

(C) 3

(D) 1

(E) -1

4.4 Answer Key

1.	E	36.	C	71.	B	106.	C	141.	B
2.	C	37.	C	72.	D	107.	E	142.	C
3.	A	38.	A	73.	C	108.	C	143.	B
4.	C	39.	C	74.	D	109.	C	144.	A
5.	C	40.	A	75.	D	110.	D	145.	D
6.	C	41.	D	76.	A	111.	E	146.	C
7.	E	42.	D	77.	C	112.	D	147.	E
8.	B	43.	D	78.	B	113.	B	148.	E
9.	C	44.	E	79.	D	114.	D	149.	C
10.	D	45.	C	80.	C	115.	E	150.	C
11.	C	46.	B	81.	D	116.	E	151.	E
12.	C	47.	E	82.	B	117.	B	152.	C
13.	B	48.	B	83.	B	118.	C	153.	D
14.	C	49.	D	84.	B	119.	B	154.	D
15.	A	50.	C	85.	B	120.	A	155.	E
16.	C	51.	C	86.	B	121.	C	156.	B
17.	E	52.	E	87.	D	122.	B	157.	D
18.	D	53.	C	88.	B	123.	A	158.	D
19.	E	54.	A	89.	C	124.	D	159.	D
20.	D	55.	B	90.	B	125.	B	160.	D
21.	C	56.	A	91.	E	126.	C	161.	C
22.	D	57.	C	92.	E	127.	B	162.	A
23.	B	58.	A	93.	A	128.	E	163.	D
24.	E	59.	D	94.	E	129.	C	164.	A
25.	A	60.	B	95.	E	130.	B	165.	D
26.	A	61.	E	96.	E	131.	C	166.	A
27.	D	62.	B	97.	E	132.	B	167.	B
28.	C	63.	C	98.	B	133.	D	168.	C
29.	D	64.	B	99.	B	134.	D	169.	B
30.	E	65.	D	100.	B	135.	D	170.	B
31.	E	66.	A	101.	D	136.	B	171.	B
32.	C	67.	C	102.	B	137.	B	172.	A
33.	D	68.	B	103.	B	138.	D	173.	B
34.	A	69.	A	104.	B	139.	A	174.	E
35.	C	70.	C	105.	E	140.	D	175.	E
								176.	B

4.5 Answer Explanations

The following discussion is intended to familiarize you with the most efficient and effective approaches to the kinds of problems common to problem solving questions. The particular questions in this chapter are generally representative of the kinds of problem solving questions you will encounter on the GMAT. Remember that it is the problem solving strategy that is important, not the specific details of a particular question.

1. Points A, B, C, and D, in that order, lie on a line. If AB = 3 cm, AC = 4 cm, and BD = 6 cm, what is CD, in centimeters?

    (A) 1
    (B) 2
    (C) 3
    (D) 4
    (E) 5

    Geometry Lines and segments

    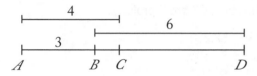

    The figure shows points A, B, C, and D as well as the given measurements. Since $AC = AB + BC$, it follows that $4 = 3 + BC$, and so $BC = 1$. Then, since $BD = BC + CD$, it follows that $6 = 1 + CD$, and so $CD = 5$.

    Alternately, $AD = AB + BD = 3 + 6 = 9$. Also, $AD = AC + CD$, so $9 = 4 + CD$ and $CD = 5$.

    The correct answer is E.

2. What is the value of $x^2yz - xyz^2$, if $x = -2$, $y = 1$, and $z = 3$?

    (A) 20
    (B) 24
    (C) 30
    (D) 32
    (E) 48

    Algebra Operations on integers

    Given that $x = -2$, $y = 1$, and $z = 3$, it follows by substitution that

$$
\begin{aligned}
x^2yz - xyz^2 &= (-2)^2(1)(3) - (-2)(1)(3^2) \\
&= (4)(1)(3) - (-2)(1)(9) \\
&= 12 - (-18) \\
&= 12 + 18 \\
&= 30
\end{aligned}
$$

The correct answer is C.

3. If x > y and y > z, which of the following represents the greatest number?

    (A) $x - z$
    (B) $x - y$
    (C) $y - x$
    (D) $z - y$
    (E) $z - x$

    Algebra Inequalities

    From $x > y$ and $y > z$, it follows that $x > z$. These inequalities imply the following about the differences that are given in the answer choices:

Answer choice	Difference	Algebraic sign	Reason
(A)	$x - z$	positive	$x > z$ implies $x - z > 0$
(B)	$x - y$	positive	$x > y$ implies $x - y > 0$
(C)	$y - x$	negative	$x - y > 0$ implies $y - x < 0$
(D)	$z - y$	negative	$y > z$ implies $0 > z - y$
(E)	$z - x$	negative	$x - z > 0$ implies $z - x < 0$

Since the expressions in A and B represent positive numbers and the expressions in C, D, and E represent negative numbers, the latter can be eliminated because every negative number is less than every positive number. To determine which of $x - z$ and $x - y$ is greater, consider the placement of points with coordinates x, y, and z on the number line.

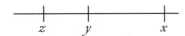

The distance between x and z (that is, $x - z$) is the sum of the distance between x and y (that is, $x - y$) and the distance between y and z (that is, $y - z$). Therefore, $(x - z) > (x - y)$, which means that $x - z$ represents the greater of the numbers represented by $(x - z)$ and $(x - y)$. Thus, $x - z$ represents the greatest of the numbers represented by the answer choices.

Alternatively,

$y > z$	given
$-y < -z$	multiply both sides by -1
$x - y < x - z$	add x to both sides

Thus, $x - z$ represents the greater of the numbers represented by $(x - z)$ and $(x - y)$. Therefore, $x - z$ represents the greatest of the numbers represented by the answer choices.

The correct answer is A.

4. To order certain plants from a catalog, it costs $3.00 per plant, plus a 5 percent sales tax, plus $6.95 for shipping and handling regardless of the number of plants ordered. If Company C ordered these plants from the catalog at the total cost of $69.95, how many plants did Company C order?

(A) 22
(B) 21
(C) 20
(D) 19
(E) 18

Algebra First-degree equations

Letting x represent the number of plants Company C bought from the catalog, then, in dollars, $3.00x$ is the cost of the plants,

$(0.05)(3.00x)$ is the sales tax, and 6.95 is the shipping and handling fee. It follows that

$3.00x + (0.05)(3.00x) + 6.95 =$	69.95	plants + tax + shipping = total
$(3.00x)(1.05) + 6.95 =$	69.95	add like terms
$(3.00x)(1.05) =$	63.00	subtract 6.95 from both sides
$x =$	20	divide both sides by $(3.00)(1.05)$

Therefore, Company C bought 20 plants from the catalog.

The correct answer is C.

5. Company C produces toy trucks at a cost of $5.00 each for the first 100 trucks and $3.50 for each additional truck. If 500 toy trucks were produced by Company C and sold for $10.00 each, what was Company C's gross profit?

(A) $2,250
(B) $2,500
(C) $3,100
(D) $3,250
(E) $3,500

Arithmetic Applied problems

The company's gross profit on the 500 toy trucks is the company's revenue from selling the trucks minus the company's cost of producing the trucks. The revenue is $(500)($10.00) = $5,000$. The cost for the first 100 trucks is $(100)($5.00) = 500, and the cost for the other 400 trucks is $(400)($3.50) = $1,400$ for a total cost of $500 + $1,400 = $1,900$. Thus, the company's gross profit is $5,000 - $1,900 = $3,100$.

The correct answer is C.

6. A group of store managers must assemble 280 displays for an upcoming sale. If they assemble 25 percent of the displays during the first hour and 40 percent of the remaining displays during the second hour, how many of the displays will <u>not</u> have been assembled by the end of the second hour?

    (A)   70
    (B)   98
    (C)   126
    (D)   168
    (E)   182

Arithmetic Percents

If, during the first hour, 25 percent of the total displays were assembled, then $280(0.25) = 70$ displays were assembled, leaving $280 - 70 = 210$ displays remaining to be assembled. Since 40 percent of the remaining displays were assembled during the second hour, $0.40(210) = 84$ displays were assembled during the second hour. Thus, $70 + 84 = 154$ displays were assembled during the first two hours and $280 - 154 = 126$ displays had not been assembled by the end of the second hour.

The correct answer is C.

7. Of the following, which is least?

    A. $\dfrac{0.03}{0.00071}$

    B. $\dfrac{0.03}{0.0071}$

    C. $\dfrac{0.03}{0.071}$

    D. $\dfrac{0.03}{0.71}$

    E. $\dfrac{0.03}{7.1}$

Arithmetic Operations on rational numbers

Since the numerator of all of the fractions in the answer choices is 0.03, the least of the fractions will be the fraction with the greatest denominator. The greatest denominator is 7.1,

and so the least of the fractions is $\dfrac{0.03}{7.1}$.

The correct answer is E.

8. The maximum recommended pulse rate R, when exercising, for a person who is x years of age is given by the equation $R = 176 - 0.8x$. What is the age, in years, of a person whose maximum recommended pulse rate when exercising is 140 ?

    (A)   40
    (B)   45
    (C)   50
    (D)   55
    (E)   60

Algebra Substitution; Operations with rational numbers

Substitute 140 for R in the given equation and solve for x.

$$140 = 176 - 0.8x$$

$$-36 = -0.8x$$

$$\frac{-36}{-0.8} = x$$

$$45 = x$$

The correct answer is B.

9. There are five sales agents in a certain real estate office. One month Andy sold twice as many properties as Ellen, Bob sold 3 more than Ellen, Cary sold twice as many as Bob, and Dora sold as many as Bob and Ellen together. Who sold the most properties that month?

    (A)   Andy
    (B)   Bob
    (C)   Cary
    (D)   Dora
    (E)   Ellen

Algebra Order

Let x represent the number of properties that Ellen sold, where $x \geq 0$. Then, since Andy sold twice as many properties as Ellen, $2x$ represents the number of properties that Andy sold. Bob sold 3 more properties than Ellen, so $(x + 3)$ represents the number of properties that Bob sold. Cary sold twice as many properties as Bob, so $2(x + 3) = (2x + 6)$ represents the number of properties that Cary sold. Finally, Dora sold as many properties as Bob and Ellen combined, so $[(x + 3) + x] = (2x + 3)$ represents the number of properties that Dora sold. The following table summarizes these results.

Agent	Properties sold
Andy	$2x$
Bob	$x + 3$
Cary	$2x + 6$
Dora	$2x + 3$
Ellen	x

Since $x \geq 0$, clearly $2x + 6$ exceeds x, $x + 3$, $2x$, and $2x + 3$. Therefore, Cary sold the most properties.

The correct answer is C.

10. Which of the following represent positive numbers?

   I. $-3 - (-5)$

   II. $(-3)(-5)$

   III. $-5 - (-3)$

(A) I only
(B) II only
(C) III only
(D) I and II
(E) II and III

Arithmetic Operations on integers

Find the value of each expression to determine if it is positive.

  I. $-3 - (-5) = -3 + 5 = 2$, which is positive.

  II. $(-3)(-5) = 15$, which is positive.

  III. $-5 - (-3) = -5 + 3 = -2$, which is not positive.

The correct answer is D.

11. If $\frac{x}{4}$ is 2 more than $\frac{x}{8}$, then $x =$

(A) 4
(B) 8
(C) 16
(D) 32
(E) 64

Algebra First-degree equations

Write an equation for the given information and solve for x.

$$\frac{x}{4} = 2 + \frac{x}{8}$$

$$(8)\left(\frac{x}{4}\right) = (8)\left(2 + \frac{x}{8}\right)$$

$$2x = 16 + x$$

$$x = 16$$

The correct answer is C.

12. If Mario was 32 years old 8 years ago, how old was he x years ago?

(A) $x - 40$
(B) $x - 24$
(C) $40 - x$
(D) $24 - x$
(E) $24 + x$

Arithmetic Operations on rational numbers

Since Mario was 32 years old 8 years ago, his age now is $32 + 8 = 40$ years old. Therefore, x years ago Mario was $40 - x$ years old.

The correct answer is C.

13. The toll T, in dollars, for a truck using a certain bridge is given by the formula $T = 1.50 + 0.50(x - 2)$, where x is the number of axles on the truck. What is the toll for an 18-wheel truck that has 2 wheels on its front axle and 4 wheels on each of its other axles?

(A) $2.50
(B) $3.00
(C) $3.50
(D) $4.00
(E) $5.00

Algebra Operations on rational numbers

The 18-wheel truck has 2 wheels on its front axle and 4 wheels on each of its other axles, and so if A represents the number of axles on the truck in addition to the front axle, then $2 + 4A = 18$, from which it follows that $4A = 16$ and $A = 4$.

Therefore, the total number of axles on the truck is $1 + A = 1 + 4 = 5$. Then, using $T = 1.50 + 0.50(x - 2)$, where x is the number of axles on the truck and $x = 5$, it follows that $T = 1.50 + 0.50(5 - 2) = 1.50 + 1.50 = 3.00$. Therefore, the toll for the truck is \$3.00.

The correct answer is B.

14. If $\left(b - 3\right)\left(4 + \dfrac{2}{b}\right) = 0$ and $b \neq 3$, then $b =$

(A) -8

(B) -2

(C) $-\dfrac{1}{2}$

(D) $\dfrac{1}{2}$

(E) 2

Algebra Second-degree equations

If $\left(b - 3\right)\left(4 + \dfrac{2}{b}\right) = 0$, then $b - 3 = 0$ or $4 + \dfrac{2}{b} = 0$. Since $b \neq 3$, then $b - 3 \neq 0$ and so $4 + \dfrac{2}{b} = 0$. Solve for b.

$$4 + \frac{2}{b} = 0$$
$$\frac{2}{b} = -4$$
$$2 = -4b$$
$$-\frac{1}{2} = b$$

The correct answer is C.

15. For what value of x between -4 and 4, inclusive, is the value of $x^2 - 10x + 16$ the greatest?

(A) -4
(B) -2
(C) 0
(D) 2
(E) 4

Algebra Second-degree equations

Given the expression $x^2 - 10x + 16$, a table of values can be created for the corresponding function $f(x) = x^2 - 10x + 16$ and the graph in the standard (x,y) coordinate plane can be sketched by plotting selected points:

x	$f(x)$
-4	72
-3	55
-2	40
-1	27
0	16
1	7
2	0
3	-5
4	-8
5	-9
6	-8
7	-5
8	0
9	7

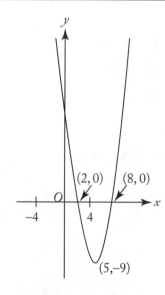

It is clear from both the table of values and the sketch of the graph that as the value of x increases from -4 to 4, the values of $x^2 - 10x + 16$ decrease. Therefore, the value of $x^2 - 10x + 16$ is greatest when $x = -4$.

Alternatively, the given expression, $x^2 - 10x + 16$, has the form $ax^2 + bx + c$, where $a = 1$, $b = -10$, and $c = 16$. The graph in the standard (x,y) coordinate plane of the corresponding function $f(x) = ax^2 + bx + c$ is a parabola with vertex at $x = -\dfrac{b}{2a}$, and so the vertex of the graph of $f(x) = x^2 - 10x + 16$ is at

$$x = -\left(\frac{-10}{2(1)}\right) = 5.$$

Because $a = 1$ and 1 is positive, this parabola opens upward and values of $x^2 - 10x + 16$ decrease as x increases from -4 to 4. Therefore, the greatest value of $x^2 - 10x + 16$ for all values of x between -4 and 4, inclusive, is at $x = -4$.

The correct answer is A.

16. The number $2 - 0.5$ is how many times the number $1 - 0.5$?

(A) 2
(B) 2.5
(C) 3
(D) 3.5
(E) 4

Arithmetic Operations on rational numbers

Set up an equation in the order given in the problem, and solve for x.

$$\left(2 - 0.5\right) = \left(1 - 0.5\right)x$$

$$1.5 = 0.5x$$

$$3 = x$$

The correct answer is C.

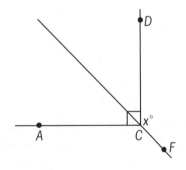

17. In the figure above, if F is a point on the line that bisects angle ACD and the measure of angle DCF is $x°$, which of the following is true of x?

(A) $90 \le x < 100$
(B) $100 \le x < 110$
(C) $110 \le x < 120$
(D) $120 \le x < 130$
(E) $130 \le x < 140$

Geometry Angles

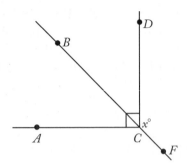

As shown in the figure above, if B is on the line that bisects $\angle ACD$, then the degree measure of $\angle DCB$ is $\dfrac{90}{2} = 45$. Then because B, C, and F are collinear, the sum of the degree measures of $\angle BCD$ and $\angle DCF$ is 180. Therefore, $x = 180 - 45 = 135$ and $130 \le 135 < 140$.

The correct answer is E.

18. In which of the following pairs are the two numbers reciprocals of each other?

I.   3 and $\dfrac{1}{3}$

II. $\dfrac{1}{17}$ and $\dfrac{-1}{17}$

III. $\sqrt{3}$ and $\dfrac{\sqrt{3}}{3}$

(A)   I only
(B)   II only
(C)   I and II
(D)   I and III
(E)   II and III

Arithmetic Properties of numbers (reciprocals)

Two numbers are reciprocals of each other if and only if their product is 1.

I. $3\left(\dfrac{1}{3}\right) = 1$ reciprocals

II. $\left(\dfrac{1}{17}\right)\left(-\dfrac{1}{17}\right) = -\dfrac{1}{(17)(17)}$ not reciprocals

III. $\left(\sqrt{3}\right)\left(\dfrac{\sqrt{3}}{3}\right) = \dfrac{3}{3} = 1$ reciprocals

The correct answer is D.

19. A rope 20.6 meters long is cut into two pieces. If the length of one piece of rope is 2.8 meters shorter than the length of the other, what is the length, in meters, of the longer piece of rope?

    (A)   7.5
    (B)   8.9
    (C)   9.9
    (D)   10.3
    (E)   11.7

Algebra First-order equations

If x represents the length of the longer piece of rope, then $x - 2.8$ represents the length of the shorter piece, where both lengths are in meters. The total length of the two pieces of rope is 20.6 meters so,

$$
\begin{aligned}
x + (x - 2.8) &= 20.6 && \text{given} \\
2x - 2.8 &= 20.6 && \text{add like terms} \\
2x &= 23.4 && \text{add 2.8 to both sides} \\
x &= 11.7 && \text{divide both sides by 2}
\end{aligned}
$$

Thus, the length of the longer piece of rope is 11.7 meters.

The correct answer is E.

20. What is the perimeter, in meters, of a rectangular garden 6 meters wide that has the same area as a rectangular playground 16 meters long and 12 meters wide?

    (A)   48
    (B)   56
    (C)   60
    (D)   76
    (E)   192

Geometry Perimeter and area

Let L represent the length, in meters, of the rectangular garden. It is given that the width of the garden is 6 meters and the area of the garden is the same as the area of a rectangular playground that is 16 meters long and 12 meters wide. It follows that $6L = (16)(12)$, and so $L = 32$. The perimeter of the garden is, then, $2(32 + 6) = 2(38) = 76$ meters.

The correct answer is D.

21. Of the total amount that Jill spent on a shopping trip, excluding taxes, she spent 50 percent on clothing, 20 percent on food, and 30 percent on other items. If Jill paid a 4 percent tax on the clothing, no tax on the food, and an 8 percent tax on all other items, then the total tax that she paid was what percent of the total amount that she spent, excluding taxes?

    (A)   2.8%
    (B)   3.6%
    (C)   4.4%
    (D)   5.2%
    (E)   6.0%

Arithmetic Applied problems

Let T represent the total amount Jill spent, excluding taxes. Jill paid a 4% tax on the clothing she bought, which accounted for 50% of the total amount she spent, and so the tax she paid on the clothing was $(0.04)(0.5T)$. Jill paid an 8% tax on the other items she bought, which accounted for 30% of the total amount she spent, and so the tax she paid on the other items was $(0.08)(0.3T)$. Therefore, the total amount of tax Jill paid was $(0.04)(0.5T) + (0.08)(0.3T) = 0.02T + 0.024T = 0.044T$. The tax as a percent of the total amount Jill spent, excluding taxes, was

$$
\left(\frac{0.044T}{T} \times 100 \right) \% = 4.4\%.
$$

The correct answer is C.

22. At the opening of a trading day at a certain stock exchange, the price per share of stock K was $8. If the price per share of stock K was $9 at the closing of the day, what was the percent increase in the price per share of stock K for that day?

    (A)   1.4%
    (B)   5.9%
    (C)   11.1%
    (D)   12.5%
    (E)   23.6%

Arithmetic Percents

An increase from $8 to $9 represents an increase of $\left(\frac{9-8}{8} \times 100 \right)\% = \frac{100}{8} \% = 12.5\%.$

The correct answer is D.

23. The price of a certain television set is discounted by 10 percent, and the reduced price is then discounted by 10 percent. This series of successive discounts is equivalent to a single discount of

(A) 20%
(B) 19%
(C) 18%
(D) 11%
(E) 10%

Arithmetic Percents

If P represents the original price of the television, then after a discount of 10 percent, the reduced price is $(1 - 0.10)P = 0.90P$. When the reduced price is discounted by 10 percent, the resulting price is $(1 - 0.10)(0.90P) = (0.90)(0.90P) = 0.81P = (1 - 0.19)P$. This price is the original price of the television discounted by 19 percent.

The correct answer is B.

24. The number of rooms at Hotel G is 10 less than twice the number of rooms at Hotel H. If the total number of rooms at Hotel G and Hotel H is 425, what is the number of rooms at Hotel G ?

(A) 140
(B) 180
(C) 200
(D) 240
(E) 280

Algebra Simultaneous equations

Let G be the number of rooms in Hotel G and let H be the number of rooms in Hotel H. Expressed in symbols, the given information is the following system of equations

$$\begin{cases} G = 2H - 10 \\ 425 = G + H \end{cases}$$

Solving the second equation for H gives $H = 425 - G$. Then, substituting $425 - G$ for H in the first equation gives

$$G = 2(425 - G) - 10$$
$$G = 850 - 2G - 10$$
$$G = 840 - 2G$$

$$3G = 840$$
$$G = 280$$

The correct answer is E.

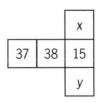

25. In the figure above, the sum of the three numbers in the horizontal row equals the product of the three numbers in the vertical column. What is the value of xy ?

(A) 6
(B) 15
(C) 35
(D) 75
(E) 90

Arithmetic Operations on rational numbers

The sum of the three numbers in the horizontal row is $37 + 38 + 15$, or 90. The product of the three numbers in the vertical column is $15xy$. Thus, $15xy = 90$, or the value of $xy = 6$.

The correct answer is A.

26. $(1 + \sqrt{5})(1 - \sqrt{5}) =$

(A) -4
(B) 2
(C) 6
(D) $-4 - 2\sqrt{5}$
(E) $6 - 2\sqrt{5}$

Arithmetic Operations on radical expressions

Work the problem.

$$(1 + \sqrt{5})(1 - \sqrt{5}) = 1^2 + \sqrt{5} - \sqrt{5} - (\sqrt{5})^2 =$$
$$1 - (\sqrt{5})^2 = 1 - 5 = -4$$

The correct answer is A.

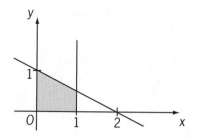

27. In the rectangular coordinate system above, the shaded region is bounded by straight lines. Which of the following is NOT an equation of one of the boundary lines?

(A) $x = 0$
(B) $y = 0$
(C) $x = 1$
(D) $x - y = 0$
(E) $x + 2y = 2$

Geometry Simple coordinate geometry

The left boundary of the shaded region is the y-axis, which has equation $x = 0$. The bottom boundary of the shaded region is the x-axis, which has equation $y = 0$. The right boundary of the shaded region is the vertical line that has equation $x = 1$ since it goes through $(1,0)$. The top boundary of the shaded region is the line that goes through $(0,1)$ and $(2,0)$. The equation of this line CANNOT be $x - y = 0$ because $0 - 1 \neq 0$ and also $2 - 0 \neq 0$. The equation of this line is $x + 2y = 2$ since both $(0,1)$ and $(2,0)$ are on this line (i.e., $0 + 2(1) = 2$ and $2 + 2(0) = 2$).

The correct answer is D.

28. A certain population of bacteria doubles every 10 minutes. If the number of bacteria in the population initially was 10^4, what was the number in the population 1 hour later?

(A) $2(10^4)$
(B) $6(10^4)$
(C) $(2^6)(10^4)$
(D) $(10^6)(10^4)$
(E) $(10^4)^6$

Arithmetic Operations on rational numbers

If the population of bacteria doubles every 10 minutes, it doubles 6 times in one hour. This doubling action can be expressed as $(2)(2)(2)(2)(2)(2)$ or 2^6. Thus, if the initial population is 10^4, the population will be $(2^6)(10^4)$ after one hour.

The correct answer is C.

29. If the perimeter of a rectangular garden plot is 34 feet and its area is 60 square feet, what is the length of each of the longer sides?

(A) 5 ft
(B) 6 ft
(C) 10 ft
(D) 12 ft
(E) 15 ft

Geometry; Algebra Perimeter; Area; Simultaneous equations

Letting x represent the length of the rectangular garden and y represent the width of the garden in the formulas for calculating perimeter and area, the given information can be expressed as:

Perimeter $= 2\big(\text{length}\big) + 2\big(\text{width}\big)$ $\qquad 34 = 2x + 2y$

or

$17 = x + y$

Area $= \big(\text{length}\big)\big(\text{width}\big)$ $\qquad 60 = xy$

This reduces the problem to finding two numbers whose sum is 17 and whose product is 60. It can be seen by inspection that the two numbers are 5 and 12, so the length of each of the longer sides of the garden is 12 ft.

It is also possible to solve $x + y = 17$ for y and substitute the value of $y = 17 - x$ in the equation for the area and solve for x:

$$xy = 60$$
$$x\big(17 - x\big) = 60$$
$$17x - x^2 = 60$$
$$0 = x^2 - 17x + 60$$
$$0 = \big(x - 12\big)\big(x - 5\big)$$

$$x = 12 \text{ or } 5$$
$$y = 5 \text{ or } 12$$

Thus, the length of each of the longer sides of the garden must be 12 ft.

The correct answer is D.

30. In a poll of 66,000 physicians, only 20 percent responded; of these, 10 percent disclosed their preference for pain reliever X. How many of the physicians who responded did <u>not</u> disclose a preference for pain reliever X ?

    (A)   1,320
    (B)   5,280
    (C)   6,600
    (D)   10,560
    (E)   11,880

Arithmetic Percents

The number of physicians who responded to the poll was $0.2(66,000) = 13,200$. If 10 percent of the respondents disclosed a preference for X, then 90 percent did not disclose a preference for X. Thus, the number of respondents who did not disclose a preference is $0.9(13,200) = 11,880$.

The correct answer is E.

31. $\dfrac{3}{100} + \dfrac{5}{1,000} + \dfrac{7}{100,000} =$

    (A)   0.357
    (B)   0.3507
    (C)   0.35007
    (D)   0.0357
    (E)   0.03507

Arithmetic Operations on rational numbers

If each fraction is written in decimal form, the sum to be found is

$$0.03$$
$$0.005$$
$$+\ 0.00007$$
$$0.03507$$

The correct answer is E.

32. Which of the following fractions is equal to the decimal 0.0625 ?

    (A) $\dfrac{5}{8}$

    (B) $\dfrac{3}{8}$

    (C) $\dfrac{1}{16}$

    (D) $\dfrac{1}{18}$

    (E) $\dfrac{3}{80}$

Arithmetic Operations on rational numbers

Work the problem.

$$0.0625 = \frac{625}{10,000} = \frac{1}{16}$$

The correct answer is C.

33. If r and s are positive integers such that $(2^r)(4^s) = 16$, then $2r + s =$

    (A)   2
    (B)   3
    (C)   4
    (D)   5
    (E)   6

Algebra Exponents

Using the rules of exponents,

$$
\begin{aligned}
(2^r)(4^s) &= 16 & &\text{given} \\
(2^r)(2^{2s}) &= 2^4 & &4^s = (2^2)^s = 2^{2s},\ 16 = 2^4 \\
2^{r+2s} &= 2^4 & &\text{addition property of exponents}
\end{aligned}
$$

Thus, $r + 2s = 4$. However, the problem asks for the value of $2r + s$. Since r and s are positive integers, $s < 2$; otherwise, r would not be positive.

Therefore, $s = 1$, and it follows that $r + (2)(1) = 4$, or $r = 2$. The value of $2r + s$ is $(2)(2) + 1 = 5$.

Alternatively, since $(2^r)(4^s) = 16$ and both r and s are positive, it follows that $s < 2$; otherwise, $4^s \geq 16$ and r would not be positive. Therefore, $s = 1$ and $(2^r)(4) = 16$. It follows that $2^r = 4$ and $r = 2$. The value of $2r + s$ is $(2)(2) + 1 = 5$.

The correct answer is D.

34. If positive integers x and y are not both odd, which of the following must be even?

   (A) xy
   (B) $x + y$
   (C) $x - y$
   (D) $x + y - 1$
   (E) $2(x + y) - 1$

Arithmetic Properties of numbers

Since it is given that x and y are NOT both odd, either both x and y are even or one is even and the other one is odd. The following table clearly shows that only the product of x and y must be even.

	Both x and y even	One of x or y even, the other odd
xy	Even	Even
$x + y$	Even	Odd
$x - y$	Even	Odd
$x + y - 1$	Odd	Even
$2(x + y) - 1$	Odd	Odd

The correct answer is A.

35. The annual budget of a certain college is to be shown on a circle graph. If the size of each sector of the graph is to be proportional to the amount of the budget it represents, how many degrees of the circle should be used to represent an item that is 15 percent of the budget?

   (A) $15°$
   (B) $36°$
   (C) $54°$
   (D) $90°$
   (E) $150°$

Arithmetic Percents; Interpretation of graphs

Since there are 360 degrees in a circle, the measure of the central angle in the circle should be $0.15(360°) = 54°$.

The correct answer is C.

36. During a two-week period, the price of an ounce of silver increased by 25 percent by the end of the first week and then decreased by 20 percent of this new price by the end of the second week. If the price of silver was x dollars per ounce at the beginning of the two-week period, what was the price, in dollars per ounce, by the end of the period?

   (A) $0.8x$
   (B) $0.95x$
   (C) x
   (D) $1.05x$
   (E) $1.25x$

Arithmetic Percents

At the end of the first week the price of an ounce of silver was $1.25x$. At the end of the second week, the price was 20 percent less than this, or 80 percent of $1.25x$, which is $(0.80)(1.25)x$, which is in turn equal to x.

The correct answer is C.

37. In a certain pond, 50 fish were caught, tagged, and returned to the pond. A few days later, 50 fish were caught again, of which 2 were found to have been tagged. If the percent of tagged fish in the second catch approximates the percent of tagged fish in the pond, what is the approximate number of fish in the pond?

   (A) 400
   (B) 625
   (C) 1,250
   (D) 2,500
   (E) 10,000

Algebra Applied problems

To solve this problem, it is necessary to determine two fractions: the fraction of fish tagged and the fraction of fish then caught that were already tagged. These two fractions can then be set equal in a proportion, and the problem can be solved.

Letting N be the approximate total number of fish in the pond, then $\dfrac{50}{N}$ is the fraction of fish in the pond that were tagged in the first catch. Then, the fraction of tagged fish in the sample of 50 that were caught in the second catch can be expressed as $\dfrac{2}{50}$, or $\dfrac{1}{25}$. Therefore, $\dfrac{50}{N} = \dfrac{1}{25}$, or $N = (50)(25) = 1{,}250.$

The correct answer is C.

38. $\sqrt{16+16} =$

 (A) $4\sqrt{2}$
 (B) $8\sqrt{2}$
 (C) $16\sqrt{2}$
 (D) 8
 (E) 16

Arithmetic Operations on radical expressions

Working this problem gives

$$\sqrt{16+16} = \sqrt{(16)(2)} = \left(\sqrt{16}\right)\left(\sqrt{2}\right) = 4\sqrt{2}$$

The correct answer is A.

39. The organizers of a fair projected a 25 percent increase in attendance this year over that of last year, but attendance this year actually decreased by 20 percent. What percent of the projected attendance was the actual attendance?

 (A) 45%
 (B) 56%
 (C) 64%
 (D) 75%
 (E) 80%

Arithmetic Percents

Letting A be last year's attendance, set up the given information, and work the problem.

$$\frac{\text{Actual Attendance}}{\text{Projected Attendance}} = \frac{0.80A}{1.25A} = 0.64 = 64\%$$

The correct answer is C.

40. What is the ratio of $\dfrac{3}{4}$ to the product $4\left(\dfrac{3}{4}\right)$?

 (A) $\dfrac{1}{4}$
 (B) $\dfrac{1}{3}$
 (C) $\dfrac{4}{9}$
 (D) $\dfrac{9}{4}$
 (E) 4

Arithmetic Operations on rational numbers

Work the problem.

$$\frac{\dfrac{3}{4}}{4\left(\dfrac{3}{4}\right)} = \frac{\dfrac{3}{4}}{\dfrac{12}{4}} = \frac{\dfrac{3}{4}}{3} = \frac{3}{4} \times \frac{1}{3} = \frac{1}{4}$$

The correct answer is A.

41. If $3 - x = 2x - 3$, then $4x =$

 (A) -24
 (B) -8
 (C) 0
 (D) 8
 (E) 24

Algebra First-degree equations

Work the problem.

$$3 - x = 2x - 3$$
$$6 = 3x \qquad \text{add 3 to both sides;}$$
$$\qquad\qquad \text{add } x \text{ to both sides}$$
$$2 = x \qquad \text{divide both sides by 3}$$

Therefore, $4x = 4(2) = 8.$

The correct answer is D.

$$2x + 2y = -4$$
$$4x + y = 1$$

42. In the system of equations above, what is the value of x ?

(A) -3

(B) -1

(C) $\dfrac{2}{5}$

(D) 1

(E) $1\dfrac{3}{4}$

Algebra Simultaneous equations

Solving the second equation for y gives $y = 1 - 4x$. Then, substituting $1 - 4x$ for y in the first equation gives

$$2x + 2(1 - 4x) = -4$$
$$2x + 2 - 8x = -4$$
$$-6x + 2 = -4$$
$$-6x = -6$$
$$x = 1$$

The correct answer is D.

43. If $x > 3{,}000$, then the value of $\dfrac{x}{2x+1}$ is closest to

(A) $\dfrac{1}{6}$

(B) $\dfrac{1}{3}$

(C) $\dfrac{10}{21}$

(D) $\dfrac{1}{2}$

(E) $\dfrac{3}{2}$

Algebra Simplifying algebraic expressions

For all large values of x, the value of $\dfrac{x}{2x+1}$ is

going to be very close to the value of $\dfrac{x}{2x}$, which

is equal to $\dfrac{1}{2}$.

The correct answer is D.

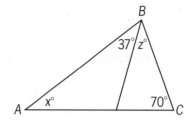

44. In $\triangle ABC$ above, what is x in terms of z ?

(A) $z + 73$

(B) $z - 73$

(C) $70 - z$

(D) $z - 70$

(E) $73 - z$

Geometry Angle measure in degrees

Since the sum of the degree measures of the angles in a triangle equals $180°$, $x + 37 + z + 70 = 180$. Solve this equation for x.

$$x + 37 + z + 70 = 180$$
$$x + z + 107 = 180$$
$$x + z = 73$$
$$x = 73 - z$$

The correct answer is E.

45. What is the maximum number of $1\dfrac{1}{4}$ foot pieces of wire that can be cut from a wire that is 24 feet long?

(A) 11

(B) 18

(C) 19

(D) 20

(E) 30

Arithmetic Operations on rational numbers

In working the problem,

$24 \div 1\dfrac{1}{4} = 24 \div \dfrac{5}{4} = 24 \times \dfrac{4}{5} = \dfrac{96}{5} = 19.2$. Since full

$1\dfrac{1}{4}$ foot pieces of wire are needed, 19 pieces can

be cut.

The correct answer is C.

$$\frac{61.24 \times (0.998)^2}{\sqrt{403}}$$

46. The expression above is approximately equal to

    (A) 1
    (B) 3
    (C) 4
    (D) 5
    (E) 6

    Arithmetic Operations on radical expressions

    Simplify the expression using approximations.

    $$\frac{61.24 \times (0.998)^2}{\sqrt{403}} \approx \frac{60 \times 1^2}{\sqrt{400}} = \frac{60}{20} = 3$$

    The correct answer is B.

47. If the numbers $\frac{17}{24}$, $\frac{1}{2}$, $\frac{3}{8}$, $\frac{3}{4}$, and $\frac{9}{16}$ were ordered from greatest to least, the middle number of the resulting sequence would be

    (A) $\frac{17}{24}$

    (B) $\frac{1}{2}$

    (C) $\frac{3}{8}$

    (D) $\frac{3}{4}$

    (E) $\frac{9}{16}$

    Arithmetic Operations on rational numbers

    The least common denominator for all the fractions in the problem is 48. Work out their equivalencies to see clearly their relative values:

    $$\frac{17}{24} = \frac{34}{48}, \frac{1}{2} = \frac{24}{48}, \frac{3}{8} = \frac{18}{48}, \frac{3}{4} = \frac{36}{48}, \frac{9}{16} = \frac{27}{48}$$

    In descending order, they are

    $$\frac{36}{48}, \frac{34}{48}, \frac{27}{48}, \frac{24}{48}, \frac{18}{48}, \text{ and the middle}$$

    number is $\frac{27}{48} = \frac{9}{16}$.

    The correct answer is E.

48. Last week Jack worked 70 hours and earned $1,260. If he earned his regular hourly wage for the first 40 hours worked, $1\frac{1}{2}$ times his regular hourly wage for the next 20 hours worked, and 2 times his regular hourly wage for the remaining 10 hours worked, what was his regular hourly wage?

    A. $7.00
    B. $14.00
    C. $18.00
    D. $22.00
    E. $31.50

    Algebra First-degree equations

    If w represents Jack's regular hourly wage, then Jack's earnings for the week can be represented by the sum of the following amounts, in dollars: $40w$ (his earnings for the first 40 hours he worked), $(20)(1.5w)$ (his earnings for the next 20 hours he worked), and $(10)(2w)$ (his earnings for the last 10 hours he worked). Therefore,

    $$40w + (20)(1.5w) + (10)(2w) = 1{,}260 \quad \text{given}$$
    $$90w = 1{,}260 \quad \text{add like terms}$$
    $$w = 14 \quad \text{divide both sides by 90}$$

    Jack's regular hourly wage was $14.00.

    The correct answer is B.

49. Last year if 97 percent of the revenues of a company came from domestic sources and the remaining revenues, totaling $450,000, came from foreign sources, what was the total of the company's revenues?

    (A) $1,350,000
    (B) $1,500,000
    (C) $4,500,000
    (D) $15,000,000
    (E) $150,000,000

    Arithmetic Percents

    If 97 percent of the revenues came from domestic sources, then the remaining 3 percent, totaling $450,000, came from foreign sources. Letting x

represent the total revenue, this information can be expressed as $0.03x = 450,000$, and thus

$$x = \frac{450,000}{.03} = \frac{45,000,000}{3} = 15,000,000.$$

The correct answer is D.

50. $\dfrac{2+2\sqrt{6}}{2} =$

(A) $\sqrt{6}$

(B) $2\sqrt{6}$

(C) $1+\sqrt{6}$

(D) $1+2\sqrt{6}$

(E) $2+\sqrt{6}$

Arithmetic Operations on radical expressions

Rewrite the expression to eliminate the denominator.

$$\frac{2+2\sqrt{6}}{2} = \frac{2\left(1+\sqrt{6}\right)}{2} = 1+\sqrt{6}$$

or

$$\frac{2+2\sqrt{6}}{2} = \frac{2}{2} + \frac{2\sqrt{6}}{2} = 1+\sqrt{6}$$

The correct answer is C.

51. A certain fishing boat is chartered by 6 people who are to contribute equally to the total charter cost of $480. If each person contributes equally to a $150 down payment, how much of the charter cost will each person still owe?

(A) $80

(B) $66

(C) $55

(D) $50

(E) $45

Arithmetic Operations on rational numbers

Since each of the 6 individuals contributes equally to the $150 down payment, and since it is given that the total cost of the chartered boat is $480, each person still owes $\dfrac{\$480-\$150}{6} = \$55$.

The correct answer is C.

52. Craig sells major appliances. For each appliance he sells, Craig receives a commission of $50 plus 10 percent of the selling price. During one particular week Craig sold 6 appliances for selling prices totaling $3,620. What was the total of Craig's commissions for that week?

(A) $412

(B) $526

(C) $585

(D) $605

(E) $662

Arithmetic Percents

Since Craig receives a commission of $50 on each appliance plus a 10 percent commission on total sales, his commission for that week was $6\left(\$50\right) + \left(0.1\right)\left(\$3,620\right) = \$662$.

The correct answer is E.

53. What number when multiplied by $\dfrac{4}{7}$ yields $\dfrac{6}{7}$ as the result?

(A) $\dfrac{2}{7}$

(B) $\dfrac{3}{3}$

(C) $\dfrac{3}{2}$

(D) $\dfrac{24}{7}$

(E) $\dfrac{7}{2}$

Algebra First-degree equations

Letting n represent the number, this problem can be expressed as $\dfrac{4}{7}n = \dfrac{6}{7}$, which can be solved for n by multiplying both sides by $\dfrac{7}{4}$:

$$\frac{4}{7}n = \frac{6}{7}$$

$n = \dfrac{42}{28}$ multiply both sides by $\dfrac{7}{4}$

$n = \dfrac{3}{2}$ reduce the fraction

The correct answer is C.

54. If 3 pounds of dried apricots that cost x dollars per pound are mixed with 2 pounds of prunes that cost y dollars per pound, what is the cost, in dollars, per pound of the mixture?

    (A) $\dfrac{3x+2y}{5}$

    (B) $\dfrac{3x+2y}{x+y}$

    (C) $\dfrac{3x+2y}{xy}$

    (D) $5(3x+2y)$

    (E) $3x+2y$

    Algebra Applied problems; Simplifying algebraic expressions

    The total number of pounds in the mixture is $3 + 2 = 5$ pounds, and the total cost of the mixture is $3x + 2y$ dollars. Therefore, the cost per pound of the mixture is $\dfrac{3x + 2y}{5}$ dollars.

    The correct answer is A.

55. Which of the following must be equal to zero for all real numbers x ?

    I. $-\dfrac{1}{x}$

    II. $x + (-x)$

    III. x^0

    (A) I only
    (B) II only
    (C) I and III only
    (D) II and III only
    (E) I, II, and III

    Arithmetic Properties of numbers

    Consider the numeric properties of each answer choice.

    I. $-\dfrac{1}{x} \neq 0$ for all real numbers x.

    II. $x + (-x) = 0$ for all real numbers x

III. $x^0 = 1 \neq 0$ for all nonzero real numbers x

Thus, only the expression in II must be equal to zero for all real numbers x.

The correct answer is B.

	City A	City B	City C	City D	City E	City F
City A						
City B						
City C						
City D						
City E						
City F						

56. In the table above, what is the least number of table entries that are needed to show the mileage between each city and each of the other five cities?

    (A) 15
    (B) 21
    (C) 25
    (D) 30
    (E) 36

    Arithmetic Interpretation of tables

    Since there is no mileage between a city and itself and since the mileage for each pair of cities needs to be entered only once, only those boxes below (or above) the diagonal from the upper left to the lower right need entries. This gives $1 + 2 + 3 + 4 + 5 = 15$ entries.

    The correct answer is A.

57. If $(t - 8)$ is a factor of $t^2 - kt - 48$, then $k =$

    (A) −6
    (B) −2
    (C) 2
    (D) 6
    (E) 14

Algebra Second-degree equations

If $(t - 8)$ is a factor of the expression $t^2 - kt - 48$, then $t = 8$ is a solution of the equation $t^2 - kt - 48 = 0$. So,

$$8^2 - 8k - 48 = 0$$
$$64 - 8k - 48 = 0$$
$$16 - 8k = 0$$
$$16 = 8k$$
$$2 = k$$

The correct answer is C.

58. $\dfrac{31}{125} =$

(A) 0.248
(B) 0.252
(C) 0.284
(D) 0.312
(E) 0.320

Arithmetic Operations on rational numbers

To avoid long division, multiply the given fraction by 1 using a form for 1 that will result in a power of 10 in the denominator.

$$\frac{31}{125} = \frac{31}{5^3} = \frac{31}{5^3} \times \frac{2^3}{2^3} = \frac{(31)(8)}{10^3} = \frac{248}{1,000} = 0.248$$

The correct answer is A.

59. Members of a social club met to address 280 newsletters. If they addressed $\dfrac{1}{4}$ of the newsletters during the first hour and $\dfrac{2}{5}$ of the remaining newsletters during the second hour, how many newsletters did they address during the second hour?

(A) 28
(B) 42
(C) 63
(D) 84
(E) 112

Arithmetic Operations on rational numbers

Since $\dfrac{1}{4}$ of the newsletters were addressed

during the first hour, $\dfrac{3}{4}(280) = 210$ newsletters were NOT addressed during the first hour and remained to be done in the second hour.

Therefore, $\dfrac{2}{5}(210) = 84$ newsletters were addressed during the second hour.

The correct answer is D.

60. $\dfrac{1}{3 - \dfrac{1}{3 - \dfrac{1}{3-1}}} =$

(A) $\dfrac{7}{23}$

(B) $\dfrac{5}{13}$

(C) $\dfrac{2}{3}$

(D) $\dfrac{23}{7}$

(E) $\dfrac{13}{5}$

Arithmetic Operations with rational numbers

Perform each subtraction beginning at the lowest level in the fraction and proceeding upward.

$$\frac{1}{3 - \dfrac{1}{3 - \dfrac{1}{3-1}}} = \frac{1}{3 - \dfrac{1}{3 - \dfrac{1}{2}}}$$

$$= \frac{1}{3 - \dfrac{1}{\dfrac{6}{2} - \dfrac{1}{2}}}$$

$$= \frac{1}{3 - \dfrac{1}{\dfrac{5}{2}}}$$

$$= \frac{1}{3 - \dfrac{2}{5}}$$

$$= \frac{1}{\dfrac{15}{5} - \dfrac{2}{5}}$$

$$= \frac{1}{\frac{13}{5}}$$

$$= \frac{5}{13}$$

The correct answer is B.

61. After 4,000 gallons of water were added to a large water tank that was already filled to $\frac{3}{4}$ of its capacity, the tank was then at $\frac{4}{5}$ of its capacity. How many gallons of water does the tank hold when filled to capacity?

   (A)   5,000
   (B)   6,200
   (C)   20,000
   (D)   40,000
   (E)   80,000

Algebra First-degree equations

Let C be the capacity of the tank. In symbols, the given information is $4,000 + \frac{3}{4}C = \frac{4}{5}C$. Solve for C.

$$4,000 + \frac{3}{4}C = \frac{4}{5}C$$

$$4,000 = \left(\frac{4}{5} - \frac{3}{4}\right)C$$

$$4,000 = \frac{16-15}{20}C$$

$$4,000 = \frac{1}{20}C$$

$$20(4,000) = C$$

$$80,000 = C$$

The correct answer is E.

62. The sum of three integers is 40. The largest integer is 3 times the middle integer, and the smallest integer is 23 less than the largest integer. What is the product of the three integers?

   (A)   1,104
   (B)   972
   (C)   672
   (D)   294
   (E)   192

Algebra Simultaneous equations

Let the three integers be x, y, and z, where $x < y < z$. Then, in symbols the given information is

$$\begin{cases} x + y + z = 40 \\ z = 3y \\ x = z - 23 \end{cases}$$

Substituting $3y$ for z in the third equation gives $x = 3y - 23$. Then, substituting $(3y - 23)$ for x and $3y$ for z into the first equation gives

$$(3y - 23) + y + 3y = 40$$

$$7y - 23 = 40$$

$$7y = 63$$

$$y = 9$$

From $y = 9$, it follows that $z = 3(9) = 27$ and $x = 27 - 23 = 4$. Thus, the product of x, y, and z is $(4)(9)(27) = 972$.

The correct answer is B.

63. Five machines at a certain factory operate at the same constant rate. If four of these machines, operating simultaneously, take 30 hours to fill a certain production order, how many <u>fewer</u> hours does it take all five machines, operating simultaneously, to fill the same production order?

   (A)   3
   (B)   5
   (C)   6
   (D)   16
   (E)   24

Arithmetic Applied problems

If 4 machines, working simultaneously, each work for 30 hours to fill a production order, it takes (4)(30) machine hours to fill the order. If 5 machines are working simultaneously, it will take $\dfrac{(4)(30)}{5} = 24$ hours. Thus, 5 machines working simultaneously will take $30 - 24 = 6$ fewer hours to fill the production order than 4 machines working simultaneously.

The correct answer is C.

64. If Mel saved more than $10 by purchasing a sweater at a 15 percent discount, what is the smallest amount the original price of the sweater could be, to the nearest dollar?

(A)   45
(B)   67
(C)   75
(D)   83
(E)   150

Arithmetic; Algebra Percents; Inequalities; Applied problems

Letting P be the original price of the sweater in dollars, the given information can be expressed as $(0.15)P > 10$. Solving for P gives

$$(0.15)P > 10$$

$$P > \frac{10}{0.15} = \frac{1{,}000}{15} = \frac{200}{3}$$

$$P > 66\frac{2}{3}$$

Thus, to the nearest dollar, the smallest amount P could have been is $67.

The correct answer is B.

65. If $d = 2.0453$ and d^* is the decimal obtained by rounding d to the nearest hundredth, what is the value of $d^* - d$?

(A) -0.0053
(B) -0.0003
(C) 0.0007
(D) 0.0047
(E) 0.0153

Arithmetic Operations on rational numbers

Since $d = 2.0453$ rounded to the nearest hundredth is 2.05, $d^* = 2.05$; therefore, $d^* - d = 2.05 - 2.0453 = 0.0047$.

The correct answer is D.

66. At a monthly meeting, $\frac{2}{5}$ of the attendees were males and $\frac{7}{8}$ of the male attendees arrived on time. If $\frac{9}{10}$ of the female attendees arrived on time, what fraction of the attendees at the monthly meeting did _not_ arrive on time?

(A) $\dfrac{11}{100}$

(B) $\dfrac{3}{25}$

(C) $\dfrac{7}{50}$

(D) $\dfrac{3}{20}$

(E) $\dfrac{4}{25}$

Arithmetic Operations with rational numbers

Let T be the total number of attendees at the meeting. Then, $\frac{2}{5}T$ is the number of male attendees. Of these, $\frac{7}{8}$ arrived on time, so $\frac{7}{8}\left(\frac{2}{5}T\right) = \frac{7}{20}T$ is the number of male attendees who arrived on time. Since $\frac{2}{5}T$ of the attendees were male, the number of female attendees is $T - \frac{2}{5}T = \frac{3}{5}T$. Of these $\frac{9}{10}$ arrived on time, so $\frac{9}{10}\left(\frac{3}{5}T\right) = \frac{27}{50}T$ is the number of female attendees who arrived on time. The total number of attendees who arrived on time is therefore

$\frac{7}{20}T + \frac{27}{50}T = \left(\frac{35+54}{100}\right)T = \frac{89}{100}T$. Thus, the number of attendees who did NOT arrive on time is $T - \frac{89}{100}T = \frac{11}{100}T$, so the fraction of attendees who did not arrive on time is $\frac{11}{100}$.

The correct answer is A.

67. The sequence a_1, a_2, a_3, a_4, a_5 is such that $a_n = a_{n-1} + 5$ for $2 \le n \le 5$. If $a_5 = 31$, what is the value of a_1?

    (A) 1
    (B) 6
    (C) 11
    (D) 16
    (E) 21

    Algebra Sequences

    Since $a_n = a_{n-1} + 5$, then $a_n - a_{n-1} = 5$. So,

    $a_5 - a_4 = 5$

    $a_4 - a_3 = 5$

    $a_3 - a_2 = 5$

    $a_2 - a_1 = 5$

    Adding the equations gives

    $a_5 - a_4 + a_4 - a_3 + a_3 - a_2 + a_2 - a_1 = 5 + 5 + 5 + 5$

    $$a_5 - a_1 = 20$$

    and substituting 31 for a_5 gives

    $31 - a_1 = 20$

    $a_1 = 11$.

    The correct answer is C.

68. A certain bridge is 4,024 feet long. Approximately how many minutes does it take to cross this bridge at a constant speed of 20 miles per hour? (1 mile = 5,280 feet)

    (A) 1
    (B) 2
    (C) 4
    (D) 6
    (E) 7

Arithmetic Applied problems

First, convert 4,024 feet to miles since the speed is given in miles per hour: $4{,}024 \text{ ft} \times \frac{1 \text{ mi}}{5{,}280 \text{ ft}} = \frac{4{,}024}{5{,}280}$ mi. Now, divide by 20 mph: $\frac{4{,}024}{5{,}280}$ mi $\div$

$\frac{20 \text{ mi}}{1 \text{ hr}} = \frac{4{,}024 \text{ mi}}{5{,}280} \times \frac{1 \text{ hr}}{20 \text{ mi}} = \frac{4{,}024 \text{ hr}}{(5{,}280)(20)}$.

Last, convert $\frac{4{,}024 \text{ hr}}{(5{,}280)(20)}$ to minutes:

$\frac{4{,}024 \text{ hr}}{(5{,}280)(20)} \times \frac{60 \text{ min}}{1 \text{ hr}} = \frac{(4{,}024)(60)\text{min}}{(5{,}280)(20)} \approx$

$\frac{4{,}000}{5{,}000} \times \frac{60}{20}$ min. Then, $\frac{4{,}000}{5{,}000} \times \frac{60}{20}$ min $=$

0.8×3 min ≈ 2 min. Thus, at a constant speed of 20 miles per hour, it takes approximately 2 minutes to cross the bridge.

The correct answer is B.

69. If $S = \{0, 4, 5, 2, 11, 8\}$, how much greater than the median of the numbers in S is the mean of the numbers in S?

    (A) 0.5
    (B) 1.0
    (C) 1.5
    (D) 2.0
    (E) 2.5

Arithmetic; Algebra Statistics; Concepts of sets

The median of S is found by ordering the values according to size (0, 2, 4, 5, 8, 11) and taking the average of the two middle numbers: $\frac{4+5}{2} = 4.5$.

The mean is $\frac{\text{sum of } n \text{ values}}{n} =$

$\frac{0 + 4 + 5 + 2 + 11 + 8}{6} = 5$.

The difference between the mean and the median is $5 - 4.5 = 0.5$.

The correct answer is A.

70. A total of 5 liters of gasoline is to be poured into two empty containers with capacities of 2 liters and 6 liters, respectively, such that both containers will be filled to the same percent of their respective capacities. What amount of gasoline, in liters, must be poured into the 6-liter container?

(A) $4\frac{1}{2}$

(B) 4

(C) $3\frac{3}{4}$

(D) 3

(E) $1\frac{1}{4}$

Algebra Ratio and proportion

If x represents the amount, in liters, of gasoline poured into the 6-liter container, then $5 - x$ represents the amount, in liters, of gasoline poured into the 2-liter container. After the gasoline is poured into the containers, the 6-liter container will be filled to $\left(\frac{x}{6} \times 100\right)$% of its capacity and the 2-liter container will be filled to $\left(\frac{5-x}{2} \times 100\right)$% of its capacity. Because these two percents are equal,

$$\frac{x}{6} = \frac{5-x}{2} \quad \text{given}$$
$$2x = 6(5 - x) \quad \text{multiply both sides by 12}$$
$$2x = 30 - 6x \quad \text{use distributive property}$$
$$8x = 30 \quad \text{add } 6x \text{ to both sides}$$
$$x = 3\frac{3}{4} \quad \text{divide both sides by 8}$$

Therefore, $3\frac{3}{4}$ liters of gasoline must be poured into the 6-liter container.

The correct answer is C.

71. When positive integer n is divided by 5, the remainder is 1. When n is divided by 7, the remainder is 3. What is the smallest positive integer k such that $k + n$ is a multiple of 35 ?

(A) 3
(B) 4
(C) 12
(D) 32
(E) 35

Arithmetic Properties of numbers

Given that the remainder is 1 when the positive integer n is divided by 5, it follows that $n = 5p + 1$ for some positive integer p. Likewise, the remainder is 3 when n is divided by 7, so $n = 7q + 3$ for some positive integer q. Equating the two expressions for n gives $5p + 1 = 7q + 3$ or $5p = 7q + 2$. Since the units digit of each multiple of 5 is either 5 or 0, the units digit of $7q + 2$ must be 5 or 0 and the units digit of $7q$ must be 3 or 8. Therefore, $7q = 28, 63, 98, 133, \ldots$, and so $q = 4, 9, 14, 19, \ldots$. Thus, $q = 5m + 4$ for some positive integer m. Then, $n = 7q + 3 = 7(5m + 4) + 3 = 35m + 28 + 3 = 35m + 31$. Therefore, if k is a positive integer, $n + k$ is a multiple of 35 when $k = 4, 39, 74, \ldots$ and the smallest of these values of k is 4.

The correct answer is B.

72. List S consists of 10 consecutive odd integers, and list T consists of 5 consecutive even integers. If the least integer in S is 7 more than the least integer in T, how much greater is the average (arithmetic mean) of the integers in S than the average of the integers in T ?

(A) 2
(B) 7
(C) 8
(D) 12
(E) 22

Arithmetic Statistics

Let the integers in S be $s, s + 2, s + 4, \ldots, s + 18$, where s is odd. Let the integers in T be $t, t + 2, t + 4, t + 6, t + 8$, where t is even. Given that $s = t + 7$, it follows that $s - t = 7$. The average of the integers in S is $\frac{10s + 90}{10} = s + 9$, and, similarly, the average of the integers in T is $\dfrac{5t+20}{5} = t+4$.

The difference in these averages is

$(s+9)-(t+4)=(s-t)+(9-4)=7+5=12.$ Thus, the average of the integers in S is 12 greater than the average of the integers in T.

The correct answer is D.

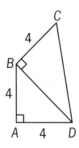

73. In the figure above, what is the area of triangular region BCD ?

   (A) $4\sqrt{2}$
   (B)   8
   (C) $8\sqrt{2}$
   (D)   16
   (E) $16\sqrt{2}$

Geometry Triangles; Area

By the Pythagorean theorem, $BD = \sqrt{4^2+4^2} = 4\sqrt{2}.$

Then the area of $\triangle BCD$ is $\dfrac{1}{2}\left(4\sqrt{2}\right)(4) = 8\sqrt{2}.$

The correct answer is C.

74. Of the goose eggs laid at a certain pond, $\dfrac{2}{3}$ hatched, and $\dfrac{3}{4}$ of the geese that hatched from those eggs survived the first month. Of the geese that survived the first month, $\dfrac{3}{5}$ did <u>not</u> survive the first year. If 120 geese survived the first year and if no more than one goose hatched from each egg, how many goose eggs were laid at the pond?

   (A)   280
   (B)   400
   (C)   540
   (D)   600
   (E)   840

Arithmetic Operations with rational numbers

Let N represent the number of eggs laid at the pond. Then $\dfrac{2}{3}N$ eggs hatched and $\dfrac{3}{4}\left(\dfrac{2}{3}N\right)$ goslings (baby geese) survived the first month.

Since $\dfrac{3}{5}$ of these goslings did not survive the first year, then $\dfrac{2}{5}$ did survive the first year. This means that $\dfrac{2}{5}\left(\dfrac{3}{4}\left(\dfrac{2}{3}N\right)\right)$ goslings survived the first year.

But this number is 120 and so, $\dfrac{2}{5}\left(\dfrac{3}{4}\left(\dfrac{2}{3}N\right)\right) = 120,$

$\dfrac{1}{5}N = 120,$ and $N = 5(120) = 600.$

The correct answer is D.

75. If $x^2-2x-15=0$ and $x>0$, which of the following must be equal to 0 ?

   I. x^2-6x+9
   II. $x^2-7x+10$
   III. $x^2-10x+25$

   (A)   I only
   (B)   II only
   (C)   III only
   (D)   II and III only
   (E)   I, II, and III

Algebra Second-degree equations

Since $x^2-2x-15=0$, then $(x-5)(x+3)=0$, so $x=5$ or $x=-3$. Since $x>0$, then $x=5$.

   I. $5^2-6(5)+9 = 25-30+9 = 4 \neq 0$

   II. $5^2-7(5)+10 = 25-35+10 = 0$

   III. $5^2-10(5)+25 = 25-50+25 = 0$

The correct answer is D.

76. If a square region has area n, what is the length of the diagonal of the square in terms of n ?

   (A) $\sqrt{2n}$
   (B) $\sqrt{n}$
   (C) $2\sqrt{n}$
   (D) $2n$
   (E) $2n^2$

Geometry Area; Pythagorean theorem

If s represents the side length of the square, then $n = s^2$. By the Pythagorean theorem, the length of the diagonal of the square is $\sqrt{s^2 + s^2} = \sqrt{n + n} = \sqrt{2n}$.

The correct answer is A.

77. The "prime sum" of an integer n greater than 1 is the sum of all the prime factors of n, including repetitions. For example, the prime sum of 12 is 7, since $12 = 2 \times 2 \times 3$ and $2 + 2 + 3 = 7$. For which of the following integers is the prime sum greater than 35 ?

(A) 440
(B) 512
(C) 620
(D) 700
(E) 750

Arithmetic Properties of numbers

A   Since $440 = 2 \times 2 \times 2 \times 5 \times 11$, the prime sum of 440 is $2 + 2 + 2 + 5 + 11 = 22$, which is not greater than 35.

B   Since $512 = 2^9$, the prime sum of 512 is $9(2) = 18$, which is not greater than 35.

C   Since $620 = 2 \times 2 \times 5 \times 31$, the prime sum of 620 is $2 + 2 + 5 + 31 = 40$, which is greater than 35.

Because there can be only one correct answer, D and E need not be checked. However, for completeness,

D   Since $700 = 2 \times 2 \times 5 \times 5 \times 7$, the prime sum of 700 is $2 + 2 + 5 + 5 + 7 = 21$, which is not greater than 35.

E   Since $750 = 2 \times 3 \times 5 \times 5 \times 5$, the prime sum of 750 is $2 + 3 + 5 + 5 + 5 = 20$, which is not greater than 35.

The correct answer is C.

78. At a garage sale, all of the prices of the items sold were different. If the price of a radio sold at the garage sale was both the 15th highest price and the 20th lowest price among the prices of the items sold, how many items were sold at the garage sale?

(A) 33
(B) 34
(C) 35
(D) 36
(E) 37

Arithmetic Operations with integers

If the price of the radio was the 15th highest price, there were 14 items that sold for prices higher than the price of the radio. If the price of the radio was the 20th lowest price, there were 19 items that sold for prices lower than the price of the radio. Therefore, the total number of items sold is $14 + 1 + 19 = 34$.

The correct answer is B.

79. For all positive integers m and v, the expression $m \ominus v$ represents the remainder when m is divided by v. What is the value of $((98 \ominus 33) \ominus 17) - (98 \ominus (33 \ominus 17))$?

(A) −10
(B) −2
(C)   8
(D) 13
(E) 17

Arithmetic Operations with integers

First, for $((98 \ominus 33) \ominus 17)$, determine $98 \ominus 33$, which equals 32, since 32 is the remainder when 98 is divided by 33 ($98 = 2(33) + 32$). Then, determine $32 \ominus 17$, which equals 15, since 15 is the remainder when 32 is divided by 17 ($32 = 1(17) + 15$). Thus, $((98 \ominus 33) \ominus 17) = 15$.

Next, for $(98 \ominus (33 \ominus 17))$, determine $33 \ominus 17$, which equals 16, since 16 is the remainder when 33 is divided by 17 ($33 = 1(17) + 16$). Then, determine $98 \ominus 16$, which equals 2, since 2 is the remainder when 98 is divided by 16 ($98 = 6(16) + 2$). Thus, $(98 \ominus (33 \ominus 17)) = 2$.

Finally, $((98 \ominus 33) \ominus 17) - (98 \ominus (33 \ominus 17)) = 15 - 2 = 13$.

The correct answer is D.

80. In a certain sequence, each term after the first term is one-half the previous term. If the tenth term of the sequence is between 0.0001 and 0.001, then the twelfth term of the sequence is between

   (A)   0.0025 and 0.025
   (B)   0.00025 and 0.0025
   (C)   0.000025 and 0.00025
   (D)   0.0000025 and 0.000025
   (E)   0.00000025 and 0.0000025

Arithmetic Sequences

Let a_n represent the nth term of the sequence. It is given that each term after the first term is $\frac{1}{2}$ the previous term and that $0.0001 < a_{10} < 0.001$. Then, for a_{11}, $\frac{0.0001}{2} < a_{11} < \frac{0.001}{2}$, or $0.00005 < a_{11} < 0.0005$. For a_{12}, $\frac{0.00005}{2} < a_{12} < \frac{0.0005}{2}$, or $0.000025 < a_{12} < 0.00025$. Thus, the twelfth term of the sequence is between 0.000025 and 0.00025.

The correct answer is C.

81. Ada and Paul received their scores on three tests. On the first test, Ada's score was 10 points higher than Paul's score. On the second test, Ada's score was 4 points higher than Paul's score. If Paul's average (arithmetic mean) score on the three tests was 3 points higher than Ada's average score on the three tests, then Paul's score on the third test was how many points higher than Ada's score?

   (A)   9
   (B)   14
   (C)   17
   (D)   23
   (E)   25

Algebra Statistics

Let a_1, a_2, and a_3 be Ada's scores on the first, second, and third tests, respectively, and let p_1, p_2, and p_3 be Paul's scores on the first, second, and third tests, respectively. Then, Ada's average score is $\frac{a_1 + a_2 + a_3}{3}$ and Paul's average score is $\frac{p_1 + p_2 + p_3}{3}$. But, Paul's average score is 3 points higher than Ada's average score, so

$\frac{p_1 + p_2 + p_3}{3} = \frac{a_1 + a_2 + a_3}{3} + 3$. Also, it is given that $a_1 = p_1 + 10$ and $a_2 = p_2 + 4$, so by substitution,

$\frac{p_1 + p_2 + p_3}{3} = \frac{\left(p_1 + 10\right) + \left(p_2 + 4\right) + a_3}{3} + 3$. Then, $p_1 + p_2 + p_3 = \left(p_1 + 10\right) + \left(p_2 + 4\right) + a_3 + 9$ and so $p_3 = a_3 + 23$. On the third test, Paul's score was 23 points higher than Ada's score.

The correct answer is D.

82. The price of a certain stock increased by 0.25 of 1 percent on a certain day. By what fraction did the price of the stock increase that day?

   (A) $\frac{1}{2,500}$

   (B) $\frac{1}{400}$

   (C) $\frac{1}{40}$

   (D) $\frac{1}{25}$

   (E) $\frac{1}{4}$

Arithmetic Percents

It is given that the price of a certain stock increased by 0.25 of 1 percent on a certain day. This is equivalent to an increase of $\frac{1}{4}$ of $\frac{1}{100}$, which is $\left(\frac{1}{4}\right)\left(\frac{1}{100}\right)$, and $\left(\frac{1}{4}\right)\left(\frac{1}{100}\right) = \frac{1}{400}$.

The correct answer is B.

83. Three business partners, Q, R, and S, agree to divide their total profit for a certain year in the ratios 2:5:8, respectively. If Q's share was $4,000, what was the total profit of the business partners for the year?

   (A) $26,000
   (B) $30,000
   (C) $52,000
   (D) $60,000
   (E) $300,000

Algebra Applied problems

Letting T represent the total profit and using the given ratios, Q's share is $\dfrac{2}{2+5+8}T = \dfrac{2}{15}T$. Since Q's share is \$4,000, then $\dfrac{2}{15}T = 4,000$ and $T = \dfrac{15}{2}(4,000) = 30,000$.

The correct answer is B.

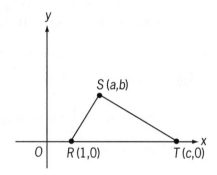

84. In the rectangular coordinate system above, the area of $\triangle RST$ is

(A) $\dfrac{bc}{2}$

(B) $\dfrac{b(c-1)}{2}$

(C) $\dfrac{c(b-1)}{2}$

(D) $\dfrac{a(c-1)}{2}$

(E) $\dfrac{c(a-1)}{2}$

Geometry Simple-coordinate geometry

Letting $\overline{RT}$ be the base of the triangle, since $RT = c - 1$, the length of the base of $\triangle RST$ is $c - 1$. The altitude to the base $\overline{RT}$ is a perpendicular dropped from S to the x-axis. The length of this perpendicular is $b - 0 = b$. Using the formula for the area, A, of a triangle, $A = \dfrac{1}{2}bh$, where b is the length of the base and h is the length of the altitude to that base, the area of $\triangle RST$ is

$\dfrac{1}{2}(c-1)(b)$ or $\dfrac{b(c-1)}{2}$.

The correct answer is B.

85. What is the largest integer n such that $\dfrac{1}{2^n} > 0.01$?

(A) 5
(B) 6
(C) 7
(D) 10
(E) 51

Arithmetic Exponents; Operations with rational numbers

Since $\dfrac{1}{2^n} > 0.01$ is equivalent to $2^n < 100$, find the largest integer n such that $2^n < 100$. Using trial and error, $2^6 = 64$ and $64 < 100$, but $2^7 = 128$ and $128 > 100$. Therefore, 6 is the largest integer such that $\dfrac{1}{2^n} > 0.01$.

The correct answer is B.

86. The average (arithmetic mean) length per film for a group of 21 films is t minutes. If a film that runs for 66 minutes is removed from the group and replaced by one that runs for 52 minutes, what is the average length per film, in minutes, for the new group of films, in terms of t?

(A) $t + \dfrac{2}{3}$

(B) $t - \dfrac{2}{3}$

(C) $21t + 14$

(D) $t + \dfrac{3}{2}$

(E) $t - \dfrac{3}{2}$

Arithmetic Statistics

Let S denote the sum of the lengths, in minutes, of the 21 films in the original group. Since the average length is t minutes, it follows that $\dfrac{S}{21} = t$. If a 66-minute film is replaced by a 52-minute film, then the sum of the lengths of the 21 films in the resulting group is $S - 66 + 52 = S - 14$. Therefore, the average length of the resulting 21 films is $\dfrac{S - 14}{21} = \dfrac{S}{21} - \dfrac{14}{21} = t - \dfrac{2}{3}$.

The correct answer is B.

87. If $x = -|w|$, which of the following must be true?

A. $x = -w$
B. $x = w$
C. $x^2 = w$
D. $x^2 = w^2$
E. $x^3 = w^3$

Algebra Absolute value

Squaring both sides of $x = -|w|$ gives $x^2 = (-|w|)^2$, or $x^2 = |w|^2 = w^2$.

Alternatively, if (x, w) is equal to either of the pairs $(-1,1)$ or $(-1,-1)$, then $x = -|w|$ is true. However, each of the answer choices except $x^2 = w^2$ is false for at least one of these two pairs.

The correct answer is D.

88. Which of the following lines in the xy-plane does <u>not</u> contain any point with integers as both coordinates?

(A) $y = x$

(B) $y = x + \dfrac{1}{2}$

(C) $y = x + 5$

(D) $y = \dfrac{1}{2}x$

(E) $y = \dfrac{1}{2}x + 5$

Algebra; Arithmetic Substitution; Operations with rational numbers

A   If x is an integer, y is an integer since $y = x$. Thus, the line given by $y = x$ contains points with integers as both coordinates.

B   If x is an integer, then if y were an integer, then $y - x$ would be an integer. But,

$y - x = \dfrac{1}{2}$ and $\dfrac{1}{2}$ is NOT an integer. Since assuming that y is an integer leads to a contradiction, then y cannot be an integer

and the line given by $y = x + \dfrac{1}{2}$ does NOT contain any points with integers as both coordinates.

Since there can be only one correct answer, the lines in C, D, and E need not be checked, but for completeness,

C   If x is an integer, $x + 5$ is an integer and so y is an integer since $y = x + 5$. Thus, the line given by $y = x + 5$ contains points with integers as both coordinates.

D   If x is an even integer, $\dfrac{1}{2}x$ is an integer and so y is an integer since $y = \dfrac{1}{2}x$. Thus, the line given by $y = \dfrac{1}{2}x$ contains points with integers as both coordinates.

E   If x is an even integer, $\dfrac{1}{2}x$ is an integer and $\dfrac{1}{2}x + 5$ is also an integer so y is an integer since $y = \dfrac{1}{2}x + 5$. Thus, the line given by $y = \dfrac{1}{2}x + 5$ contains points with integers as both coordinates.

The correct answer is B.

89. One inlet pipe fills an empty tank in 5 hours. A second inlet pipe fills the same tank in 3 hours. If both pipes are used together, how long will it take to fill $\dfrac{2}{3}$ of the tank?

(A) $\dfrac{8}{15}$ hr

(B) $\dfrac{3}{4}$ hr

(C) $\dfrac{5}{4}$ hr

(D) $\dfrac{15}{8}$ hr

(E) $\dfrac{8}{3}$ hr

Algebra Applied problems

If the first pipe fills the tank in 5 hours, then it fills $\dfrac{1}{5}$ of the tank in one hour. If the second pipe fills the tank in 3 hours, then it fills $\dfrac{1}{3}$ of the tank in one hour. Together, the two pipes fill

$\dfrac{1}{5} + \dfrac{1}{3} = \dfrac{8}{15}$ of the tank in one hour, which means they fill the whole tank in $\frac{15}{8}$ hours. To fill $\frac{2}{3}$ of the tank at this constant rate would then take

$$\left(\frac{2}{3}\right)\left(\frac{15}{8}\right) = \frac{5}{4} \text{ hours.}$$

The correct answer is C.

90. $\left(\frac{1}{5}\right)^2 - \left(\frac{1}{5}\right)\left(\frac{1}{4}\right) =$

(A) $-\frac{1}{20}$

(B) $-\frac{1}{100}$

(C) $\frac{1}{100}$

(D) $\frac{1}{20}$

(E) $\frac{1}{5}$

Arithmetic Operations on rational numbers

$$\left(\frac{1}{5}\right)^2 - \left(\frac{1}{5}\right)\left(\frac{1}{4}\right) = \frac{1}{25} - \frac{1}{20}$$

$$= \frac{4}{100} - \frac{5}{100}$$

$$= -\frac{1}{100}$$

The correct answer is B.

91. If the length and width of a rectangular garden plot were each increased by 20 percent, what would be the percent increase in the area of the plot?

(A) 20%
(B) 24%
(C) 36%
(D) 40%
(E) 44%

Geometry Area

If L represents the length of the original plot and W represents the width of the original plot, the area of the original plot is LW. To get the dimensions of the plot after the increase, multiply

each dimension of the original plot by $(1 + 0.2) = 1.2$ to reflect the 20 percent increase.

Then, the area of the plot after the increase is $(1.2L)(1.2W) = 1.44LW$ or 144 percent of the area of the original plot, which is an increase of 44 percent over the area of the original plot.

The correct answer is E.

92. The population of a bacteria culture doubles every 2 minutes. Approximately how many minutes will it take for the population to grow from 1,000 to 500,000 bacteria?

(A) 10
(B) 12
(C) 14
(D) 16
(E) 18

Arithmetic Estimation

Set up a table of values to see how the culture grows.

Number of Minutes	Bacteria Population
0	1,000
2	2,000
4	4,000
6	8,000
8	16,000
10	32,000
12	64,000
14	128,000
16	256,000
18	512,000

At 18 minutes, the population of bacteria is just over 500,000.

The correct answer is E.

93. For a light that has an intensity of 60 candles at its source, the intensity in candles, S, of the light at a point d feet from the source is given by the formula $S = \dfrac{60k}{d^2}$, where k is a constant. If the intensity of the light is 30 candles at a distance of 2 feet from the source, what is the intensity of the light at a distance of 20 feet from the source?

    (A) $\dfrac{3}{10}$ candle

    (B) $\dfrac{1}{2}$ candle

    (C) 1 candle

    (D) 2 candles

    (E) 3 candles

Algebra Applied problems

First, solve the equation for the constant k using the values where both the intensity (S) and distance (d) are known.

$$S = \frac{60k}{d^2}$$

$$30 = \frac{60k}{2^2} \qquad \text{substitute } S = 30 \text{ candles and } d = 2 \text{ feet}$$

$$120 = 60k \qquad \text{solve for } k$$

$$2 = k$$

Then, with this known value of k, solve the equation for S where only the distance (d) is known.

$$S = \frac{60k}{d^2}$$

$$S = \frac{60(2)}{20^2} \qquad \text{substitute } k = 2 \text{ and } d = 20 \text{ feet}$$

$$S = \frac{120}{400} = \frac{3}{10}$$

The correct answer is A.

$$\begin{array}{r} AB \\ + \ BA \\ \hline AAC \end{array}$$

94. In the correctly worked addition problem shown, where the sum of the two-digit positive integers AB and BA is the three-digit integer AAC, and A, B, and C are different digits, what is the units digit of the integer AAC?

    (A) 9
    (B) 6
    (C) 3
    (D) 2
    (E) 0

Arithmetic Place value

Determine the value of C.

It is given that $(10A + B) + (10B + A) = 100A + 10A + C$, or $11A + 11B = 110A + C$. Thus, $11B - 99A = C$, or $11(B - 9A) = C$. Therefore, C is divisible by 11, and 0 is the only digit that is divisible by 11.

The correct answer is E.

$$3r \le 4s + 5$$

$$|s| \le 5$$

95. Given the inequalities above, which of the following CANNOT be the value of r?

    (A) -20
    (B) -5
    (C) 0
    (D) 5
    (E) 20

Algebra Inequalities

Since $|s| \le 5$, it follows that $-5 \le s \le 5$. Therefore, $-20 \le 4s \le 20$, and hence $-15 \le 4s + 5 \le 25$. Since $3r \le 4s + 5$ (given) and $4s + 5 \le 25$ (end of previous sentence), it follows that $3r \le 25$. Among the answer choices, $3r \le 25$ is false only for $r = 20$.

The correct answer is E.

96. A positive integer is divisible by 9 if and only if the sum of its digits is divisible by 9. If n is a positive integer, for which of the following values of k is $25 \times 10^n + k \times 10^{2n}$ divisible by 9 ?

    (A)   9
    (B)   16
    (C)   23
    (D)   35
    (E)   47

Arithmetic Properties of numbers

Since n can be any positive integer, let $n = 2$. Then $25 \times 10^n = 2{,}500$, so its digits consist of the digits 2 and 5 followed by two digits of 0. Also, $k \times 10^{2n} = k \times 10{,}000$, so its digits consist of the digits of k followed by four digits of 0. Therefore, the digits of $(25 \times 10^n) + (k \times 10^{2n})$ consist of the digits of k followed by the digits 2 and 5, followed by two digits of 0. The table below shows this for $n = 2$ and $k = 35$:

$$25 \times 10^n = 2{,}500$$
$$35 \times 10^{2n} = 350{,}000$$
$$(25 \times 10^n) + (35 \times 10^{2n}) = 352{,}500$$

Thus, when $n = 2$, the sum of the digits of $(25 \times 10^n) + (k \times 10^{2n})$ will be $2 + 5 = 7$ plus the sum of the digits of k. Of the answer choices, this sum of digits is divisible by 9 only for $k = 47$, which gives $2 + 5 + 4 + 7 = 18$. It can also be verified that, for each positive integer n, the only such answer choice is $k = 47$, although this additional verification is not necessary to obtain the correct answer.

The correct answer is E.

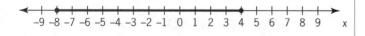

97. On the number line, the shaded interval is the graph of which of the following inequalities?

    (A) $|x| \leq 4$
    (B) $|x| \leq 8$
    (C) $|x - 2| \leq 4$
    (D) $|x - 2| \leq 6$
    (E) $|x + 2| \leq 6$

Algebra Inequalities; Absolute value

The midpoint of the interval from -8 to 4, inclusive, is $\dfrac{-8+4}{2} = -2$ and the length of the interval from -8 to 4, inclusive, is $4 - (-8) = 12$, so the interval consists of all numbers within a distance of $\dfrac{12}{2} = 6$ from -2. Using an inequality involving absolute values, this can be described by $|x - (-2)| \leq 6$, or $|x + 2| \leq 6$.

Alternatively, the inequality $-8 \leq x \leq 4$ can be written as the conjunction $-8 \leq x$ and $x \leq 4$. Rewrite this conjunction so that the lower value, -8, and the upper value, 4, are shifted to values that have the same magnitude. This can be done by adding 2 to each side of each inequality, which gives $-6 \leq x + 2$ and $x + 2 \leq 6$. Thus, $x + 2$ lies between -6 and 6, inclusive, and it follows that $|x + 2| \leq 6$.

The correct answer is E.

98. Of all the students in a certain dormitory, $\dfrac{1}{2}$ are first-year students and the rest are second-year students. If $\dfrac{4}{5}$ of the first-year students have <u>not</u> declared a major and if the fraction of second-year students who have declared a major is 3 times the fraction of first-year students who have declared a major, what fraction of all the students in the dormitory are second-year students who have <u>not</u> declared a major?

    (A) $\dfrac{1}{15}$
    (B) $\dfrac{1}{5}$
    (C) $\dfrac{4}{15}$
    (D) $\dfrac{1}{3}$
    (E) $\dfrac{2}{5}$

Arithmetic Applied problems

Consider the table below in which T represents the total number of students in the dormitory. Since $\dfrac{1}{2}$ of the students are first-year students and the rest are second-year students, it follows that $\frac{1}{2}$ of the students are second-year students, and so the totals for the first-year and second-year columns are both $0.5T$. Since $\frac{4}{5}$ of the first-year students have not declared a major, it follows that the middle entry in the first-year column is $\frac{4}{5}(0.5T) = 0.4T$ and the first entry in the first-year column is $0.5T - 0.4T = 0.1T$. Since the fraction of second-year students who have declared a major is 3 times the fraction of first-year students who have declared a major, it follows that the first entry in the second-year column is $3(0.1T) = 0.3T$ and the second entry in the second-year column is $0.5T - 0.3T = 0.2T$. Thus, the fraction of students that are second-year students who have not declared a major is $\frac{0.2T}{T} = 0.2 = \frac{1}{5}$.

	First-year	Second-year	Total
Declared major	$0.1T$	$0.3T$	$0.4T$
Not declared major	$0.4T$	$0.2T$	$0.6T$
Total	$0.5T$	$0.5T$	T

The correct answer is B.

99. If the average (arithmetic mean) of x, y, and z is $7x$ and $x \neq 0$, what is the ratio of x to the sum of y and z?

   (A)   1:21
   (B)   1:20
   (C)   1:6
   (D)   6:1
   (E)   20:1

Algebra Ratio and proportion

Given that the average of x, y, and z is $7x$, it follows that $\frac{x+y+z}{3} = 7x$, or $x + y + z = 21x$, or $y + z = 20x$. Dividing both sides of the last equation by $20(y + z)$ gives $\frac{1}{20} = \frac{x}{y+z}$, so the ratio of x to the sum of y and z is 1:20.

The correct answer is B.

100. $\dfrac{(-1.5)(1.2) - (4.5)(0.4)}{30} =$

   (A) -1.2
   (B) -0.12
   (C) 0
   (D) 0.12
   (E) 1.2

Arithmetic Operations on rational numbers

Simplify the expression.

$$\frac{(-1.5)(1.2) - (4.5)(0.4)}{30} =$$
$$\frac{-1.80 - 1.80}{30} = \frac{-3.60}{30} = -0.12$$

The correct answer is B.

101. René earns $8.50 per hour on days other than Sundays and twice that rate on Sundays. Last week she worked a total of 40 hours, including 8 hours on Sunday. What were her earnings for the week?

   (A) $272
   (B) $340
   (C) $398
   (D) $408
   (E) $476

Arithmetic Operations on rational numbers

René worked a total of $40 - 8 = 32$ hours at a rate of $8.50 per hour during the week. On Sunday she worked 8 hours at a rate of $\$8.50(2) = \$17.00$ per hour. Her total earnings for the week were thus $32(\$8.50) + 8(\$17) = \$408$.

The correct answer is D.

102. In a shipment of 120 machine parts, 5 percent were defective. In a shipment of 80 machine parts, 10 percent were defective. For the two shipments combined, what percent of the machine parts were defective?

   (A)   6.5%
   (B)   7.0%
   (C)   7.5%
   (D)   8.0%
   (E)   8.5%

Arithmetic Percents

The number of defective parts in the first shipment was $120(0.05) = 6$. The number of defective parts in the second shipment was $80(0.10) = 8$. The percent of machine parts that were defective in the two shipments combined was therefore

$$\frac{6+8}{120+80} = \frac{14}{200} = \frac{7}{100} = 7\%.$$

The correct answer is B.

---

103. If $8^{2x+3} = 2^{3x+6}$, then $x =$

   (A) -3
   (B) -1
   (C) 0
   (D) 1
   (E) 3

Algebra First-degree equations

To work the problem, create a common base so that the exponents can be set equal to each other.

$$8^{2x+3} = 2^{3x+6}$$
$$\left(2^3\right)^{2x+3} = 2^{3x+6} \quad \text{since } 8 = 2 \times 2 \times 2, \text{ can be expressed as } 2^3$$
$$2^{6x+9} = 2^{3x+6} \quad \text{multiply exponents}$$
$$6x+9 = 3x+6 \quad \text{set exponents equal since they are on a common base (2)}$$
$$3x = -3 \quad \text{solve for } x$$
$$x = -1$$

The correct answer is B.

---

104. Of the following, the closest approximation to $\sqrt{\dfrac{5.98(601.5)}{15.79}}$ is

   (A) 5
   (B) 15
   (C) 20
   (D) 25
   (E) 225

Arithmetic Estimation

$$\sqrt{\frac{5.98(601.5)}{15.79}} \approx \sqrt{\frac{6(600)}{16}} =$$
$$\sqrt{\frac{3{,}600}{16}} = \frac{\sqrt{3{,}600}}{\sqrt{16}} = \frac{60}{4} = 15$$

The correct answer is B.

---

105. Which of the following CANNOT be the greatest common divisor of two positive integers x and y?

   (A) 1
   (B) x
   (C) y
   (D) $x - y$
   (E) $x + y$

Arithmetic Properties of numbers

One example is sufficient to show that a statement CAN be true.

A   The greatest common divisor (gcd) of $x = 3$ and $y = 2$ is 1 and, therefore, 1 can be the gcd of the two positive integers x and y.

B   The greatest common divisor (gcd) of $x = 3$ and $y = 6$ is 3 and therefore x can be the gcd of the two positive integers x and y.

C   The greatest common divisor (gcd) of $x = 6$ and $y = 3$ is 3 and therefore y can be the gcd of the two positive integers x and y.

D   The greatest common divisor (gcd) of $x = 3$ and $y = 2$ is 1. Since $3 - 2 = 1$, $x - y$ can be the gcd of the two positive integers x and y.

By the process of elimination, $x + y$ CANNOT be the gcd of the two positive integers x and y.

Algebraically, since $x > 0$, $x + y > y$. Also, since $y > 0$, $x + y > x$. The greatest divisor of x is x, so $x + y$ cannot be a divisor of x. Likewise, the greatest divisor of y is y, so $x + y$ cannot be a divisor of y. Therefore, $x + y$ cannot be a divisor of either x or y and thus cannot be a common divisor of x and y.

The correct answer is E.

106. Last year Carlos saved 10 percent of his annual earnings. This year he earned 5 percent more than last year and he saved 12 percent of his annual earnings. The amount saved this year was what percent of the amount saved last year?

(A) 122%
(B) 124%
(C) 126%
(D) 128%
(E) 130%

Arithmetic Percents

Let x represent the amount of Carlos's annual earnings last year.

Carlos's savings last year = $0.1x$

Carlos's earnings this year = $1.05x$

Carlos's savings this year = $(1.05x)(0.12) = 0.126x$

The amount saved this year as a percent of the amount saved last year is $\dfrac{0.126x}{0.1x} = 1.26 = 126\%$.

The correct answer is C.

107. A corporation that had $115.19 billion in profits for the year paid out $230.10 million in employee benefits. Approximately what percent of the profits were the employee benefits? (Note: 1 billion $= 10^9$)

(A) 50%
(B) 20%
(C) 5%
(D) 2%
(E) 0.2%

Arithmetic Percents; Estimation

The employee benefits as a fraction of profits can be expressed as

$$\frac{230.10 \times 10^6}{115.19 \times 10^9} \approx \frac{230 \times 10^6}{115 \times 10^9}$$

$$= \frac{230}{115} \times \frac{10^6}{10^9}$$

$$= 2 \times 10^{-3}$$

$$= 0.002$$

$$= 0.2\%$$

The correct answer is E.

108. In the coordinate plane, line k passes through the origin and has slope 2. If points $(3,y)$ and $(x,4)$ are on line k, then $x + y =$

(A) 3.5
(B) 7
(C) 8
(D) 10
(E) 14

Algebra Simple coordinate geometry

Since line k has slope 2 and passes through the origin, the equation of line k is $y = 2x$. If the point $(3,y)$ is on line k, then $y = 2(3) = 6$. If the point $(x,4)$ is on line k, then $4 = 2x$ and so $x = 2$. Therefore, $x + y = 2 + 6 = 8$.

The correct answer is C.

109. If a, b, and c are constants, $a > b > c$, and $x^3 - x = (x-a)(x-b)(x-c)$ for all numbers x, what is the value of b?

(A) -3
(B) -1
(C) 0
(D) 1
(E) 3

Algebra Simplifying algebraic expressions

Since $(x-a)(x-b)(x-c) = x^3 - x = x(x^2 - 1)$ $= x(x+1)(x-1) = (x-0)(x-1)(x+1)$ then a, b, and c are 0, 1, and -1 in some order. Since $a > b > c$, it follows that $a = 1$, $b = 0$, and $c = -1$.

The correct answer is C.

110. On the number line, if $r < s$, if p is halfway between r and s, and if t is halfway between p and r, then $\dfrac{s-t}{t-r} =$

    (A) $\dfrac{1}{4}$

    (B) $\dfrac{1}{3}$

    (C) $\dfrac{4}{3}$

    (D) 3

    (E) 4

Algebra Factoring; Simplifying algebraic expressions

Using a number line makes it possible to see these relationships more readily:

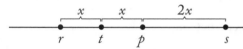

The given relative distances between r, s, t, and p are shown in the number line above. The distance between s and t can be expressed as $s - t$, or as $x + 2x$. The distance between t and r can be expressed as $t - r$, or as x. Thus, by substitution into the given equation:

$$\frac{s-t}{t-r} = \frac{x+2x}{x} = \frac{3x}{x} = 3.$$

The correct answer is D.

111. Company K's earnings were $12 million last year. If this year's earnings are projected to be 150 percent greater than last year's earnings, what are Company K's projected earnings this year?

    (A) $13.5 million
    (B) $15 million
    (C) $18 million
    (D) $27 million
    (E) $30 million

Arithmetic Percents

If one quantity x is p percent **greater** than another quantity y, then $x = y + \left(\dfrac{p}{100}\right)y$. Let y represent last year's earnings and x represent this year's earnings, which are projected to be 150 percent greater than last year's earnings. Then, $x = y + \left(\dfrac{150}{100}\right)y = y + 1.5\,y = 2.5\,y$. Since last year's earnings were $12 million, this year's earnings are projected to be $2.5\big(\$12\,\text{million}\big) = \$30\,\text{million}$.

The correct answer is E.

112. If $\dfrac{3}{x} = 2$ and $\dfrac{y}{4} = 3$, then $\dfrac{3+y}{x+4} =$

    (A) $\dfrac{10}{9}$

    (B) $\dfrac{3}{2}$

    (C) $\dfrac{20}{11}$

    (D) $\dfrac{30}{11}$

    (E) 5

Algebra First-degree equations; Simplifying algebraic expressions

Solving $\dfrac{3}{x} = 2$ and $\dfrac{y}{4} = 3$ for x and y, respectively, gives $x = \dfrac{3}{2}$ and $y = 12$. Then substituting these into the given expression gives

$$\frac{3+y}{x+4} = \frac{3+12}{\frac{3}{2}+4} = \frac{3+12}{\frac{3}{2}+\frac{8}{2}} = \frac{15}{\frac{11}{2}} = \frac{15\times 2}{11} = \frac{30}{11}$$

The correct answer is D.

113. $17^3 + 17^4 =$

    (A) 17^7
    (B) $17^3(18)$
    (C) $17^6(18)$
    (D) $2(17^3) + 17$
    (E) $2(17^3) - 17$

Arithmetic Exponents

Since $17^3 = 17^3 \times 1$ and $17^4 = 17^3 \times 17$, then 17^3 may be factored out of each term. It follows that $17^3 + 17^4 = 17^3(1 + 17) = 17^3(18)$.

The correct answer is B.

114. A certain clock marks every hour by striking a number of times equal to the hour, and the time required for a stroke is exactly equal to the time interval between strokes. At 6:00 the time lapse between the beginning of the first stroke and the end of the last stroke is 22 seconds. At 12:00, how many seconds elapse between the beginning of the first stroke and the end of the last stroke?

    (A)   72
    (B)   50
    (C)   48
    (D)   46
    (E)   44

Arithmetic Operations on rational numbers

At 6:00 there are 6 strokes and 5 intervals between strokes. Thus, there are 11 equal time intervals in the 22 seconds between the beginning of the first stroke and the end of the last stroke. Therefore, each time interval is $\frac{22}{11} = 2$ seconds long. At 12:00 there are 12 strokes and 11 intervals between strokes. Thus, there are 23 equal 2-second time intervals, or $23 \times 2 = 46$ seconds, between the beginning of the first stroke and the end of the last stroke.

The correct answer is D.

115. What is the greatest number of identical bouquets that can be made out of 21 white and 91 red tulips if no flowers are to be left out? (Two bouquets are identical whenever the number of red tulips in the two bouquets is equal and the number of white tulips in the two bouquets is equal.)

    (A)   3
    (B)   4
    (C)   5
    (D)   6
    (E)   7

Arithmetic Properties of numbers

Since the question asks for the greatest number of bouquets that can be made using all of the flowers, the number of bouquets will need to be the greatest common factor of 21 and 91. Since $21 = (3)(7)$ and $91 = (7)(13)$, the greatest common factor of 21 and 91 is 7. Therefore, 7 bouquets can be made, each with 3 white tulips and 13 red tulips.

The correct answer is E.

116. In the xy-plane, the points (c,d), $(c,-d)$, and $(-c,-d)$ are three vertices of a certain square. If $c < 0$ and $d > 0$, which of the following points is in the same quadrant as the fourth vertex of the square?

    (A) $(-5,-3)$
    (B) $(-5,3)$
    (C) $(5,-3)$
    (D) $(3,-5)$
    (E) $(3,5)$

Geometry Coordinate geometry

Because the points (c,d) and $(c,-d)$ lie on the same vertical line (the line with equation $x = c$), one side of the square has length $2d$ and is vertical. Therefore, the side of the square opposite this side has length $2d$, is vertical, and contains the vertex $(-c,-d)$. From this it follows that the remaining vertex is $(-c,d)$, because $(-c,d)$ lies on the same vertical line as $(-c,-d)$ (the line with equation $x = -c$) and these two vertices are a distance $2d$ apart. Because $c < 0$ and $d > 0$, the point $(-c,d)$ has positive x-coordinate and positive y-coordinate. Thus, the point $(-c,d)$ is in Quadrant I. Of the answer choices, only $(3,5)$ is in Quadrant I.

The correct answer is E.

117. For all numbers s and t, the operation $*$ is defined by $s * t = (s - 1)(t + 1)$. If $(-2) * x = -12$, then $x =$

    (A)   2
    (B)   3
    (C)   5
    (D)   6
    (E)   11

Algebra First-degree equations

The equivalent values established for this problem are $s = -2$ and $t = x$. So, substitute -2 for s and x for t in the given equation:

$$-2 * x = -12$$
$$(-2 - 1)(x + 1) = -12$$
$$(-3)(x + 1) = -12$$
$$x + 1 = 4$$
$$x = 3$$

The correct answer is B.

118. Salesperson A's compensation for any week is $360 plus 6 percent of the portion of A's total sales above $1,000 for that week. Salesperson B's compensation for any week is 8 percent of B's total sales for that week. For what amount of total weekly sales would both salespeople earn the same compensation?

    (A) $21,000
    (B) $18,000
    (C) $15,000
    (D) $4,500
    (E) $4,000

Algebra Applied problems; Simultaneous equations

Let x represent the total weekly sales amount at which both salespersons earn the same compensation. Then, the given information regarding when Salesperson A's weekly pay equals Salesperson B's weekly pay can be expressed as:

$$360 + 0.06(x - 1,000) = 0.08x$$
$$360 + 0.06x - 60 = 0.08x \quad \text{solve for } x$$
$$300 = 0.02x$$
$$15,000 = x$$

The correct answer is C.

119. If $\dfrac{3}{10^4} = x\%$, then $x =$

    (A)   0.3
    (B)   0.03
    (C)   0.003
    (D)   0.0003
    (E)   0.00003

Arithmetic Percents

Given that $\dfrac{3}{10^4} = x\%$, and writing $x\%$ as $\dfrac{x}{100}$, it follows that $\dfrac{3}{10^4} = \dfrac{x}{100}$. Multiplying both sides by 100 gives $x = \dfrac{300}{10^4} = \dfrac{300}{10,000} = \dfrac{3}{100} = 0.03$

The correct answer is B.

120. If a basketball team scores an average (arithmetic mean) of x points per game for n games and then scores y points in its next game, what is the team's average score for the $n + 1$ games?

    (A) $\dfrac{nx + y}{n + 1}$

    (B) $x + \dfrac{y}{n + 1}$

    (C) $x + \dfrac{y}{n}$

    (D) $\dfrac{n(x + y)}{n + 1}$

    (E) $\dfrac{x + ny}{n + 1}$

Arithmetic Statistics

Using the formula $\text{average} = \dfrac{\text{total points}}{\text{number of games}}$, the average number of points per game for the first n games can be expressed as $x = \dfrac{\text{total points for } n \text{ games}}{n}$. Solving this equation shows that the total points for n games $= nx$. Then, the total points for $n + 1$ games can be expressed as $nx + y$, and the average number of points for $n + 1$ games $= \dfrac{nx + y}{n + 1}$.

The correct answer is A.

121. If $xy > 0$ and $yz < 0$, which of the following must be negative?

    (A) xyz

    (B) xyz^2

    (C) xy^2z

    (D) xy^2z^2

    (E) $x^2y^2z^2$

Arithmetic Properties of numbers

Since $xy > 0$ and $yz < 0$, $(xy)(yz) = xy^2z < 0$, and xy^2z is the expression given in answer choice C. Alternatively, the chart below shows all possibilities for the algebraic signs of x, y, and z. Those satisfying $xy > 0$ are checked in the fourth column of the chart, and those satisfying $yz < 0$ are checked in the fifth column of the chart.

x	y	z	$xy > 0$	$yz < 0$
+	+	+	✓	
+	+	−	✓	✓
+	−	+		✓
+	−	−		
−	+	+		
−	+	−		✓
−	−	+	✓	✓
−	−	−	✓	

The chart below shows only the possibilities that satisfy both $xy > 0$ and $yz < 0$. Noting that the expression in answer choice E is the product of the squares of three nonzero numbers, which is always positive, extend the chart to include the algebraic sign of each of the other answer choices.

x	y	z	xyz	xyz^2	xy^2z	xy^2z^2
+	+	−	−	+	−	+
−	−	+	+	+	−	−

Only xy^2z is negative in both cases.

The correct answer is C.

122. At a certain pizzeria, $\frac{1}{8}$ of the pizzas sold in one week were mushroom and $\frac{1}{3}$ of the remaining pizzas sold were pepperoni. If n of the pizzas sold were pepperoni, how many were mushroom?

    (A) $\frac{3}{8}n$

    (B) $\frac{3}{7}n$

    (C) $\frac{7}{16}n$

    (D) $\frac{7}{8}n$

    (E) $3n$

Algebra Simplifying algebraic expressions

Let t represent the total number of pizzas sold. Then $\frac{1}{8}t$ represents the number of mushroom pizzas sold, $\frac{7}{8}t$ represents the number of remaining pizzas sold, and $\frac{1}{3}\left(\frac{7}{8}t\right) = \frac{7}{24}t$ represents the number of pepperoni pizzas sold.

Then $n = \frac{7}{24}t$, $t = \frac{24}{7}n$, and $\frac{1}{8}t = \frac{1}{8}\left(\frac{24}{7}n\right) = \frac{3}{7}n$.

Thus, $\frac{3}{7}n$ mushroom pizzas were sold.

The correct answer is B.

123. Two trains, X and Y, started simultaneously from opposite ends of a 100-mile route and traveled toward each other on parallel tracks. Train X, traveling at a constant rate, completed the 100-mile trip in 5 hours; Train Y, traveling at a constant rate, completed the 100-mile trip in 3 hours. How many miles had Train X traveled when it met Train Y ?

    (A) 37.5

    (B) 40.0

    (C) 60.0

    (D) 62.5

    (E) 77.5

Algebra Applied problems

To solve this problem, use the formula distance = rate × time and its two equivalent forms rate = $\dfrac{\text{distance}}{\text{time}}$ and time = $\dfrac{\text{distance}}{\text{rate}}$. Train X

traveled 100 miles in 5 hours so its rate was

$\dfrac{100}{5}$ = 20 miles per hour. Train Y traveled

100 miles in 3 hours so its rate was $\dfrac{100}{3}$ miles per

hour. If t represents the number of hours the
trains took to meet, then when the trains met,
Train X had traveled a distance of $20t$ miles and

Train Y had traveled a distance of $\dfrac{100}{3}t$ miles.

Since the trains started at opposite ends of the
100-mile route, the sum of the distances they had
traveled when they met was 100 miles. Therefore,

$$20t + \frac{100}{3}t = 100$$

$$\frac{160}{3}t = 100$$

$$t = 100\left(\frac{3}{160}\right)$$

$$= \frac{300}{160}$$

$$= \frac{15}{8}$$

Thus, Train X had traveled

$20t = 20\left(\dfrac{15}{8}\right) = \dfrac{75}{2} = 37.5$ miles when it met
Train Y.

The correct answer is A.

124. What is the value of $2x^2 - 2.4x - 1.7$ for $x = 0.7$?

(A) -0.72
(B) -1.42
(C) -1.98
(D) -2.40
(E) -2.89

Algebra Simplifying algebraic expressions

Work the problem by substituting $x = 0.7$.

$2x^2 - 2.4x - 1.7$

$= 2(0.7)^2 - 2.4(0.7) - 1.7$

$= 2(0.49) - 1.68 - 1.7$

$= 0.98 - 1.68 - 1.7$

$= -2.40$

The correct answer is D.

125. What is the remainder when 3^{24} is divided by 5?

(A) 0
(B) 1
(C) 2
(D) 3
(E) 4

Arithmetic Properties of numbers

A pattern in the units digits of the numbers 3, $3^2 = 9$, $3^3 = 27$, $3^4 = 81$, $3^5 = 243$, etc., can be found by observing that the units digit of a product of two integers is the same as the units digit of the product of the units digit of the two integers. For example, the units digit of $3^5 = 3 \times 3^4 = 3 \times 81$ is 3 since the units digit of 3×1 is 3, and the units digit of $3^6 = 3 \times 3^5 = 3 \times 243$ is 9 since the units digit of 3×3 is 9. From this it follows that the units digit of the powers of 3 follow the pattern 3, 9, 7, 1, 3, 9, 7, 1, etc., with a units digit of 1 for 3^4, 3^8, 3^{12}, ..., 3^{24}, ... Therefore, the units digit of 3^{24} is 1. Thus, 3^{24} is 1 more than a multiple of 10, and hence 3^{24} is 1 more than a multiple of 5, and so the remainder when 3^{24} is divided by 5 is 1.

The correct answer is B.

126. If the volume of a ball is 32,490 cubic millimeters, what is the volume of the ball in cubic centimeters? (1 millimeter = 0.1 centimeter)

(A) 0.3249
(B) 3.249
(C) 32.49
(D) 324.9
(E) 3,249

Arithmetic Measurement conversion

Since 1 mm = 0.1 cm, it follows that
$1 \text{ mm}^3 = (0.1)^3 \text{ cm}^3 = 0.001 \text{ cm}^3$. Therefore,
$32{,}490 \text{ mm}^3 = (32{,}490)(0.001) \text{ cm}^3 = 32.49 \text{ cm}^3$.

The correct answer is C.

127. David used part of $100,000 to purchase a house. Of the remaining portion, he invested $\frac{1}{3}$ of it at 4 percent simple annual interest and $\frac{2}{3}$ of it at 6 percent simple annual interest. If after a year the income from the two investments totaled $320, what was the purchase price of the house?

(A) $96,000
(B) $94,000
(C) $88,000
(D) $75,000
(E) $40,000

Algebra Applied problems; Percents

Let x be the amount, in dollars, that David used to purchase the house. Then David invested $(100{,}000 - x)$ dollars, $\frac{1}{3}$ at 4% simple annual interest and $\frac{2}{3}$ at 6% simple annual interest. After one year the total interest, in dollars, on this investment was
$\frac{1}{3}(100{,}000 - x)(0.04) + \frac{2}{3}(100{,}000 - x)(0.06) = 320$.
Solve this equation to find the value of x.

$\frac{1}{3}(100{,}000 - x)(0.04) +$		
$\frac{2}{3}(100{,}000 - x)(0.06) = 320$	given	
$(100{,}000 - x)(0.04) +$		
$2(100{,}000 - x)(0.06) = 960$	multiply both sides by 3	
$4{,}000 - 0.04x +$		
$12{,}000 - 0.12x = 960$	distributive property	
$16{,}000 - 0.16x = 960$	combine like terms	

$16{,}000 - 960 = 0.16x$	add $0.16x - 960$ to both sides	
$100{,}000 - 6{,}000 = x$	divide both sides by 0.16	
$94{,}000 = x$		

Therefore, the purchase price of the house was $94,000.

The correct answer is B.

128. The cost to rent a small bus for a trip is x dollars, which is to be shared equally among the people taking the trip. If 10 people take the trip rather than 16, how many more dollars, in terms of x, will it cost per person?

(A) $\dfrac{x}{6}$

(B) $\dfrac{x}{10}$

(C) $\dfrac{x}{16}$

(D) $\dfrac{3x}{40}$

(E) $\dfrac{3x}{80}$

Algebra Applied problems

If 16 take the trip, the cost per person would be $\frac{x}{16}$ dollars. If 10 take the trip, the cost per person would be $\frac{x}{10}$ dollars. (Note that the lowest common multiple of 10 and 16 is 80.)

Thus, if 10 take the trip, the increase in dollars per person would be $\frac{x}{10} - \frac{x}{16} = \frac{8x}{80} - \frac{5x}{80} = \frac{3x}{80}$.

The correct answer is E.

129. If x is an integer and $y = 3x + 2$, which of the following CANNOT be a divisor of y?

    (A)   4
    (B)   5
    (C)   6
    (D)   7
    (E)   8

    Arithmetic Properties of numbers

    Although $3x$ is always divisible by 3, $3x + 2$ cannot be divisible by 3 since 2 is not divisible by 3. Thus, $3x + 2$ cannot be divisible by any multiple of 3, including 6.

    The correct answer is C.

130. A certain electronic component is sold in boxes of 54 for $16.20 and in boxes of 27 for $13.20. A customer who needed only 54 components for a project had to buy 2 boxes of 27 because boxes of 54 were unavailable. Approximately how much more did the customer pay for each component due to the unavailability of the larger boxes?

    (A) $0.33
    (B) $0.19
    (C) $0.11
    (D) $0.06
    (E) $0.03

    Arithmetic Operations of rational numbers

    The customer paid $2\left(\$13.20\right) = \$26.40$ for the 2 boxes of 27 components. This is $\$26.40 - \$16.20 = \$10.20$ more than the cost of a single box of 54 components. So, the extra cost per component is $\dfrac{\$10.20}{54} = \$0.19$.

    The correct answer is B.

131. As a salesperson, Phyllis can choose one of two methods of annual payment: either an annual salary of $35,000 with no commission or an annual salary of $10,000 plus a 20 percent commission on her total annual sales. What must her total annual sales be to give her the same annual pay with either method?

    (A) $100,000
    (B) $120,000
    (C) $125,000
    (D) $130,000
    (E) $132,000

    Algebra Applied problems

    Letting s be Phyllis's total annual sales needed to generate the same annual pay with either method, the given information can be expressed as $\$35,000 = \$10,000 + 0.2s$. Solve this equation for s.

    $$\$35,000 = \$10,000 + 0.2s$$

    $$\$25,000 = 0.2s$$

    $$\$125,000 = s$$

    The correct answer is C.

132. Last year Department Store X had a sales total for December that was 4 times the average (arithmetic mean) of the monthly sales totals for January through November. The sales total for December was what fraction of the sales total for the year?

    (A) $\dfrac{1}{4}$

    (B) $\dfrac{4}{15}$

    (C) $\dfrac{1}{3}$

    (D) $\dfrac{4}{11}$

    (E) $\dfrac{4}{5}$

    Algebra; Arithmetic Applied problems; Statistics

    Let A equal the average sales per month for the first 11 months. The given information about the total sales for the year can then be expressed as

$11A + 4A = 15A$. Thus, $4A = (F)(15A)$, where F is the fraction of the sales total for the year that the sales total for December represents. Then

$$F = \frac{4A}{15A} = \frac{4}{15}.$$

The correct answer is B.

133. Working alone, Printers X, Y, and Z can do a certain printing job, consisting of a large number of pages, in 12, 15, and 18 hours, respectively. What is the ratio of the time it takes Printer X to do the job, working alone at its rate, to the time it takes Printers Y and Z to do the job, working together at their individual rates?

(A) $\dfrac{4}{11}$

(B) $\dfrac{1}{2}$

(C) $\dfrac{15}{22}$

(D) $\dfrac{22}{15}$

(E) $\dfrac{11}{4}$

Arithmetic Operations on rational numbers

Since Printer Y can do the job in 15 hours, it can do $\dfrac{1}{15}$ of the job in 1 hour. Since Printer Z can do the job in 18 hours, it can do $\dfrac{1}{18}$ of the job in 1 hour. Together, Printers Y and Z can do

$$\left(\frac{1}{15} + \frac{1}{18}\right) = \left(\frac{6}{90} + \frac{5}{90}\right) = \frac{11}{90}$$ of the job in 1 hour,

which means that it takes them $\dfrac{90}{11}$ hours to complete the job. Since Printer X completes the job in 12 hours, the ratio of the time required for X to do the job to the time required for Y and Z working together to do the job is

$$\frac{12}{\frac{90}{11}} = \frac{12(11)}{90} = \frac{2(11)}{15} = \frac{22}{15}.$$

The correct answer is D.

134. In the sequence x_0, x_1, x_2, ..., x_n, each term from x_1 to x_k is 3 greater than the previous term, and each term from x_{k+1} to x_n is 3 less than the previous term, where n and k are positive integers and $k < n$. If $x_0 = x_n = 0$ and if $x_k = 15$, what is the value of n?

(A) 5
(B) 6
(C) 9
(D) 10
(E) 15

Algebra Sequences

Since $x_0 = 0$ and each term from x_1 to x_k is 3 greater than the previous term, then $x_k = 0 + (k)(3)$. Since $x_k = 15$, then $15 = 3k$ and $k = 5$. Since each term from x_{k+1} to x_n is 3 less than the previous term, then $x_n = x_k - (n-k)(3)$. Substituting the known values for x_k, x_n, and k gives $0 = 15 - (n-5)(3)$, from which it follows that $3n = 30$ and $n = 10$.

The correct answer is D.

135. If $x \neq 2$, then $\dfrac{3x^2(x-2) - x + 2}{x-2} =$

(A) $3x^2 - x + 2$
(B) $3x^2 + 1$
(C) $3x^2$
(D) $3x^2 - 1$
(E) $3x^2 - 2$

Algebra Simplifying algebraic expressions

When simplifying this expression, it is important to note that, as a first step, the numerator must be factored so that the numerator is the product of two or more expressions, one of which is $(x-2)$. This can be accomplished by rewriting the last two terms of the numerator as $(-1)(x-2)$. Then

$$\frac{3x^2(x-2)-x+2}{x-2} = \frac{3x^2(x-2)+(-1)(x-2)}{x-2}$$

$$= \frac{(x-2)(3x^2+(-1))}{x-2}$$

$$= 3x^2+(-1)$$

$$= 3x^2-1$$

The correct answer is D.

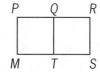

Note: Not drawn to scale.

136. In the figure shown above, line segment QR has length 12, and rectangle $MPQT$ is a square. If the area of rectangular region $MPRS$ is 540, what is the area of rectangular region $TQRS$?

(A) 144
(B) 216
(C) 324
(D) 360
(E) 396

Geometry; Algebra Area; Second-degree equations

Since $MPQT$ is a square, let $MP = PQ = x$. Then $PR = PQ + QR = x + 12$. The area of $MPRS$ can be expressed as $x(x+12)$. Since the area of $MPRS$ is given to be 540,

$$x(x+12) = 540$$

$$x^2 + 12x = 540$$

$$x^2 + 12x - 540 = 0$$

$$(x-18)(x+30) = 0$$

$$x = 18 \text{ or } x = -30$$

Since x represents a length and must be positive, $x = 18$. The area of $TQRS$ is then $(12)(18) = 216$.

As an alternative to solving the quadratic equation, look for a pair of positive numbers such that their product is 540 and one is 12 greater than the other. The pair is 18 and 30, so $x = 18$ and the area of $TQRS$ is then $(12)(18) = 216$.

The correct answer is B.

137. A train travels from New York City to Chicago, a distance of approximately 840 miles, at an average rate of 60 miles per hour and arrives in Chicago at 6:00 in the evening, Chicago time. At what hour in the morning, New York City time, did the train depart for Chicago? (Note: Chicago time is one hour earlier than New York City time.)

(A) 4:00
(B) 5:00
(C) 6:00
(D) 7:00
(E) 8:00

Arithmetic Operations on rational numbers

Using the formula $\frac{\text{distance}}{\text{rate}} = \text{time}$,

it can be calculated that it took the train

$\frac{840 \text{ miles}}{60 \text{ miles per hour}} = 14$ hours to travel from

New York City to Chicago. The train arrived in Chicago at 6:00 in the evening. Since it had departed 14 hours before that, it had therefore departed at 4:00 a.m. Chicago time. Then, since it is given that Chicago time is one hour earlier than New York City time, it had departed at 5:00 a.m. New York City time.

The correct answer is B.

138. Last year Manfred received 26 paychecks. Each of his first 6 paychecks was $750; each of his remaining paychecks was $30 more than each of his first 6 paychecks. To the nearest dollar, what was the average (arithmetic mean) amount of his paychecks for the year?

(A) $752
(B) $755
(C) $765
(D) $773
(E) $775

Arithmetic Statistics

In addition to the first 6 paychecks for $750 each, Manfred received $26 - 6 = 20$ paychecks for $750 + $30 or $780 each. Applying the formula

$$\frac{\text{sum of values}}{\text{number of values}} = \text{average},$$ this information

can be expressed in the following equation:

$$\frac{6(750) + 20(780)}{26} = \frac{20,100}{26} = 773.08$$

The correct answer is D.

139. Machines A and B always operate independently and at their respective constant rates. When working alone, Machine A can fill a production lot in 5 hours, and Machine B can fill the same lot in x hours. When the two machines operate simultaneously to fill the production lot, it takes them 2 hours to complete the job. What is the value of x ?

   (A) $3\frac{1}{3}$

   (B) 3

   (C) $2\frac{1}{2}$

   (D) $2\frac{1}{3}$

   (E) $1\frac{1}{2}$

Algebra Applied problems

Since Machine A can fill a production lot in

5 hours, it can fill $\frac{1}{5}$ of the lot in 1 hour. Since

Machine B can fill the same production lot in

x hours, it can fill $\frac{1}{x}$ of the lot in 1 hour. The two

machines operating simultaneously can fill $\frac{1}{5} + \frac{1}{x}$

of the lot in 1 hour. Since it takes them 2 hours to

complete the lot together, they can fill $\frac{1}{2}$ of the lot

in 1 hour and so $\frac{1}{5} + \frac{1}{x} = \frac{1}{2}$, which can be solved

for x as follows:

$$\frac{1}{5} + \frac{1}{x} = \frac{1}{2}$$

$$10x\left(\frac{1}{5} + \frac{1}{x}\right) = 10x\left(\frac{1}{2}\right)$$

$$2x + 10 = 5x$$

$$10 = 3x$$

$$\frac{10}{3} = x$$

$$x = 3\frac{1}{3}$$

The correct answer is A.

140. A driver completed the first 20 miles of a 40-mile trip at an average speed of 50 miles per hour. At what average speed must the driver complete the remaining 20 miles to achieve an average speed of 60 miles per hour for the entire 40-mile trip? (Assume that the driver did not make any stops during the 40-mile trip.)

   (A)   65 mph
   (B)   68 mph
   (C)   70 mph
   (D)   75 mph
   (E)   80 mph

Algebra Applied problems

Using $D = rt$, where D represents distance, r represents average speed, and t represents time, and its equivalent formula $t = \dfrac{D}{r}$ to make a chart like the one below is often helpful in solving this type of problem.

	D	r	t
1st 20 miles	20	50	$\frac{20}{50} = \frac{2}{5}$
2nd 20 miles	20	r	$\frac{20}{r}$
Total trip	40	60	$\frac{40}{60} = \frac{2}{3}$

The total time for the trip is the sum of the times for the first 20 miles and the second 20 miles, so

$$\frac{2}{5} + \frac{20}{r} = \frac{2}{3}$$

$$(15r)\left(\frac{2}{5} + \frac{20}{r}\right) = (15r)\left(\frac{2}{3}\right)$$

$$6r + 300 = 10r$$

$$300 = 4r$$

$$75 = r$$

The correct answer is D.

141. The figure shown above consists of three identical circles that are tangent to each other. If the area of the shaded region is $64\sqrt{3} - 32\pi$, what is the radius of each circle?

(A) 4
(B) 8
(C) 16
(D) 24
(E) 32

Geometry Circles; Triangles; Area

Let r represent the radius of each circle. Then the triangle shown dashed in the figure is equilateral with sides $2r$ units long. The interior of the triangle is composed of the shaded region and three circular sectors. The area of the shaded region can be found as the area of the triangle minus the sum of the areas of the three sectors. Since the triangle is equilateral, its side lengths are in the proportions as shown in the following diagram. The area of the interior of the triangle is $\frac{1}{2}(2r)(r\sqrt{3}) = r^2\sqrt{3}$.

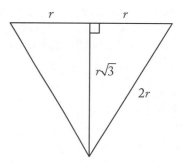

Each of the three sectors has a central angle of $60°$ because the central angle is an angle of the equilateral triangle. Therefore, the area of each sector is $\frac{60}{360} = \frac{1}{6}$ of the area of the circle. The sum of the areas of the three sectors is then

$3\left(\frac{1}{6}\pi r^2\right) = \frac{1}{2}\pi r^2$. Thus, the area of the shaded region is $r^2\sqrt{3} - \frac{1}{2}\pi r^2 = r^2\left(\sqrt{3} - \frac{1}{2}\pi\right)$. But, this area is given as $64\sqrt{3} - 32\pi = 64\left(\sqrt{3} - \frac{1}{2}\pi\right)$. Thus $r^2 = 64$, and $r = 8$.

The correct answer is B.

142. A positive integer n is a perfect number provided that the sum of all the positive factors of n, including 1 and n, is equal to $2n$. What is the sum of the reciprocals of all the positive factors of the perfect number 28 ?

(A) $\frac{1}{4}$

(B) $\frac{56}{27}$

(C) 2

(D) 3

(E) 4

Arithmetic Properties of numbers

The factors of 28 are 1, 2, 4, 7, 14, and 28. Therefore, the sum of the reciprocals of the factors of 28 is $\frac{1}{1} + \frac{1}{2} + \frac{1}{4} + \frac{1}{7} + \frac{1}{14} + \frac{1}{28} =$

$\frac{28}{28} + \frac{14}{28} + \frac{7}{28} + \frac{4}{28} + \frac{2}{28} + \frac{1}{28} =$

$\frac{28 + 14 + 7 + 4 + 2 + 1}{28} = \frac{56}{28} = 2.$

The correct answer is C.

143. The infinite sequence $a_1, a_2, \ldots, a_n, \ldots$ is such that $a_1 = 2$, $a_2 = -3$, $a_3 = 5$, $a_4 = -1$, and $a_n = a_{n-4}$ for $n > 4$. What is the sum of the first 97 terms of the sequence?

    (A) 72
    (B) 74
    (C) 75
    (D) 78
    (E) 80

Arithmetic Sequences and series

Because $a_n = a_{n-4}$ for $n > 4$, it follows that the terms of the sequence repeat in groups of 4 terms:

Values for n	Values for a_n
1, 2, 3, 4	2, −3, 5, −1
5, 6, 7, 8	2, −3, 5, −1
9, 10, 11, 12	2, −3, 5, −1
13, 14, 15, 16	2, −3, 5, −1

Thus, since $97 = 24(4) + 1$, the sum of the first 97 terms can be grouped into 24 groups of 4 terms each, with one remaining term, which allows the sum to be easily found:

$(a_1 + a_2 + a_3 + a_4) + (a_5 + a_6 + a_7 + a_8) + \ldots + (a_{93} + a_{94} + a_{95} + a_{96}) + a_{97}$

$= (2 - 3 + 5 - 1) + (2 - 3 + 5 - 1) + \ldots + (2 - 3 + 5 - 1) + 2$

$= 24(2 - 3 + 5 - 1) + 2 = 24(3) + 2 = 74$

The correct answer is B.

144. The sequence $a_1, a_2, \ldots, a_n, \ldots$ is such that $a_n = 2a_{n-1} - x$ for all positive integers $n \geq 2$ and for a certain number x. If $a_5 = 99$ and $a_3 = 27$, what is the value of x ?

    (A) 3
    (B) 9
    (C) 18
    (D) 36
    (E) 45

Algebra Sequences and series

An expression for a_5 that involves x can be obtained using $a_3 = 27$ and applying the equation $a_n = 2a_{n-1} - x$ twice, once for $n = 4$ and once for $n = 5$.

$a_4 = 2a_3 - x$	using $a_n = 2a_{n-1} - x$ for $n = 4$
$= 2(27) - x$	using $a_3 = 27$
$a_5 = 2a_4 - x$	using $a_n = 2a_{n-1} - x$ for $n = 5$
$= 2[2(27) - x] - x$	using $a_4 = 2(27) - x$
$= 4(27) - 3x$	combine like terms

Therefore, using $a_5 = 99$, we have

$99 = 4(27) - 3x$	given
$3x = 4(27) - 99$	adding $(3x - 99)$ to both sides
$x = 4(9) - 33$	dividing both sides by 3
$x = 3$	arithmetic

The correct answer is A.

145. A window is in the shape of a regular hexagon with each side of length 80 centimeters. If a diagonal through the center of the hexagon is w centimeters long, then $w =$

    (A) 80
    (B) 120
    (C) 150
    (D) 160
    (E) 240

Geometry Polygons

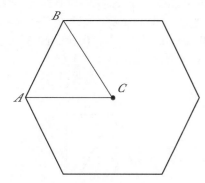

Let A and B be the endpoints of one of the sides of the hexagon and let C be the center of the hexagon. Then the degree measure of $\angle ACB$ is $\frac{360}{6} = 60$ and the sum of the degree measures of $\angle ABC$ and $\angle BAC$ is $180 - 60 = 120$. Also, since $AC = BC$, the degree measures of $\angle ABC$ and $\angle BAC$ are equal. Therefore, the degree measure of each of $\angle ABC$ and $\angle BAC$ is 60. Thus, $\triangle ABC$ is an equilateral triangle with side length $AB = 80$. It follows that the length of a diagonal through the center of the hexagon is $2(AC) = 2(80) = 160$.

The correct answer is D.

146. On a certain transatlantic crossing, 20 percent of a ship's passengers held round-trip tickets and also took their cars aboard the ship. If 60 percent of the passengers with round-trip tickets did <u>not</u> take their cars aboard the ship, what percent of the ship's passengers held round-trip tickets?

(A) $33\frac{1}{3}\%$
(B) 40%
(C) 50%
(D) 60%
(E) $66\frac{2}{3}\%$

Arithmetic Percents

Since the number of passengers on the ship is immaterial, let the number of passengers on the ship be 100 for convenience. Let x be the number of passengers that held round-trip tickets. Then, since 20 percent of the passengers held a round-trip ticket and took their cars aboard the ship, $0.20(100) = 20$ passengers held round-trip tickets and took their cars aboard the ship. The remaining passengers with round-trip tickets did not take

their cars aboard, and they represent $0.6x$ (that is, 60 percent of the passengers with round-trip tickets). Thus, $0.6x + 20 = x$, from which it follows that $20 = 0.4x$, and so $x = 50$. The percent of passengers with round-trip tickets is, then, $\frac{50}{100} = 50\%$.

The correct answer is C.

147. If x and k are integers and $\left(12^x\right)\left(4^{2x+1}\right) = \left(2^k\right)\left(3^2\right)$, what is the value of k?

(A) 5
(B) 7
(C) 10
(D) 12
(E) 14

Arithmetic Exponents

Rewrite the expression on the left so that it is a product of powers of 2 and 3.

$$\left(12^x\right)\left(4^{2x+1}\right) = \left[\left(3 \cdot 2^2\right)^x\right]\left[\left(2^2\right)^{2x+1}\right]$$

$$= \left(3^x\right)\left[\left(2^2\right)^x\right]\left[2^{2(2x+1)}\right]$$

$$= \left(3^x\right)\left(2^{2x}\right)\left(2^{4x+2}\right)$$

$$= \left(3^x\right)\left(2^{6x+2}\right)$$

Then, since $\left(12^x\right)\left(4^{2x+1}\right) = \left(2^k\right)\left(3^2\right)$, it follows that $\left(3^x\right)\left(2^{6x+2}\right) = \left(2^k\right)\left(3^2\right) = \left(3^2\right)\left(2^k\right)$, so $x = 2$ and $k = 6x + 2$. Substituting 2 for x gives $k = 6(2) + 2 = 14$.

The correct answer is E.

148. For every even positive integer m, $f(m)$ represents the product of all even integers from 2 to m, inclusive. For example, $f(12) = 2 \times 4 \times 6 \times 8 \times 10 \times 12$. What is the greatest prime factor of $f(24)$?

(A) 23
(B) 19
(C) 17
(D) 13
(E) 11

Arithmetic Properties of numbers

Rewriting $f(24) = 2 \times 4 \times 6 \times 8 \times 10 \times 12 \times 14 \times \ldots \times 20 \times 22 \times 24$ as $2 \times 4 \times 2(3) \times 8 \times 2(5) \times 12 \times 2(7) \times \ldots \times 20 \times 2(11) \times 24$ shows that all of the prime numbers from 2 through 11 are factors of $f(24)$. The next prime number is 13, but 13 is not a factor of $f(24)$ because none of the even integers from 2 through 24 has 13 as a factor. Therefore, the largest prime factor of $f(24)$ is 11.

The correct answer is E.

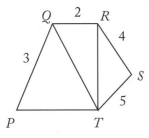

Note: Not drawn to scale.

149. In pentagon *PQRST*, $PQ = 3$, $QR = 2$, $RS = 4$, and $ST = 5$. Which of the lengths 5, 10, and 15 could be the value of *PT*?

   (A)   5 only
   (B)   15 only
   (C)   5 and 10 only
   (D)   10 and 15 only
   (E)   5, 10, and 15

Geometry Polygons; Triangles

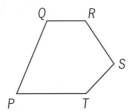

Note: Not drawn to scale.

In the figure above, diagonals $\overline{TQ}$ and $\overline{TR}$ have been drawn in to show $\triangle TRS$ and $\triangle TRQ$. Because the length of any side of a triangle must be less than the sum of the lengths of the other two sides, $RT < 5 + 4 = 9$ in $\triangle TRS$, and $QT < RT + 2$ in

$\triangle TRQ$. Since $RT < 9$, then $RT + 2 < 9 + 2 = 11$, which then implies $QT < 11$. Now, $PT < QT + 3$ in $\triangle TQP$, and since $QT < 11$, $QT + 3 < 11 + 3 = 14$. It follows that $PT < 14$. Therefore, 15 cannot be the length of $\overline{PT}$ since $15 \not< 14$.

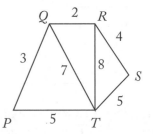

Note: Not drawn to scale.

To show that 5 can be the length of $\overline{PT}$, consider the figure above. For $\triangle TQP$, the length of any side is less than the sum of the lengths of the other two sides as shown below.

$$QT = 7 < 8 = 5 + 3 = PT + PQ$$
$$PQ = 3 < 12 = 5 + 7 = PT + TQ$$
$$PT = 5 < 10 = 3 + 7 = PQ + TQ$$

For $\triangle RQT$, the length of any side is less than the sum of the lengths of the other two sides as shown below.

$$RT = 8 < 9 = 7 + 2 = QT + QR$$
$$RQ = 2 < 15 = 7 + 8 = QT + RT$$
$$QT = 7 < 10 = 2 + 8 = QR + RT$$

For $\triangle RST$, the length of any side is less than the sum of the lengths of the other two sides as shown below.

$$RS = 4 < 13 = 8 + 5 = TR + TS$$
$$RT = 8 < 9 = 5 + 4 = ST + SR$$
$$ST = 5 < 12 = 8 + 4 = TR + RS$$

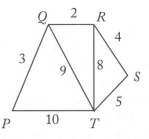

Note: Not drawn to scale.

To show that 10 can be the length of $\overline{PT}$, consider the figure above. For ΔTQP, the length of any side is less than the sum of the lengths of the other two sides as shown below.

$$QT = 9 < 13 = 10 + 3 = PT + PQ$$

$$PQ = 3 < 19 = 10 + 9 = PT + TQ$$

$$PT = 10 < 12 = 3 + 9 = PQ + TQ$$

For ΔRQT, the length of any side is less than the sum of the lengths of the other two sides as shown below.

$$RT = 8 < 11 = 9 + 2 = QT + QR$$

$$RQ = 2 < 17 = 9 + 8 = QT + RT$$

$$QT = 9 < 10 = 2 + 8 = QR + RT$$

For ΔRST, the length of any side is less than the sum of the lengths of the other two sides as shown below.

$$RS = 4 < 13 = 8 + 5 = TR + TS$$

$$RT = 8 < 9 = 5 + 4 = ST + SR$$

$$ST = 5 < 12 = 8 + 4 = TR + RS$$

Therefore, 5 and 10 can be the length of $\overline{PT}$, and 15 cannot be the length of $\overline{PT}$.

The correct answer is C.

$$3,\ k,\ 2,\ 8,\ m,\ 3$$

150. The arithmetic mean of the list of numbers above is 4. If k and m are integers and $k \neq m$, what is the median of the list?

(A)   2
(B)   2.5
(C)   3
(D)   3.5
(E)   4

Arithmetic Statistics

Since the arithmetic mean $= \dfrac{\text{sum of values}}{\text{number of values}}$,

then $\dfrac{3 + k + 2 + 8 + m + 3}{6} = 4$, and so

$\dfrac{16 + k + m}{6} = 4$, $16 + k + m = 24$, $k + m = 8$. Since

$k \neq m$, then either $k < 4$ and $m > 4$ or $k > 4$ and

$m < 4$. Because k and m are integers, either $k \leq 3$ and $5 \geq m$ or $k \geq 5$ and $m \leq 3$.

Case (i):   If $k \leq 2$, then $m \geq 6$ and the six integers in ascending order are k, 2, 3, 3, m, 8 or k, 2, 3, 3, 8, m. The two middle integers are both 3 so the median is $\dfrac{3 + 3}{2} = 3$.

Case (ii):   If $k = 3$, then $m = 5$ and the six integers in ascending order are 2, k, 3, 3, m, 8. The two middle integers are both 3 so the median is $\dfrac{3 + 3}{2} = 3$.

Case (iii):   If $k = 5$, then $m = 3$ and the six integers in ascending order are 2, m, 3, 3, k, 8. The two middle integers are both 3 so the median is $\dfrac{3 + 3}{2} = 3$.

Case (iv):   If $k \geq 6$, then $m \leq 2$ and the six integers in ascending order are m, 2, 3, 3, k, 8 or m, 2, 3, 3, 8, k. The two middle integers are both 3 so the median is $\dfrac{3 + 3}{2} = 3$.

The correct answer is C.

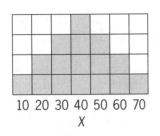

10 20 30 40 50 60 70

X

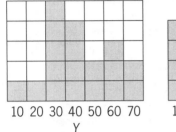

10 20 30 40 50 60 70

Y

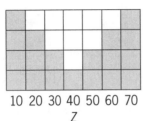

10 20 30 40 50 60 70

Z

151. If the variables X, Y, and Z take on only the values 10, 20, 30, 40, 50, 60, or 70 with frequencies indicated by the shaded regions above, for which of the frequency distributions is the mean equal to the median?

(A)   X only
(B)   Y only
(C)   Z only
(D)   X and Y
(E)   X and Z

Arithmetic Statistics

The frequency distributions for both X and Z are symmetric about 40, and thus both X and Z have mean = median = 40. Therefore, any answer choice that does not include both X and Z can be eliminated. This leaves only answer choice E.

The correct answer is E.

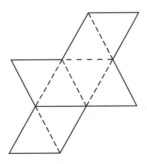

152. When the figure above is cut along the solid lines, folded along the dashed lines, and taped along the solid lines, the result is a model of a geometric solid. This geometric solid consists of 2 pyramids, each with a square base that they share. What is the sum of the number of edges and the number of faces of this geometric solid?

(A)   10
(B)   18
(C)   20
(D)   24
(E)   25

Geometry Solids

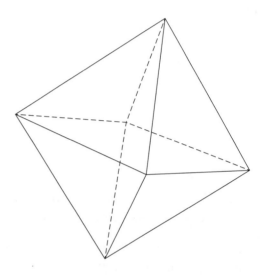

A geometric solid consisting of 2 pyramids, each with a square base that they share, is shown in the figure above. From the figure it can be seen that the solid has 12 edges and 8 faces. Therefore, the sum of the number of edges and the number of faces of the solid is $12 + 8 = 20$.

Alternatively, the solid has $7 + 5 = 12$ edges because each edge in the solid is generated from either a dashed segment (there are 7 dashed segments) or from a pair of solid segments taped together (there are $\frac{10}{2} = 5$ such pairs of solid segments), and the solid has 8 faces because there are 8 small triangles in the given figure. Therefore, the sum of the number of edges and the number of faces of the solid is $12 + 8 = 20$.

The correct answer is C.

$$2x + y = 12$$
$$|y| \le 12$$

153. For how many ordered pairs (x, y) that are solutions of the system above are x and y both integers?

(A) 7
(B) 10
(C) 12
(D) 13
(E) 14

Algebra Absolute value

From $|y| \le 12$, if y must be an integer, then y must be in the set
$S = \{\pm 12, \ \pm 11, \ \pm 10, \ \ldots, \ \pm 3, \ \pm 2, \ \pm 1, \ 0\}$.
Since $2x + y = 12$, then $x = \dfrac{12 - y}{2}$. If x must be an integer, then $12 - y$ must be divisible by 2; that is, $12 - y$ must be even. Since 12 is even, $12 - y$ is even if and only if y is even. This eliminates all odd integers from S, leaving only the even integers $\pm 12, \pm 10, \pm 8, \pm 6, \pm 4, \pm 2$, and 0. Thus, there are 13 possible integer y-values, each with a corresponding integer x-value and, therefore, there are 13 ordered pairs (x, y), where x and y are both integers, that solve the system.

The correct answer is D.

154. The points R, T, and U lie on a circle that has radius 4. If the length of arc RTU is $\dfrac{4\pi}{3}$, what is the length of line segment RU?

(A) $\dfrac{4}{3}$

(B) $\dfrac{8}{3}$

(C) 3
(D) 4
(E) 6

Geometry Circles; Triangles; Circumference

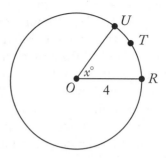

In the figure above, O is the center of the circle that contains R, T, and U and x is the degree measure of $\angle ROU$. Since the circumference of the circle is $2\pi(4) = 8\pi$ and there are $360°$ in the circle, the ratio of the length of arc RTU to the circumference of the circle is the same as the ratio of x to 360. Therefore, $\dfrac{\frac{4\pi}{3}}{8\pi} = \dfrac{x}{360}$. Then
$x = \dfrac{\frac{4\pi}{3}(360)}{8\pi} = \dfrac{480\pi}{8\pi} = 60$. This means that $\triangle ROU$ is an isosceles triangle with side lengths $OR = OU = 4$ and vertex angle measuring $60°$. The base angles of $\triangle ROU$ must have equal measures and the sum of their measures must be $180° - 60° = 120°$. Therefore, each base angle measures $60°$, $\triangle ROU$ is equilateral, and $RU = 4$.

The correct answer is D.

155. A certain university will select 1 of 7 candidates eligible to fill a position in the mathematics department and 2 of 10 candidates eligible to fill 2 identical positions in the computer science department. If none of the candidates is eligible for a position in both departments, how many different sets of 3 candidates are there to fill the 3 positions?

(A) 42
(B) 70
(C) 140
(D) 165
(E) 315

Arithmetic Elementary combinatorics

To fill the position in the math department, 1 candidate will be selected from a group of 7 eligible candidates, and so there are 7 sets of 1 candidate each to fill the position in the math department. To fill the positions in the computer science department, any one of the 10 eligible candidates can be chosen for the first position and any of the remaining 9 eligible candidates can be chosen for the second position, making a total of $10 \times 9 = 90$ sets of 2 candidates to fill the computer science positions. But, this number includes the set in which Candidate A was chosen to fill the first position and Candidate B was chosen to fill the second position as well as the set in which Candidate B was chosen for the first position and Candidate A was chosen for the second position. These sets are not different essentially since the positions are identical and in both sets Candidates A and B are chosen to fill the 2 positions. Therefore, there are $\frac{90}{2} = 45$ sets of 2 candidates to fill the computer science positions. Then, using the multiplication principle, there are $7 \times 45 = 315$ different sets of 3 candidates to fill the 3 positions.

The correct answer is E.

156. A survey of employers found that during 1993 employment costs rose 3.5 percent, where employment costs consist of salary costs and fringe-benefit costs. If salary costs rose 3 percent and fringe-benefit costs rose 5.5 percent during 1993, then fringe-benefit costs represented what percent of employment costs at the beginning of 1993 ?

    (A) 16.5%
    (B) 20%
    (C) 35%
    (D) 55%
    (E) 65%

    ### Algebra; Arithmetic First-degree equations; Percents

    Let E represent employment costs, S represent salary costs, and F represent fringe-benefit costs. Then $E = S + F$. An increase of 3 percent in salary costs and a 5.5 percent increase in fringe-benefit costs resulted in a 3.5 percent increase in employment costs. Therefore $1.03S + 1.055F = 1.035E$. But, $E = S + F$, so

$$1.03S + 1.055F = 1.035(S + F) = 1.035S + 1.035F.$$

Combining like terms gives

$$(1.055 - 1.035)F = (1.035 - 1.03)S \text{ or}$$

$0.02F = 0.005S$. Then, $S = \dfrac{0.02}{0.005}F = 4F$. Thus, since $E = S + F$, it follows that $E = 4F + F = 5F$.

Then, F as a percent of E is $\dfrac{F}{E} = \dfrac{F}{5F} = \dfrac{1}{5} = 20\%$.

The correct answer is B.

157. The subsets of the set {w, x, y} are {w}, {x}, {y}, {w, x}, {w, y}, {x, y}, {w, x, y}, and { } (the empty subset). How many subsets of the set {w, x, y, z} contain w ?

    (A) Four
    (B) Five
    (C) Seven
    (D) Eight
    (E) Sixteen

Arithmetic Sets

As shown in the table, the subsets of $\{w, x, y, z\}$ can be organized into two columns, those subsets of $\{w, x, y, z\}$ that do not contain w (left column) and the corresponding subsets of $\{w, x, y, z\}$ that contain w (right column), and each of these collections has the same number of sets. Therefore, there are 8 subsets of $\{w, x, y, z\}$ that contain w.

subsets not containing w	subsets containing w
{ }	{w}
{x}	{w, x}
{y}	{w, y}
{z}	{w, z}
{x, y}	{w, x, y}
{x, z}	{w, x, z}
{y, z}	{w, y, z}
{x, y, z}	{w, x, y, z}

The correct answer is D.

158. There are 10 books on a shelf, of which 4 are paperbacks and 6 are hardbacks. How many possible selections of 5 books from the shelf contain at least one paperback and at least one hardback?

    (A)   75
    (B)   120
    (C)   210
    (D)   246
    (E)   252

Arithmetic Elementary combinatorics

The number of selections of 5 books containing at least one paperback and at least one hardback is equal to $T - N$, where T is the total number of selections of 5 books and N is the number of selections that do not contain both a paperback and a hardback. The value of T is

$$\binom{10}{5} = \frac{10!}{5!\left(10 - 5\right)!} = \frac{(6)(7)(8)(9)(10)}{(1)(2)(3)(4)(5)}$$
$$= (7)(2)(9)(2) = 252.$$

To find the value of N, first note that no selection of 5 books can contain all paperbacks, since there are only 4 paperback books. Thus, the value of N is equal to the number of selections of 5 books that contain all hardbacks, which is equal to 6 since there are 6 ways that a single hardback can be left out when choosing the 5 hardback books. It follows that the number of selections of 5 books containing at least one paperback and at least one hardback is $T - N = 252 - 6 = 246$.

The correct answer is D.

159. If x is to be chosen at random from the set {1, 2, 3, 4} and y is to be chosen at random from the set {5, 6, 7}, what is the probability that xy will be even?

    (A) $\frac{1}{6}$

    (B) $\frac{1}{3}$

    (C) $\frac{1}{2}$

    (D) $\frac{2}{3}$

    (E) $\frac{5}{6}$

Arithmetic; Algebra Probability; Concepts of sets

By the principle of multiplication, since there are 4 elements in the first set and 3 elements in the second set, there are $\left(4\right)\left(3\right) = 12$ possible products of xy, where x is chosen from the first set and y is chosen from the second set. These products will be even EXCEPT when both x and y are odd. Since there are 2 odd numbers in the first set and 2 odd numbers in the second set, there are $\left(2\right)\left(2\right) = 4$ products of x and y that are odd. This means that the remaining $12 - 4 = 8$ products are even. Thus, the probability that xy is even is $\frac{8}{12} = \frac{2}{3}$.

The correct answer is D.

160. The function f is defined for each positive three-digit integer n by $f(n) = 2^x\, 3^y\, 5^z$, where x, y, and z are the hundreds, tens, and units digits of n, respectively. If m and v are three-digit positive integers such that $f(m) = 9f(v)$, then $m - v =$

    (A)   8
    (B)   9
    (C)   18
    (D)   20
    (E)   80

Algebra Place value

Let the hundreds, tens, and units digits of m be A, B, and C, respectively; and let the hundreds, tens, and units digits of v be a, b, and c, respectively. From $f(m) = 9f(v)$ it follows that $2^A 3^B 5^C = 9(2^a 3^b 5^c) = 3^2(2^a 3^b 5^c) = 2^a 3^{b+2} 5^c$. Therefore, $A = a$, $B = b + 2$, and $C = c$. Now calculate $m - v$.

$$m - v = (100A + 10B + C) \quad \text{place value}$$
$$ - (100a + 10b + c) \quad \text{property}$$
$$= (100a + 10(b + 2) + c) \quad \text{obtained}$$
$$ - (100a + 10b + c) \quad \text{above}$$
$$= 10(b + 2) - 10b \quad \text{combine like terms}$$
$$= 10b + 20 - 10b \quad \text{distributive property}$$
$$= 20 \quad \text{combine like terms}$$

The correct answer is D.

161. If $10^{50} - 74$ is written as an integer in base 10 notation, what is the sum of the digits in that integer?

(A) 424
(B) 433
(C) 440
(D) 449
(E) 467

Arithmetic Properties of numbers

$10^2 - 74$	$=$	$100 - 74$	$= 26$
$10^3 - 74$	$=$	$1,000 - 74$	$= 926$
$10^4 - 74$	$=$	$10,000 - 74$	$= 9,926$
$10^5 - 74$	$=$	$100,000 - 74$	$= 99,926$
$10^6 - 74$	$=$	$1,000,000 - 74$	$= 999,926$

From the table above it is clear that $10^{50} - 74$ in base 10 notation will be 48 digits of 9 followed by the digits 2 and 6. Therefore, the sum of the digits of $10^{50} - 74$ is equal to $48(9) + 2 + 6 = 440$.

The correct answer is C.

162. A certain company that sells only cars and trucks reported that revenues from car sales in 1997 were down 11 percent from 1996 and revenues from truck sales in 1997 were up 7 percent from 1996. If total revenues from car sales and truck sales in 1997 were up 1 percent from 1996, what is the ratio of revenue from car sales in 1996 to revenue from truck sales in 1996?

(A) 1:2
(B) 4:5
(C) 1:1
(D) 3:2
(E) 5:3

Algebra; Arithmetic First-degree equations; Percents

Let C_{96} and C_{97} represent revenues from car sales in 1996 and 1997, respectively, and let T_{96} and T_{97} represent revenues from truck sales in 1996 and 1997, respectively. A decrease of 11 percent in revenue from car sales from 1996 to 1997 can be represented as $(1 - 0.11)C_{96} = C_{97}$, and a 7 percent increase in revenue from truck sales from 1996 to 1997 can be represented as $(1 + 0.07)T_{96} = T_{97}$. An overall increase of 1 percent in revenue from car and truck sales from 1996 to 1997 can be represented as $C_{97} + T_{97} = (1 + 0.01)(C_{96} + T_{96})$. Then, by substitution of expressions for C_{97} and T_{97} that were derived above,

$$(1 - 0.11)C_{96} + (1 + 0.07)T_{96} = (1 + 0.01)(C_{96} + T_{96})$$

and so $0.89C_{96} + 1.07T_{96} = 1.01(C_{96} + T_{96})$ or $0.89C_{96} + 1.07T_{96} = 1.01C_{96} + 1.01T_{96}$. Then, combining like terms gives $(1.07 - 1.01)T_{96} = (1.01 - 0.89)C_{96}$ or $0.06T_{96} = 0.12C_{96}$. Thus $\dfrac{C_{96}}{T_{96}} = \dfrac{0.06}{0.12} = \dfrac{1}{2}$. The ratio of revenue from car sales in 1996 to revenue from truck sales in 1996 is 1:2.

The correct answer is A.

163. If $4 < \dfrac{7-x}{3}$, which of the following must be true?

    I. $5 < x$
    II. $|x + 3| > 2$
    III. $-(x + 5)$ is positive.

    (A) II only
    (B) III only
    (C) I and II only
    (D) II and III only
    (E) I, II, and III

Algebra Inequalities

Given that $4 < \dfrac{7-x}{3}$, it follows that $12 < 7 - x$.

Then, $5 < -x$ or, equivalently, $x < -5$.

I.   If $4 < \dfrac{7-x}{3}$, then $x < -5$. If $5 < x$ were true then, by combining $5 < x$ and $x < -5$, it would follow that $5 < -5$, which cannot be true.

Therefore, it is not the case that, if $4 < \dfrac{7-x}{3}$, then Statement I must be true. In fact, Statement I is never true.

II. If $4 < \dfrac{7-x}{3}$, then $x < -5$, and it follows that $x + 3 < -2$. Since $-2 < 0$, then $x + 3 < 0$ and $|x + 3| = -(x + 3)$. If $x + 3 < -2$, then $-(x + 3) > 2$ and by substitution, $|x + 3| > 2$. Therefore, Statement II must be true for every value of x such that $x < -5$. Therefore, Statement II must be true if $4 < \dfrac{7-x}{3}$.

III. If $4 < \dfrac{7-x}{3}$, then $x < -5$ and $x + 5 < 0$. But, if $x + 5 < 0$, then it follows that $-(x + 5) > 0$ and so $-(x + 5)$ is positive. Therefore Statement III must be true if $4 < \dfrac{7-x}{3}$.

The correct answer is D.

164. A certain right triangle has sides of length x, y, and z, where $x < y < z$. If the area of this triangular region is 1, which of the following indicates all of the possible values of y?

    (A) $y > \sqrt{2}$

    (B) $\dfrac{\sqrt{3}}{2} < y < \sqrt{2}$

    (C) $\dfrac{\sqrt{2}}{3} < y < \dfrac{\sqrt{3}}{2}$

    (D) $\dfrac{\sqrt{3}}{4} < y < \dfrac{\sqrt{2}}{3}$

    (E) $y < \dfrac{\sqrt{3}}{4}$

Geometry; Algebra Triangles; Area; Inequalities

Since x, y, and z are the side lengths of a right triangle and $x < y < z$, it follows that x and y are the lengths of the legs of the triangle and so the area of the triangle is $\dfrac{1}{2}xy$. But, it is given that the area is 1 and so $\dfrac{1}{2}xy = 1$. Then, $xy = 2$ and $y = \dfrac{2}{x}$. Under the assumption that x, y, and z are all positive since they are the side lengths of a triangle, $x < y$ implies $\dfrac{1}{x} > \dfrac{1}{y}$ and then $\dfrac{2}{x} > \dfrac{2}{y}$. But, $y = \dfrac{2}{x}$, so by substitution, $y > \dfrac{2}{y}$, which implies that $y^2 > 2$ since y is positive. Thus, $y > \sqrt{2}$.

Alternatively, if $x < \sqrt{2}$ and $y < \sqrt{2}$, then $xy < 2$. If $x > \sqrt{2}$ and $y > \sqrt{2}$, then $xy > 2$. But, $xy = 2$ so one of x or y must be less than $\sqrt{2}$ and the other must be greater than $\sqrt{2}$. Since $x < y$, it follows that $x < \sqrt{2} < y$ and $y > \sqrt{2}$.

The correct answer is A.

165. A set of numbers has the property that for any number t in the set, $t + 2$ is in the set. If -1 is in the set, which of the following must also be in the set?

> I. -3
> II. 1
> III. 5

(A) I only
(B) II only
(C) I and II only
(D) II and III only
(E) I, II, and III

Arithmetic Properties of numbers

It is given that -1 is in the set and, if t is in the set, then $t + 2$ is in the set.

I. Since $\{-1, 1, 3, 5, 7, 9, 11, …\}$ contains -1 and satisfies the property that if t is in the set, then $t + 2$ is in the set, it is not true that -3 must be in the set.

II. Since -1 is in the set, $-1 + 2 = 1$ is in the set. Therefore, it must be true that 1 is in the set.

III. Since -1 is in the set, $-1 + 2 = 1$ is in the set. Since 1 is in the set, $1 + 2 = 3$ is in the set. Since 3 is in the set, $3 + 2 = 5$ is in the set. Therefore, it must be true that 5 is in the set.

The correct answer is D.

166. A couple decides to have 4 children. If they succeed in having 4 children and each child is equally likely to be a boy or a girl, what is the probability that they will have exactly 2 girls and 2 boys?

(A) $\dfrac{3}{8}$

(B) $\dfrac{1}{4}$

(C) $\dfrac{3}{16}$

(D) $\dfrac{1}{8}$

(E) $\dfrac{1}{16}$

Arithmetic Probability

Representing the birth order of the 4 children as a sequence of 4 letters, each of which is B for boy and G for girl, there are 2 possibilities (B or G) for the first letter, 2 for the second letter, 2 for the third letter, and 2 for the fourth letter, making a total of $2^4 = 16$ sequences. The table below categorizes some of these 16 sequences.

# of boys	# of girls	Sequences	# of sequences
0	4	GGGG	1
1	3	BGGG, GBGG, GGBG, GGGB	4
3	1	GBBB, BGBB, BBGB, BBBG	4
4	0	BBBB	1

The table accounts for $1 + 4 + 4 + 1 = 10$ sequences. The other 6 sequences will have 2Bs and 2Gs. Therefore the probability that the couple will have exactly 2 boys and 2 girls is $\dfrac{6}{16} = \dfrac{3}{8}$.

For the mathematically inclined, if it is assumed that a couple has a fixed number of children, that the probability of having a girl each time is p, and that the sex of each child is independent of the sex of the other children, then the number of girls, x, born to a couple with n children is a random variable having the binomial probability distribution. The probability of having exactly x girls born to a couple with n children is given by the formula $\binom{n}{x} p^x (1 - p)^{n - x}$. For the problem at hand, it is given that each child is equally likely to be a boy or a girl, and so $p = \dfrac{1}{2}$. Thus, the probability of having exactly 2 girls born to a couple with 4 children is

$$\binom{4}{2}\left(\frac{1}{2}\right)^2\left(\frac{1}{2}\right)^2 = \frac{4!}{2!2!}\left(\frac{1}{2}\right)^2\left(\frac{1}{2}\right)^2 =$$

$$(6)\left(\frac{1}{4}\right)\left(\frac{1}{4}\right) = \frac{6}{16} = \frac{3}{8}.$$

The correct answer is A.

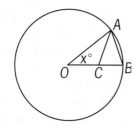

167. In the figure above, point O is the center of the circle and $OC = AC = AB$. What is the value of x ?

(A) 40
(B) 36
(C) 34
(D) 32
(E) 30

Geometry Angles

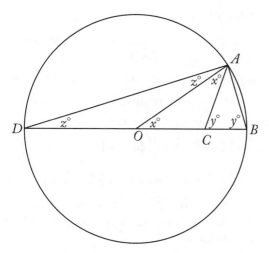

Consider the figure above, where $\overline{DB}$ is a diameter of the circle with center O and $\overline{AD}$ is a chord. Since $OC = AC$, ΔOCA is isosceles and so the base angles, $\angle AOC$ and $\angle OAC$, have the same degree measure. The measure of $\angle AOC$ is given as $x°$, so

the measure of $\angle OAC$ is $x°$. Since $AC = AB$, ΔCAB is isosceles and so the base angles, $\angle ACB$ and $\angle ABC$, have the same degree measure. The measure of each is marked as $y°$. Likewise, since $\overline{OD}$ and $\overline{OA}$ are radii of the circle, $OD = OA$, and ΔDOA is isosceles with base angles, $\angle ADO$ and $\angle DAO$, each measuring $z°$. Each of the following statements is true:

(i)   The measure of $\angle CAB$ is $180 - 2y$ since the sum of the measures of the angles of ΔCAB is 180.

(ii) $\angle DAB$ is a right angle (because $\overline{DB}$ is a diameter of the circle) and so $z + x + (180 - 2y) = 90$, or, equivalently, $2y - x - z = 90$.

(iii) $z + 90 + y = 180$ since the sum of the measures of the angles of right triangle ΔDAB is 180, or, equivalently, $z = 90 - y$.

(iv) $x = 2z$ because the measure of exterior angle $\angle AOC$ to ΔAOD is the sum of the measures of the two opposite interior angles, $\angle ODA$ and $\angle OAD$.

(v) $y = 2x$ because the measure of exterior angle $\angle ACB$ to ΔOCA is the sum of the measures of the two opposite interior angles, $\angle COA$ and $\angle CAO$.

Multiplying the final equation in (iii) by 2 gives $2z = 180 - 2y$. But, $x = 2z$ in (iv), so $x = 180 - 2y$. Finally, the sum of the measures of the angles of ΔCAB is 180 and so $y + y + x = 180$. Then from (v), $2x + 2x + x = 180$, $5x = 180$, and $x = 36$.

The correct answer is B.

168. When 10 is divided by the positive integer n, the remainder is $n - 4$. Which of the following could be the value of n?

    (A) 3
    (B) 4
    (C) 7
    (D) 8
    (E) 12

Algebra Properties of numbers

If q is the quotient and $n - 4$ is the remainder when 10 is divided by the positive integer n, then $10 = qn + (n - 4)$. So, $14 = qn + n = n(q + 1)$. This means that n must be a factor of 14 and so $n = 1$, $n = 2$, $n = 7$, or $n = 14$ since n is a positive integer and the only positive integer factors of 14 are 1, 2, 7, and 14. The only positive integer factor of 14 given in the answer choices is 7.

The correct answer is C.

169. An airline passenger is planning a trip that involves three connecting flights that leave from Airports A, B, and C, respectively. The first flight leaves Airport A every hour, beginning at 8:00 a.m., and arrives at Airport B $2\frac{1}{2}$ hours later. The second flight leaves Airport B every 20 minutes, beginning at 8:00 a.m., and arrives at Airport C $1\frac{1}{6}$ hours later. The third flight leaves Airport C every hour, beginning at 8:45 a.m. What is the least total amount of time the passenger must spend between flights if all flights keep to their schedules?

    (A) 25 min
    (B) 1 hr 5 min
    (C) 1 hr 15 min
    (D) 2 hr 20 min
    (E) 3 hr 40 min

Arithmetic Operations on rational numbers

Since the flight schedules at each of Airports A, B, and C are the same hour after hour, assume that the passenger leaves Airport A at 8:00 and arrives at Airport B at 10:30. Since flights from Airport B leave at 20-minute intervals beginning on the hour, the passenger must wait 10 minutes at Airport B for the flight that leaves at 10:40 and arrives at Airport C $1\frac{1}{6}$ hours or 1 hour 10 minutes later. Thus, the passenger arrives at Airport C at 11:50. Having arrived too late for the 11:45 flight from Airport C, the passenger must wait 55 minutes for the 12:45 flight. Thus, the least total amount of time the passenger must spend waiting between flights is $10 + 55 = 65$ minutes, or 1 hour 5 minutes.

The correct answer is B.

170. If n is a positive integer and n^2 is divisible by 72, then the largest positive integer that must divide n is

    (A) 6
    (B) 12
    (C) 24
    (D) 36
    (E) 48

Arithmetic Properties of numbers

Since n^2 is divisible by 72, $n^2 = 72k$ for some positive integer k. Since $n^2 = 72k$, then $72k$ must be a perfect square. Since $72k = (2^3)(3^2)k$, then $k = 2m^2$ for some positive integer m in order for $72k$ to be a perfect square. Then,

$$n^2 = 72k = (2^3)(3^2)(2m^2) = (2^4)(3^2)m^2$$
$$= \left[(2^2)(3)(m)\right]^2, \text{ and } n = (2^2)(3)(m). \text{ The positive}$$

integers that MUST divide n are 1, 2, 3, 4, 6, and 12. Therefore, the largest positive integer that must divide n is 12.

The correct answer is B.

171. If n is a positive integer and $k+2=3^n$, which of the following could NOT be a value of k ?

(A) 1
(B) 4
(C) 7
(D) 25
(E) 79

Arithmetic Operations on rational numbers

For a number to equal 3^n, the number must be a power of 3. Substitute the answer choices for k in the equation given, and determine which one does not yield a power of 3.

A $1+2=3$ power of 3 (3^1)

B $4+2=6$ multiple of 3, but NOT a power of 3

C $7+2=9$ power of 3 (3^2)

D $25+2=27$ power of 3 (3^3)

E $79+2=81$ power of 3 (3^4)

The correct answer is B.

172. A certain grocery purchased x pounds of produce for p dollars per pound. If y pounds of the produce had to be discarded due to spoilage and the grocery sold the rest for s dollars per pound, which of the following represents the gross profit on the sale of the produce?

(A) $(x-y)s-xp$
(B) $(x-y)p-ys$
(C) $(s-p)y-xp$
(D) $xp-ys$
(E) $(x-y)(s-p)$

Algebra Simplifying algebraic expressions; Applied problems

Since the grocery bought x pounds of produce for p dollars per pound, the total cost of the produce was xp dollars. Since y pounds of the produce was discarded, the grocery sold $x-y$ pounds of produce at the price of s dollars per pound, yielding a total revenue of $(x-y)s$ dollars. Then, the grocery's gross profit on the sale of the produce is its total revenue minus its total cost or $(x-y)s-xp$ dollars.

The correct answer is A.

173. If x, y, and z are positive integers such that x is a factor of y, and x is a multiple of z, which of the following is NOT necessarily an integer?

(A) $\dfrac{x+z}{z}$

(B) $\dfrac{y+z}{x}$

(C) $\dfrac{x+y}{z}$

(D) $\dfrac{xy}{z}$

(E) $\dfrac{yz}{x}$

Arithmetic Properties of numbers

Since the positive integer x is a factor of y, then $y=kx$ for some positive integer k. Since x is a multiple of the positive integer z, then $x=mz$ for some positive integer m.

Substitute these expressions for x and/or y into each answer choice to find the one expression that is NOT necessarily an integer.

A $\dfrac{x+z}{z}=\dfrac{mz+z}{z}=\dfrac{(m+1)z}{z}=m+1$, which MUST be an integer

B $\dfrac{y+z}{x}=\dfrac{y}{x}+\dfrac{z}{x}=\dfrac{kx}{x}+\dfrac{z}{mz}=k+\dfrac{1}{m}$, which NEED NOT be an integer

Because only one of the five expressions need not be an integer, the expressions given in C, D, and E need not be tested. However, for completeness,

C $\dfrac{x+y}{z}=\dfrac{mz+kx}{z}=\dfrac{mz+k(mz)}{z}=\dfrac{mz(1+k)}{z}$ $=m(1+k)$, which MUST be an integer

D $\dfrac{xy}{z}=\dfrac{(mz)y}{z}=my$, which MUST be an integer

E $\dfrac{yz}{x}=\dfrac{(kx)(z)}{x}=kz$, which MUST be an integer

The correct answer is B.

174. Running at their respective constant rates, Machine X takes 2 days longer to produce w widgets than Machine Y. At these rates, if the two machines together produce $\frac{5}{4}w$ widgets in 3 days, how many days would it take Machine X alone to produce $2w$ widgets?

(A) 4
(B) 6
(C) 8
(D) 10
(E) 12

Algebra; Applied problems

If x, where $x > 2$, represents the number of days Machine X takes to produce w widgets, then Machine Y takes $x - 2$ days to produce w widgets. It follows that Machines X and Y can produce $\frac{w}{x}$ and $\frac{w}{x-2}$ widgets, respectively, in 1 day and together they can produce $\frac{w}{x} + \frac{w}{x-2}$ widgets in 1 day. Since it is given that, together, they can produce $\frac{5}{4}w$ widgets in 3 days, it follows that, together, they can produce $\frac{1}{3}\left(\frac{5}{4}w\right) = \frac{5}{12}w$ widgets in 1 day. Thus,

$$\frac{w}{x} + \frac{w}{x-2} = \frac{5}{12}w$$

$$\left(\frac{1}{x} + \frac{1}{x-2}\right)w = \frac{5}{12}w$$

$$\left(\frac{1}{x} + \frac{1}{x-2}\right) = \frac{5}{12}$$

$$12x(x-2)\left(\frac{1}{x} + \frac{1}{x-2}\right) = 12x(x-2)\left(\frac{5}{12}\right)$$

$$12\left[(x-2) + x\right] = 5x(x-2)$$

$$12(2x-2) = 5x(x-2)$$

$$24x - 24 = 5x^2 - 10x$$

$$0 = 5x^2 - 34x + 24$$

$$0 = (5x - 4)(x - 6)$$

$$x = \frac{4}{5} \text{ or } 6$$

Therefore, since $x > 2$, it follows that $x = 6$. Machine X takes 6 days to produce w widgets and $2(6) = 12$ days to produce $2w$ widgets.

The correct answer is E.

175. A square wooden plaque has a square brass inlay in the center, leaving a wooden strip of uniform width around the brass square. If the ratio of the brass area to the wooden area is 25 to 39, which of the following could be the width, in inches, of the wooden strip?

I. 1
II. 3
III. 4

(A) I only
(B) II only
(C) I and II only
(D) I and III only
(E) I, II, and III

Geometry Area

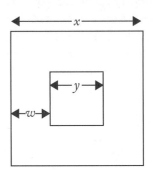

Note: Not drawn to scale.

Let x represent the side length of the entire plaque, let y represent the side length of the brass inlay, and w represent the uniform width of the wooden strip around the brass inlay, as shown in the figure above. Since the ratio of the area of the brass inlay to the area of the wooden strip is 25 to 39, the ratio of the area of the brass inlay to the area of the entire plaque is $\frac{y^2}{x^2} = \frac{25}{25+39} = \frac{25}{64}$.

Then, $\frac{y}{x} = \sqrt{\frac{25}{64}} = \frac{5}{8}$ and $y = \frac{5}{8}x$. Also, $x = y + 2w$

and $w = \dfrac{x-y}{2}$. Substituting $\dfrac{5}{8}x$ for y into this expression for w gives $w = \dfrac{x - \dfrac{5}{8}x}{2} = \dfrac{\dfrac{3}{8}x}{2} = \dfrac{3}{16}x$. Thus,

I. If the plaque were $\dfrac{16}{3}$ inches on a side, then the width of the wooden strip would be 1 inch, and so 1 inch is a possible width for the wooden strip.

II. If the plaque were 16 inches on a side, then the width of the wooden strip would be 3 inches, and so 3 inches is a possible width for the wooden strip.

III. If the plaque were $\dfrac{64}{3}$ inches on a side, then the width of the wooden strip would be 4 inches, and so 4 inches is a possible width for the wooden strip.

The correct answer is E.

176. $\dfrac{2\dfrac{3}{5} - 1\dfrac{2}{3}}{\dfrac{2}{3} - \dfrac{3}{5}} =$

(A) 16
(B) 14
(C) 3
(D) 1
(E) −1

Arithmetic Operations on rational numbers

Work the problem:

$$\dfrac{2\dfrac{3}{5} - 1\dfrac{2}{3}}{\dfrac{2}{3} - \dfrac{3}{5}} =$$

$$\dfrac{\dfrac{13}{5} - \dfrac{5}{3}}{\dfrac{2}{3} - \dfrac{3}{5}} = \dfrac{\dfrac{39-25}{15}}{\dfrac{10-9}{15}} = \dfrac{\dfrac{14}{15}}{\dfrac{1}{15}} = \dfrac{14}{15} \times \dfrac{15}{1} = 14$$

The correct answer is B.

5.0   Data Sufficiency

5.0 Data Sufficiency

Data sufficiency questions appear in the Quantitative section of the GMAT® exam. Multiple-choice data sufficiency questions are intermingled with problem solving questions throughout the section. You will have 75 minutes to complete the Quantitative section of the GMAT exam, or about 2 minutes to answer each question. These questions require knowledge of the following topics:

- Arithmetic
- Elementary algebra
- Commonly known concepts of geometry

Data sufficiency questions are designed to measure your ability to analyze a quantitative problem, recognize which given information is relevant, and determine at what point there is sufficient information to solve a problem. In these questions, you are to classify each problem according to the five fixed answer choices, rather than find a solution to the problem.

Each data sufficiency question consists of a question, often accompanied by some initial information, and two statements, labeled (1) and (2), which contain additional information. You must decide whether the information in each statement is sufficient to answer the question or—if neither statement provides enough information—whether the information in the two statements together is sufficient. It is also possible that the statements in combination do not give enough information to answer the question.

Begin by reading the initial information and the question carefully. Next, consider the first statement. Does the information provided by the first statement enable you to answer the question? Go on to the second statement. Try to ignore the information given in the first statement when you consider whether the second statement provides information that, by itself, allows you to answer the question. Now you should be able to say, for each statement, whether it is sufficient to determine the answer.

Next, consider the two statements in tandem. Do they, together, enable you to answer the question?

Look again at your answer choices. Select the one that most accurately reflects whether the statements provide the information required to answer the question.

5.1 Test-Taking Strategies

1. **Do not waste valuable time solving a problem.**
   You only need to determine whether sufficient information is given to solve it.

2. **Consider each statement separately.**
   First, decide whether each statement alone gives sufficient information to solve the problem. Be sure to disregard the information given in statement (1) when you evaluate the information given in statement (2). If either, or both, of the statements give(s) sufficient information to solve the problem, select the answer corresponding to the description of which statement(s) give(s) sufficient information to solve the problem.

3. **Judge the statements in tandem if neither statement is sufficient by itself.**
   It is possible that the two statements together do not provide sufficient information. Once you decide, select the answer corresponding to the description of whether the statements together give sufficient information to solve the problem.

4. **Answer the question asked.**
   For example, if the question asks, "What is the value of y?" for an answer statement to be sufficient, you must be able to find one and only one value for y. Being able to determine minimum or maximum values for an answer (e.g., $y = x + 2$) is not sufficient, because such answers constitute a range of values rather than the specific value of y.

5. **Be very careful not to make unwarranted assumptions based on the images represented.**
   Figures are not necessarily drawn to scale; they are generalized figures showing little more than intersecting line segments and the relationships of points, angles, and regions. So, for example, if a figure described as a rectangle looks like a square, do *not* conclude that it is, in fact, a square just by looking at the figure.

If statement 1 is sufficient, then the answer must be **A or D.**

If statement 2 is not sufficient, then the answer must be **A.**

If statement 2 is sufficient, then the answer must be **D.**

If statement 1 is not sufficient, then the answer must be **B, C, or E.**

If statement 2 is sufficient, then the answer must be **B.**

If statement 2 is not sufficient, then the answer must be **C or E.**

If both statements together are sufficient, then the answer must be **C.**

If both statements together are still not sufficient, then the answer must be **E.**

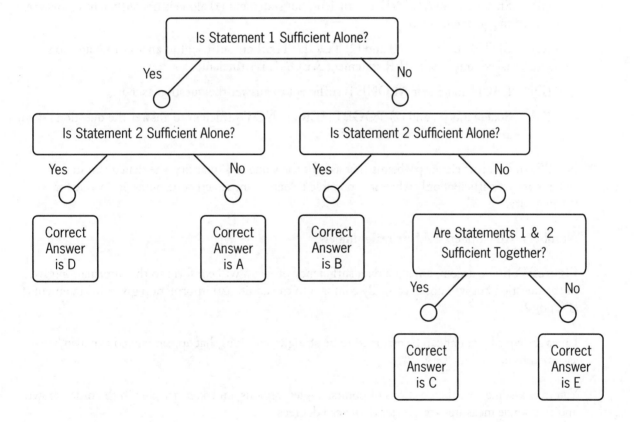

5.2 The Directions

These directions are similar to those you will see for data sufficiency questions when you take the GMAT exam. If you read the directions carefully and understand them clearly before going to sit for the test, you will not need to spend much time reviewing them when you take the GMAT exam.

Each data sufficiency problem consists of a question and two statements, labeled (1) and (2), that give data. You have to decide whether the data given in the statements are *sufficient* for answering the question. Using the data given in the statements *plus* your knowledge of mathematics and everyday facts (such as the number of days in July or the meaning of *counterclockwise*), you must indicate whether the data given in the statements are sufficient for answering the questions and then indicate one of the following answer choices:

(A)   Statement (1) ALONE is sufficient, but statement (2) alone is not sufficient to answer the question asked;

(B)   Statement (2) ALONE is sufficient, but statement (1) alone is not sufficient to answer the question asked;

(C)   BOTH statements (1) and (2) TOGETHER are sufficient to answer the question asked, but NEITHER statement ALONE is sufficient;

(D)   EACH statement ALONE is sufficient to answer the question asked;

(E)   Statements (1) and (2) TOGETHER are NOT sufficient to answer the question asked, and additional data are needed.

NOTE: In data sufficiency problems that ask for the value of a quantity, the data given in the statements are sufficient only when it is possible to determine exactly one numerical value for the quantity.

Numbers: All numbers used are real numbers.

Figures: A figure accompanying a data sufficiency problem will conform to the information given in the question but will not necessarily conform to the additional information given in statements (1) and (2).

Lines shown as straight can be assumed to be straight and lines that appear jagged can also be assumed to be straight.

You may assume that the positions of points, angles, regions, and so forth exist in the order shown and that angle measures are greater than zero degrees.

All figures lie in a plane unless otherwise indicated.

5.3 Sample Questions

Each <u>data sufficiency</u> problem consists of a question and two statements, labeled (1) and (2), which contain certain data. Using these data and your knowledge of mathematics and everyday facts (such as the number of days in July or the meaning of the word *counterclockwise*), decide whether the data given are sufficient for answering the question and then indicate one of the following answer choices:

A Statement (1) ALONE is sufficient, but statement (2) alone is not sufficient.
B Statement (2) ALONE is sufficient, but statement (1) alone is not sufficient.
C BOTH statements TOGETHER are sufficient, but NEITHER statement ALONE is sufficient.
D EACH statement ALONE is sufficient.
E Statements (1) and (2) TOGETHER are not sufficient.

<u>Note:</u> In data sufficiency problems that ask for the value of a quantity, the data given in the statements are sufficient only when it is possible to determine exactly one numerical value for the quantity.

<u>Example:</u>

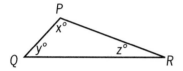

In $\triangle PQR$, what is the value of x?

(1) $PQ = PR$
(2) $y = 40$

<u>Explanation:</u> According to statement (1) $PQ = PR$; therefore, $\triangle PQR$ is isosceles and $y = z$. Since $x + y + z = 180$, it follows that $x + 2y = 180$. Since statement (1) does not give a value for y, you cannot answer the question using statement (1) alone. According to statement (2), $y = 40$; therefore, $x + z = 140$. Since statement (2) does not give a value for z, you cannot answer the question using statement (2) alone. Using both statements together, since $x + 2y = 180$ and the value of y is given, you can find the value of x. Therefore, BOTH statements (1) and (2) TOGETHER are sufficient to answer the questions, but NEITHER statement ALONE is sufficient.

<u>Numbers:</u> All numbers used are real numbers.

<u>Figures:</u>
- Figures conform to the information given in the question, but will not necessarily conform to the additional information given in statements (1) and (2).
- Lines shown as straight are straight, and lines that appear jagged are also straight.
- The positions of points, angles, regions, etc., exist in the order shown, and angle measures are greater than zero.
- All figures lie in a plane unless otherwise indicated.

1. What is the tenths digit of the number d when it is written as a decimal?

   (1) $d = \dfrac{54}{25}$

   (2) $1,000d = 2,160$

   6 in

2. A framed picture is shown above. The frame, shown shaded, is 6 inches wide and forms a border of uniform width around the picture. What are the dimensions of the viewable portion of the picture?

   (1) The area of the shaded region is 24 square inches.

   (2) The frame is 8 inches tall.

3. What is the value of the integer x ?

   (1) x rounded to the nearest hundred is 7,200.

   (2) The hundreds digit of x is 2.

4. Is $2x > 2y$?

   (1) $x > y$

   (2) $3x > 3y$

5. If p and q are positive, is $\dfrac{p}{q}$ less than 1?

   (1) p is less than 4.

   (2) q is less than 4.

6. In a certain factory, hours worked by each employee in excess of 40 hours per week are overtime hours and are paid for at $1\frac{1}{2}$ times the employee's regular hourly pay rate. If an employee worked a total of 42 hours last week, how much was the employee's gross pay for the hours worked last week?

   (1) The employee's gross pay for overtime hours worked last week was $30.

   (2) The employee's gross pay for all hours worked last week was $30 more than for the previous week.

7. If $x > 0$, what is the value of x^5 ?

   (1) $\sqrt{x} = 32$

   (2) $x^2 = 2^{20}$

8. What is the value of the integer N ?

   (1) $101 < N < 103$

   (2) $202 < 2N < 206$

9. Is zw positive?

   (1) $z + w^3 = 20$

   (2) z is positive.

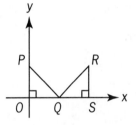

10. In the rectangular coordinate system above, if $\triangle OPQ$ and $\triangle QRS$ have equal area, what are the coordinates of point R ?

    (1) The coordinates of point P are (0,12).

    (2) $OP = OQ$ and $QS = RS$.

11. If y is greater than 110 percent of x, is y greater than 75 ?

    (1) $x > 75$

    (2) $y - x = 10$

12. What is the average (arithmetic mean) of x and y ?

    (1) The average of x and $2y$ is 10.

    (2) The average of $2x$ and $7y$ is 32.

13. What is the value of $\dfrac{r}{2} + \dfrac{s}{2}$?

    (1) $\dfrac{r + s}{2} = 5$

    (2) $r + s = 10$

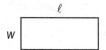

14. If ℓ and w represent the length and width, respectively, of the rectangle above, what is the perimeter?

    (1) $2\ell + w = 40$
    (2) $\ell + w = 25$

15. For all x, the expression x^* is defined to be $ax + a$, where a is a constant. What is the value of 2^* ?

    (1) $3^* = 2$
    (2) $5^* = 3$

16. Is $k + m < 0$?

    (1) $k < 0$
    (2) $km > 0$

17. A retailer purchased a television set for x percent less than its list price, and then sold it for y percent less than its list price. What was the list price of the television set?

    (1) $x = 15$
    (2) $x - y = 5$

18. If Ann saves x dollars each week and Beth saves y dollars each week, what is the total amount that they save per week?

    (1) Beth saves $5 more per week than Ann saves per week.
    (2) It takes Ann 6 weeks to save the same amount that Beth saves in 5 weeks.

19. What is the total number of executives at Company P ?

    (1) The number of male executives is $\frac{3}{5}$ the number of female executives.
    (2) There are 4 more female executives than male executives.

20. What is the ratio of c to d ?

    (1) The ratio of $3c$ to $3d$ is 3 to 4.
    (2) The ratio of $c + 3$ to $d + 3$ is 4 to 5.

21. A certain dealership has a number of cars to be sold by its salespeople. How many cars are to be sold?

    (1) If each of the salespeople sells 4 of the cars, 23 cars will remain unsold.
    (2) If each of the salespeople sells 6 of the cars, 5 cars will remain unsold.

22. Committee member W wants to schedule a one-hour meeting on Thursday for himself and three other committee members, X, Y, and Z. Is there a one-hour period on Thursday that is open for all four members?

    (1) On Thursday W and X have an open period from 9:00 a.m. to 12:00 noon.
    (2) On Thursday Y has an open period from 10:00 a.m. to 1:00 p.m. and Z has an open period from 8:00 a.m. to 11:00 a.m.

23. Some computers at a certain company are Brand X and the rest are Brand Y. If the ratio of the number of Brand Y computers to the number of Brand X computers at the company is 5 to 6, how many of the computers are Brand Y ?

    (1) There are 80 more Brand X computers than Brand Y computers at the company.
    (2) There is a total of 880 computers at the company.

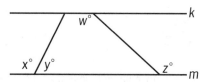

24. In the figure shown, lines k and m are parallel to each other. Is $x = z$?

    (1) $x = w$
    (2) $y = 180 - w$

25. When the wind speed is 9 miles per hour, the wind-chill factor w is given by

    $$w = -17.366 + 1.19t,$$

    where t is the temperature in degrees Fahrenheit. If at noon yesterday the wind speed was 9 miles per hour, was the wind-chill factor greater than 0 ?

    (1) The temperature at noon yesterday was greater than 10 degrees Fahrenheit.
    (2) The temperature at noon yesterday was less than 20 degrees Fahrenheit.

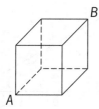

26. What is the volume of the cube above?

    (1) The surface area of the cube is 600 square inches.
    (2) The length of diagonal AB is $10\sqrt{3}$ inches.

27. Of the 230 single-family homes built in City X last year, how many were occupied at the end of the year?

    (1) Of all single-family homes in City X, 90 percent were occupied at the end of last year.
    (2) A total of 7,200 single-family homes in City X were occupied at the end of last year.

28. If J, S, and V are points on the number line, what is the distance between S and V?
    (1) The distance between J and S is 20.
    (2) The distance between J and V is 25.

29. If x is a positive integer, what is the value of x?

    (1) $x^2 = \sqrt{x}$
    (2) $\dfrac{n}{x} = n$ and $n \neq 0$.

30. During a certain bicycle ride, was Sherry's average speed faster than 24 kilometers per hour?
    (1 kilometer = 1,000 meters)

    (1) Sherry's average speed during the bicycle ride was faster than 7 meters per second.
    (2) Sherry's average speed during the bicycle ride was slower than 8 meters per second.

31. If x and y are integers, what is the value of x?

    (1) $xy = 1$
    (2) $x \neq -1$

32. If p, s, and t are positive, is $|ps - pt| > p(s - t)$?

    (1) $p < s$
    (2) $s < t$

33. What were the gross revenues from ticket sales for a certain film during the second week in which it was shown?

    (1) Gross revenues during the second week were $1.5 million less than during the first week.
    (2) Gross revenues during the third week were $2.0 million less than during the first week.

34. The total cost of an office dinner was shared equally by k of the n employees who attended the dinner. What was the total cost of the dinner?

    (1) Each of the k employees who shared the cost of the dinner paid $19.
    (2) If the total cost of the dinner had been shared equally by $k + 1$ of the n employees who attended the dinner, each of the $k + 1$ employees would have paid $18.

35. For a recent play performance, the ticket prices were $25 per adult and $15 per child. A total of 500 tickets were sold for the performance. How many of the tickets sold were for adults?

    (1) Revenue from ticket sales for this performance totaled $10,500.
    (2) The average (arithmetic mean) price per ticket sold was $21.

36. What is the value of x?

    (1) $x + 1 = 2 - 3x$
    (2) $\dfrac{1}{2x} = 2$

37. If x and y are positive integers, what is the remainder when $10^x + y$ is divided by 3?

    (1) $x = 5$
    (2) $y = 2$

38. What was the amount of money donated to a certain charity?

    (1) Of the amount donated, 40 percent came from corporate donations.
    (2) Of the amount donated, $1.5 million came from noncorporate donations.

39. What is the value of the positive integer n ?

    (1) $n^4 < 25$

    (2) $n \neq n^2$

40. If the set S consists of five consecutive positive integers, what is the sum of these five integers?

    (1) The integer 11 is in S, but 10 is not in S.

    (2) The sum of the even integers in S is 26.

41. A total of 20 amounts are entered on a spreadsheet that has 5 rows and 4 columns; each of the 20 positions in the spreadsheet contains one amount. The average (arithmetic mean) of the amounts in row i is R_i ($1 \le i \le 5$). The average of the amounts in column j is C_j ($1 \le j \le 4$). What is the average of all 20 amounts on the spreadsheet?

    (1) $R_1 + R_2 + R_3 + R_4 + R_5 = 550$

    (2) $C_1 + C_2 + C_3 + C_4 = 440$

42. Was the range of the amounts of money that Company Y budgeted for its projects last year equal to the range of the amounts of money that it budgeted for its projects this year?

    (1) Both last year and this year, Company Y budgeted money for 12 projects and the least amount of money that it budgeted for a project was $400.

    (2) Both last year and this year, the average (arithmetic mean) amount of money that Company Y budgeted per project was $2,000.

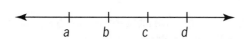

43. If a, b, c, and d are numbers on the number line shown and if the tick marks are equally spaced, what is the value of $a + c$?

    (1) $a + b = -8$

    (2) $a + d = 0$

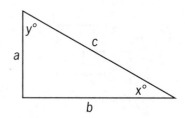

44. In the triangle above, does $a^2 + b^2 = c^2$?

    (1) $x + y = 90$

    (2) $x = y$

45. If $rs \neq 0$, is $\dfrac{1}{r} + \dfrac{1}{s} = 4$?

    (1) $r + s = 4rs$

    (2) $r = s$

46. If x, y, and z are three integers, are they consecutive integers?

    (1) $z - x = 2$

    (2) $x < y < z$

47. A collection of 36 cards consists of 4 sets of 9 cards each. The 9 cards in each set are numbered 1 through 9. If one card has been removed from the collection, what is the number on that card?

    (1) The units digit of the sum of the numbers on the remaining 35 cards is 6.

    (2) The sum of the numbers on the remaining 35 cards is 176.

48. In the xy-plane, point (r,s) lies on a circle with center at the origin. What is the value of $r^2 + s^2$?

    (1) The circle has radius 2.

    (2) The point $\left(\sqrt{2}, -\sqrt{2}\right)$ lies on the circle.

49. If r, s, and t are nonzero integers, is $r^5 s^3 t^4$ negative?

    (1) rt is negative.

    (2) s is negative.

50. If x and y are integers, what is the value of y ?

    (1) $xy = 27$

    (2) $x = y^2$

51. How many newspapers were sold at a certain newsstand today?

    (1) A total of 100 newspapers were sold at the newsstand yesterday, 10 fewer than twice the number sold today.
    (2) The number of newspapers sold at the newsstand yesterday was 45 more than the number sold today.

52. John took a test that had 60 questions numbered from 1 to 60. How many of the questions did he answer correctly?

    (1) The number of questions he answered correctly in the first half of the test was 7 more than the number he answered correctly in the second half of the test.
    (2) He answered $\frac{5}{6}$ of the odd-numbered questions correctly and $\frac{4}{5}$ of the even-numbered questions correctly.

53. If x is a positive integer, is $\sqrt{x}$ an integer?

    (1) $\sqrt{4x}$ is an integer.
    (2) $\sqrt{3x}$ is not an integer.

54. Is the value of n closer to 50 than to 75 ?

    (1) $75 - n > n - 50$
    (2) $n > 60$

55. Last year, if Elena spent a total of $720 on newspapers, magazines, and books, what amount did she spend on newspapers?

    (1) Last year, the amount that Elena spent on magazines was 80 percent of the amount that she spent on books.
    (2) Last year, the amount that Elena spent on newspapers was 60 percent of the total amount that she spent on magazines and books.

56. If p, q, x, y, and z are different positive integers, which of the five integers is the median?

    (1) $p + x < q$
    (2) $y < z$

57. If $w + z = 28$, what is the value of wz ?

    (1) w and z are positive integers.
    (2) w and z are consecutive odd integers.

58. What is the value of $a - b$?

    (1) $a = b + 4$
    (2) $(a - b)^2 = 16$

59. Machine X runs at a constant rate and produces a lot consisting of 100 cans in 2 hours. How much less time would it take to produce the lot of cans if both Machines X and Y were run simultaneously?

    (1) Both Machines X and Y produce the same number of cans per hour.
    (2) It takes Machine X twice as long to produce the lot of cans as it takes Machines X and Y running simultaneously to produce the lot.

60. Can the positive integer p be expressed as the product of two integers, each of which is greater than 1 ?

    (1) $31 < p < 37$
    (2) p is odd.

61. Is $x < y$?

    (1) $z < y$
    (2) $z < x$

62. If $abc \neq 0$, is $\dfrac{\frac{a}{b}}{c} = \dfrac{a}{\frac{b}{c}}$?

    (1) $a = 1$
    (2) $c = 1$

63. A certain list consists of 400 different numbers. Is the average (arithmetic mean) of the numbers in the list greater than the median of the numbers in the list?

    (1) Of the numbers in the list, 280 are less than the average.
    (2) Of the numbers in the list, 30 percent are greater than or equal to the average.

64. What is the area of rectangular region R ?

    (1) Each diagonal of R has length 5.
    (2) The perimeter of R is 14.

65. If Q is an integer between 10 and 100, what is the value of Q?

   (1) One of Q's digits is 3 more than the other, and the sum of its digits is 9.
   (2) $Q < 50$

66. If p and q are positive integers and $pq = 24$, what is the value of p?

   (1) $\frac{q}{6}$ is an integer.
   (2) $\frac{p}{2}$ is an integer.

67. What is the value of $x^2 - y^2$?

   (1) $x - y = y + 2$
   (2) $x - y = \dfrac{1}{x + y}$

68. How many integers n are there such that $r < n < s$?

   (1) $s - r = 5$
   (2) r and s are not integers.

69. If the total price of n equally priced shares of a certain stock was $12,000, what was the price per share of the stock?

   (1) If the price per share of the stock had been $1 more, the total price of the n shares would have been $300 more.
   (2) If the price per share of the stock had been $2 less, the total price of the n shares would have been 5 percent less.

70. If n is positive, is $\sqrt{n} > 100$?

   (1) $\sqrt{n-1} > 99$
   (2) $\sqrt{n+1} > 101$

71. Is $xy > 5$?

   (1) $1 \le x \le 3$ and $2 \le y \le 4$.
   (2) $x + y = 5$

72. In Year X, 8.7 percent of the men in the labor force were unemployed in June compared with 8.4 percent in May. If the number of men in the labor force was the same for both months, how many men were unemployed in June of that year?

   (1) In May of Year X, the number of unemployed men in the labor force was 3.36 million.
   (2) In Year X, 120,000 more men in the labor force were unemployed in June than in May.

73. If $x \ne 0$, what is the value of $\left(\dfrac{x^p}{x^q}\right)^4$?

   (1) $p = q$
   (2) $x = 3$

74. On Monday morning a certain machine ran continuously at a uniform rate to fill a production order. At what time did it completely fill the order that morning?

   (1) The machine began filling the order at 9:30 a.m.
   (2) The machine had filled $\frac{1}{2}$ of the order by 10:30 a.m. and $\frac{5}{6}$ of the order by 11:10 a.m.

75. If $kmn \ne 0$, is $\dfrac{x}{m}(m^2 + n^2 + k^2) = xm + yn + zk$?

   (1) $\dfrac{z}{k} = \dfrac{x}{m}$
   (2) $\dfrac{x}{m} = \dfrac{y}{n}$

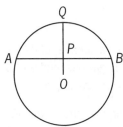

76. What is the radius of the circle above with center O?

   (1) The ratio of OP to PQ is 1 to 2.
   (2) P is the midpoint of chord AB.

77. What is the number of 360-degree rotations that a bicycle wheel made while rolling 100 meters in a straight line without slipping?

   (1) The diameter of the bicycle wheel, including the tire, was 0.5 meter.
   (2) The wheel made twenty 360-degree rotations per minute.

78. If $2x(5n) = t$, what is the value of t?

    (1) $x = n + 3$
    (2) $2x = 32$

79. In the equation $x^2 + bx + 12 = 0$, x is a variable and b is a constant. What is the value of b?

    (1) $x - 3$ is a factor of $x^2 + bx + 12$.
    (2) 4 is a root of the equation $x^2 + bx + 12 = 0$.

80. A Town T has 20,000 residents, 60 percent of whom are female. What percent of the residents were born in Town T?

    (1) The number of female residents who were born in Town T is twice the number of male residents who were <u>not</u> born in Town T.
    (2) The number of female residents who were <u>not</u> born in Town T is twice the number of female residents who were born in Town T.

81. In $\triangle XYZ$, what is the length of YZ?

    (1) The length of XY is 3.
    (2) The length of XZ is 5.

82. If the average (arithmetic mean) of n consecutive odd integers is 10, what is the least of the integers?

    (1) The range of the n integers is 14.
    (2) The greatest of the n integers is 17.

83. What was the ratio of the number of cars to the number of trucks produced by Company X last year?

    (1) Last year, if the number of cars produced by Company X had been 8 percent greater, the number of cars produced would have been 150 percent of the number of trucks produced by Company X.
    (2) Last year Company X produced 565,000 cars and 406,800 trucks.

84. If x, y, and z are positive numbers, is $x > y > z$?

    (1) $xz > yz$
    (2) $yx > yz$

85. K is a set of numbers such that

    (i) if x is in K, then $-x$ is in K, and
    (ii) if each of x and y is in K, then xy is in K.

    Is 12 in K?

    (1) 2 is in K.
    (2) 3 is in K.

86. If $x^2 + y^2 = 29$, what is the value of $(x - y)^2$?

    (1) $xy = 10$
    (2) $x = 5$

87. If x, y, and z are numbers, is $z = 18$?

    (1) The average (arithmetic mean) of x, y, and z is 6.
    (2) $x = -y$

88. After winning 50 percent of the first 20 games it played, Team A won all of the remaining games it played. What was the total number of games that Team A won?

    (1) Team A played 25 games altogether.
    (2) Team A won 60 percent of all the games it played.

89. Is x between 0 and 1?

    (1) x^2 is less than x.
    (2) x^3 is positive.

90. Is p^2 an odd integer?

    (1) p is an odd integer.
    (2) $\sqrt{p}$ is an odd integer.

91. If m and n are nonzero integers, is m^n an integer?

    (1) n^m is positive.
    (2) n^m is an integer.

92. What is the value of xy?

    (1) $x + y = 10$
    (2) $x - y = 6$

93. Is x^2 greater than x?

    (1) x^2 is greater than 1.
    (2) x is greater than -1.

94. Michael arranged all his books in a bookcase with 10 books on each shelf and no books left over. After Michael acquired 10 additional books, he arranged all his books in a new bookcase with 12 books on each shelf and no books left over. How many books did Michael have before he acquired the 10 additional books?

    (1) Before Michael acquired the 10 additional books, he had fewer than 96 books.
    (2) Before Michael acquired the 10 additional books, he had more than 24 books.

95. If $xy > 0$, does $(x-1)(y-1) = 1$?

    (1) $x + y = xy$
    (2) $x = y$

96. Last year in a group of 30 businesses, 21 reported a net profit and 15 had investments in foreign markets. How many of the businesses did not report a net profit nor invest in foreign markets last year?

    (1) Last year 12 of the 30 businesses reported a net profit and had investments in foreign markets.
    (2) Last year 24 of the 30 businesses reported a net profit or invested in foreign markets, or both.

97. If k and n are integers, is n divisible by 7?

    (1) $n - 3 = 2k$
    (2) $2k - 4$ is divisible by 7.

98. Is the perimeter of square S greater than the perimeter of equilateral triangle T?

    (1) The ratio of the length of a side of S to the length of a side of T is 4:5.
    (2) The sum of the lengths of a side of S and a side of T is 18.

99. If $x + y + z > 0$, is $z > 1$?

    (1) $z > x + y + 1$
    (2) $x + y + 1 < 0$

100. Can the positive integer n be written as the sum of two different positive prime numbers?

    (1) n is greater than 3.
    (2) n is odd.

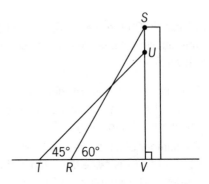

101. In the figure above, segments RS and TU represent two positions of the same ladder leaning against the side SV of a wall. The length of TV is how much greater than the length of RV?

    (1) The length of TU is 10 meters.
    (2) The length of RV is 5 meters.

Cancellation Fees	
Days Prior to Departure	Percent of Package Price
46 or more	10%
45–31	35%
30–16	50%
15–5	65%
4 or fewer	100%

102. The table above shows the cancellation fee schedule that a travel agency uses to determine the fee charged to a tourist who cancels a trip prior to departure. If a tourist canceled a trip with a package price of $1,700 and a departure date of September 4, on what day was the trip canceled?

    (1) The cancellation fee was $595.
    (2) If the trip had been canceled one day later, the cancellation fee would have been $255 more.

103. If *P* and *Q* are each circular regions, what is the radius of the larger of these regions?

    (1) The area of *P* plus the area of *Q* is equal to 90π.
    (2) The larger circular region has a radius that is 3 times the radius of the smaller circular region.

104. For all *z*, $\lceil z \rceil$ denotes the least integer greater than or equal to *z*. Is $\lceil x \rceil = 0$?

    (1) $-1 < x < -0.1$
    (2) $\lceil x + 0.5 \rceil = 1$

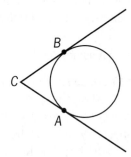

105. The circular base of an above-ground swimming pool lies in a level yard and just touches two straight sides of a fence at points *A* and *B*, as shown in the figure above. Point *C* is on the ground where the two sides of the fence meet. How far from the center of the pool's base is point *A* ?

    (1) The base has area 250 square feet.
    (2) The center of the base is 20 feet from point *C*.

106. If $xy = -6$, what is the value of $xy(x + y)$?

    (1) $x - y = 5$
    (2) $xy^2 = 18$

107. If the average (arithmetic mean) of 4 numbers is 50, how many of the numbers are greater than 50 ?

    (1) None of the four numbers is equal to 50.
    (2) Two of the numbers are equal to 25.

108. [*y*] denotes the greatest integer less than or equal to *y*. Is $d < 1$?

    (1) $d = y - [y]$
    (2) $[d] = 0$

109. If *m* is a positive integer, then m^3 has how many digits?

    (1) *m* has 3 digits.
    (2) m^2 has 5 digits.

110. For each landscaping job that takes more than 4 hours, a certain contractor charges a total of *r* dollars for the first 4 hours plus 0.2*r* dollars for each additional hour or fraction of an hour, where $r > 100$. Did a particular landscaping job take more than 10 hours?

    (1) The contractor charged a total of $288 for the job.
    (2) The contractor charged a total of 2.4*r* dollars for the job.

111. The sequence $s_1, s_2, s_3, ..., s_n, ...$ is such that $s_n = \dfrac{1}{n} - \dfrac{1}{n+1}$ for all integers $n \geq 1$. If *k* is a positive integer, is the sum of the first *k* terms of the sequence greater than $\dfrac{9}{10}$?

    (1) $k > 10$
    (2) $k < 19$

112. If *x* and *y* are nonzero integers, is $x^y < y^x$?

    (1) $x = y^2$
    (2) $y > 2$

113. In the sequence *S* of numbers, each term after the first two terms is the sum of the two immediately preceding terms. What is the 5th term of *S* ?

    (1) The 6th term of *S* minus the 4th term equals 5.
    (2) The 6th term of *S* plus the 7th term equals 21.

114. If *d* is a positive integer, is $\sqrt{d}$ an integer?

    (1) *d* is the square of an integer.
    (2) $\sqrt{d}$ is the square of an integer.

115. Is the positive integer *n* a multiple of 24 ?

    (1) *n* is a multiple of 4.
    (2) *n* is a multiple of 6.

116. If 75 percent of the guests at a certain banquet ordered dessert, what percent of the guests ordered coffee?

    (1) 60 percent of the guests who ordered dessert also ordered coffee.
    (2) 90 percent of the guests who ordered coffee also ordered dessert.

117. A tank containing water started to leak. Did the tank contain more than 30 gallons of water when it started to leak? (Note: 1 gallon = 128 ounces)

    (1) The water leaked from the tank at a constant rate of 6.4 ounces per minute.
    (2) The tank became empty less than 12 hours after it started to leak.

118. If x is an integer, is y an integer?

    (1) The average (arithmetic mean) of x, y, and y − 2 is x.
    (2) The average (arithmetic mean) of x and y is not an integer.

119. If 2 different representatives are to be selected at random from a group of 10 employees and if p is the probability that both representatives selected will be women, is $p > \frac{1}{2}$?

    (1) More than $\frac{1}{2}$ of the 10 employees are women.
    (2) The probability that both representatives selected will be men is less than $\frac{1}{10}$.

120. In the xy-plane, lines k and ℓ intersect at the point (1,1). Is the y-intercept of k greater than the y-intercept of ℓ ?

    (1) The slope of k is less than the slope of ℓ.
    (2) The slope of ℓ is positive.

121. Each of the 45 books on a shelf is written either in English or in Spanish, and each of the books is either a hardcover book or a paperback. If a book is to be selected at random from the books on the shelf, is the probability less than $\frac{1}{2}$ that the book selected will be a paperback written in Spanish?

    (1) Of the books on the shelf, 30 are paperbacks.
    (2) Of the books on the shelf, 15 are written in Spanish.

122. If S is a set of four numbers w, x, y, and z, is the range of the numbers in S greater than 2 ?

    (1) $w − z > 2$
    (2) z is the least number in S.

123. Stations X and Y are connected by two separate, straight, parallel rail lines that are 250 miles long. Train P and train Q simultaneously left Station X and Station Y, respectively, and each train traveled to the other's point of departure. The two trains passed each other after traveling for 2 hours. When the two trains passed, which train was nearer to its destination?

    (1) At the time when the two trains passed, train P had averaged a speed of 70 miles per hour.
    (2) Train Q averaged a speed of 55 miles per hour for the entire trip.

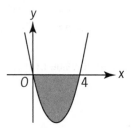

124. In the xy-plane shown, the shaded region consists of all points that lie above the graph of $y = x^2 − 4x$ and below the x-axis. Does the point (a,b) (not shown) lie in the shaded region if $b < 0$?

    (1) $0 < a < 4$
    (2) $a^2 − 4a < b$

5.4 Answer Key

1.	D	32.	B	63.	D	94.	A
2.	C	33.	E	64.	C	95.	A
3.	E	34.	C	65.	C	96.	D
4.	D	35.	D	66.	E	97.	C
5.	E	36.	D	67.	B	98.	A
6.	A	37.	B	68.	C	99.	B
7.	D	38.	C	69.	D	100.	E
8.	D	39.	C	70.	B	101.	D
9.	E	40.	D	71.	E	102.	C
10.	C	41.	D	72.	D	103.	C
11.	A	42.	E	73.	A	104.	A
12.	C	43.	C	74.	B	105.	A
13.	D	44.	A	75.	C	106.	B
14.	B	45.	A	76.	E	107.	E
15.	D	46.	C	77.	A	108.	D
16.	C	47.	D	78.	C	109.	E
17.	E	48.	D	79.	D	110.	B
18.	C	49.	E	80.	C	111.	A
19.	C	50.	C	81.	E	112.	C
20.	A	51.	A	82.	D	113.	A
21.	C	52.	B	83.	D	114.	D
22.	C	53.	A	84.	E	115.	E
23.	D	54.	A	85.	C	116.	C
24.	D	55.	B	86.	A	117.	E
25.	E	56.	E	87.	C	118.	A
26.	D	57.	B	88.	D	119.	E
27.	E	58.	A	89.	A	120.	A
28.	E	59.	D	90.	D	121.	B
29.	D	60.	A	91.	E	122.	A
30.	A	61.	E	92.	C	123.	A
31.	C	62.	B	93.	A	124.	B

5.5 Answer Explanations

The following discussion of data sufficiency is intended to familiarize you with the most efficient and effective approaches to the kinds of problems common to data sufficiency. The particular questions in this chapter are generally representative of the kinds of data sufficiency questions you will encounter on the GMAT. Remember that it is the problem solving strategy that is important, not the specific details of a particular question.

1. What is the tenths digit of the number d when it is written as a decimal?

    (1) $d = \dfrac{54}{25}$

    (2) $1{,}000d = 2{,}160$

Arithmetic Place value

(1) Given that $d = \dfrac{54}{25}$, it follows that $d = \dfrac{54}{25} \times \dfrac{4}{4} = \dfrac{216}{100} = 2.16$ and the tenths digit is 1; SUFFICIENT.

(2) Given that $1{,}000d = 2{,}160$, it follows that $d = \dfrac{2{,}160}{1{,}000} = \dfrac{216}{100} = 2.16$ and the tenths digit is 1; SUFFICIENT.

The correct answer is D; each statement alone is sufficient.

6 in

2. A framed picture is shown above. The frame, shown shaded, is 6 inches wide and forms a border of uniform width around the picture. What are the dimensions of the viewable portion of the picture?

    (1) The area of the shaded region is 24 square inches.

    (2) The frame is 8 inches tall.

Geometry Area

Let the outer dimensions of the frame be 6 inches by B inches, and let the dimensions of the viewable portion of the picture be a inches by b inches. Then the area of the frame is the area of the viewable portion and the frame combined minus the area of the viewable portion, which equals $(6B - ab)$ square inches. Determine the values of a and b.

(1) Given that $6B - ab = 24$, then it is not possible to determine the values of a and b. For example, if $B = 8$, $a = 4$, and $b = 6$, then $6B - ab = 6(8) - (4)(6) = 24$. However, if $B = 7$, $a = 3$, and $b = 6$, then $6B - ab = 6(7) - (3)(6) = 24$; NOT sufficient.

(2) Given that $B = 8$, then $6B - ab = 48 - ab$, but it is still not possible to determine the values of a and b; NOT sufficient.

Taking (1) and (2) together, it follows that $6B - ab = 24$ and $B = 8$, and therefore $48 - ab = 24$ and $ab = 24$. Also, letting the uniform width of the border be x inches, the outer dimensions of the frame are $(a + 2x)$ inches $= 6$ inches and $(b + 2x)$ inches $= 8$ inches, from which it follows by subtracting the last two equations that $b - a = 2$. Thus, $b = a + 2$, and so $ab = 24$ becomes $a(a + 2) = 24$, or $a^2 + 2a - 24 = 0$. Factoring gives $(a + 6)(a - 4) = 0$, so $a = -6$ or $a = 4$. Because no dimension of the viewable portion can be negative, it follows that $a = 4$ and $b = a + 2 = 4 + 2 = 6$.

The correct answer is C; both statements together are sufficient.

3. What is the value of the integer x?

    (1) x rounded to the nearest hundred is 7,200.
    (2) The hundreds digit of x is 2.

    Arithmetic Rounding

    (1) Given that x rounded to the nearest hundred is 7,200, the value of x cannot be determined. For example, x could be 7,200 or x could be 7,201; NOT sufficient.

    (2) Given that the hundreds digit of x is 2, the value of x cannot be determined. For example, x could be 7,200 or x could be 7,201; NOT sufficient.

    Taking (1) and (2) together is of no more help than either (1) or (2) taken separately because the same examples were used in both (1) and (2).

    The correct answer is E;
    both statements together are still not sufficient.

4. Is $2x > 2y$?

    (1) $x > y$
    (2) $3x > 3y$

    Algebra Inequalities

    (1) It is given that $x > y$. Thus, multiplying both sides by the positive number 2, it follows that $2x > 2y$; SUFFICIENT.

    (2) It is given that $3x > 3y$. Thus, multiplying both sides by the positive number $\frac{2}{3}$, it follows that $2x > 2y$; SUFFICIENT.

    The correct answer is D;
    each statement alone is sufficient.

5. If p and q are positive, is $\frac{p}{q}$ less than 1?

    (1) p is less than 4.
    (2) q is less than 4.

    Arithmetic Properties of numbers

    (1) Given that p is less than 4, then it is not possible to determine whether $\frac{p}{q}$ is less than 1. For example, if $p = 1$ and $q = 2$, then $\frac{p}{q} = \frac{1}{2}$ and $\frac{1}{2}$ is less than 1. However, if $p = 2$ and $q = 1$, then $\frac{p}{q} = 2$ and 2 is not less than 1; NOT sufficient.

    (2) Given that q is less than 4, then it is not possible to determine whether $\frac{p}{q}$ is less than 1. For example, if $p = 1$ and $q = 2$, then $\frac{p}{q} = \frac{1}{2}$ and $\frac{1}{2}$ is less than 1. However, if $p = 2$ and $q = 1$, then $\frac{p}{q} = 2$ and 2 is not less than 1; NOT sufficient.

    Taking (1) and (2) together is of no more help than either (1) or (2) taken separately because the same examples were used in both (1) and (2).

    The correct answer is E;
    both statements together are still not sufficient.

6. In a certain factory, hours worked by each employee in excess of 40 hours per week are overtime hours and are paid for at $1\frac{1}{2}$ times the employee's regular hourly pay rate. If an employee worked a total of 42 hours last week, how much was the employee's gross pay for the hours worked last week?

    (1) The employee's gross pay for overtime hours worked last week was $30.
    (2) The employee's gross pay for all hours worked last week was $30 more than for the previous week.

    Arithmetic Applied problems

    If an employee's regular hourly rate was R and the employee worked 42 hours last week, then the employee's gross pay for hours worked last week was $40R + 2(1.5R)$. Determine the value of $40R + 2(1.5R) = 43R$, or equivalently, the value of R.

(1) Given that the employee's gross pay for overtime hours worked last week was $30, it follows that $2(1.5R) = 30$ and $R = 10$; SUFFICIENT.

(2) Given that the employee's gross pay for all hours worked last week was $30 more than for the previous week, the value of R cannot be determined because nothing specific is known about the value of the employee's pay for all hours worked the previous week; NOT sufficient.

The correct answer is A; statement (1) alone is sufficient.

7. If $x > 0$, what is the value of x^5 ?

(1) $\sqrt{x} = 32$
(2) $x^2 = 2^{20}$

Algebra Exponents

(1) Given that $\sqrt{x} = 32$, it follows that $x = 32^2$ and $x^5 = (32^2)^5$; SUFFICIENT.

(2) Given that $x^2 = 2^{20}$, since x is positive, it follows that $x = \sqrt{2^{20}} = 2^{10}$ and $x^5 = (2^{10})^5$; SUFFICIENT.

The correct answer is D; each statement alone is sufficient.

8. What is the value of the integer N ?

(1) $101 < N < 103$
(2) $202 < 2N < 206$

Arithmetic Inequalities

(1) Given that N is an integer and $101 < N < 103$, it follows that $N = 102$; SUFFICIENT.

(2) Given that N is an integer and $202 < 2N < 206$, it follows that $101 < N < 103$ and $N = 102$; SUFFICIENT.

The correct answer is D; each statement alone is sufficient.

9. Is zw positive ?

(1) $z + w^3 = 20$
(2) z is positive.

Arithmetic Properties of numbers

(1) Given that $z + w^3 = 20$, if $z = 1$ and $w = \sqrt[3]{19}$, then $z + w^3 = 20$ and zw is positive. However, if $z = 20$ and $w = 0$, then $z + w^3 = 20$ and zw is not positive; NOT sufficient.

(2) Given that z is positive, if $z = 1$ and $w = \sqrt[3]{19}$, then zw is positive. However, if $z = 20$ and $w = 0$, then zw is not positive; NOT sufficient.

Taking (1) and (2) together is of no more help than either (1) or (2) taken separately because the same examples were used in both (1) and (2).

The correct answer is E; both statements together are still not sufficient.

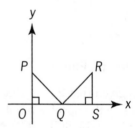

10. In the rectangular coordinate system above, if $\triangle OPQ$ and $\triangle QRS$ have equal area, what are the coordinates of point R ?

(1) The coordinates of point P are $(0,12)$.
(2) $OP = OQ$ and $QS = RS$.

Geometry Coordinate geometry; triangles

Since the area of $\triangle OPQ$ is equal to the area of $\triangle QRS$, it follows that $\frac{1}{2}(OQ)(OP) = \frac{1}{2}(QS)(SR)$, or $(OQ)(OP) = (QS)(SR)$. Also, if both OS and SR are known, then the coordinates of point R will be known.

(1)   Given that the y-coordinate of P is 12, it is not possible to determine the coordinates of point R. For example, if $OQ = QS = SR = 12$, then the equation $(OQ)(OP) = (QS)(SR)$ becomes $(12)(12) = (12)(12)$, which is true, and the x-coordinate of R is $OQ + QS = 24$ and the y-coordinate of R is $SR = 12$. However, if $OQ = 12$, $QS = 24$, and $SR = 6$, then the equation $(OQ)(OP) = (QS)(SR)$ becomes $(12)(12) = (24)(6)$, which is true, and the x-coordinate of R is $OQ + QS = 36$ and the y-coordinate of R is $SR = 6$; NOT sufficient.

(2)   Given that $OP = OQ$ and $QS = RS$, it is not possible to determine the coordinates of point R, since everything given would still be true if all the lengths were doubled, but doing this would change the coordinates of point R; NOT sufficient.

Taking (1) and (2) together, it follows that $OP = OQ = 12$. Therefore, $(OQ)(OP) = (QS)(SR)$ becomes $(12)(12) = (QS)(SR)$, or $144 = (QS)(SR)$. Using $QS = RS$ in the last equation gives $144 = (QS)^2$, or $12 = QS$. Thus, $OQ = QS = SR = 12$ and point R has coordinates (24,12).

The correct answer is C; both statements together are sufficient.

11.   If y is greater than 110 percent of x, is y greater than 75 ?

(1) $x > 75$

(2) $y - x = 10$

Arithmetic; Algebra Percents; Inequalities

(1)   It is given that $y > (110\%)x = 1.1x$ and $x > 75$. Therefore, $y > (1.1)(75)$, and so y is greater than 75; SUFFICIENT.

(2)   Although it is given that $y - x = 10$, more information is needed to determine if y is greater than 75. For example, if $x = 80$ and $y = 90$, then y is greater than 110 percent of x, $y - x = 10$, and y is greater than 75. However, if $x = 20$ and $y = 30$, then y is greater than 110 percent of x, $y - x = 10$, and y is not greater than 75; NOT sufficient.

The correct answer is A; statement 1 alone is sufficient.

12.   What is the average (arithmetic mean) of x and y ?

(1)   The average of x and $2y$ is 10.

(2)   The average of $2x$ and $7y$ is 32.

Algebra Statistics

The average of x and y is $\dfrac{x + y}{2}$, which can be determined if and only if the value of $x + y$ can be determined.

(1)   It is given that the average of x and $2y$ is 10. Therefore, $\dfrac{x + 2y}{2} = 10$, or $x + 2y = 20$. Because the value of $x + y$ is desired, rewrite the last equation as $(x + y) + y = 20$, or $x + y = 20 - y$. This shows that the value of $x + y$ can vary. For example, if $x = 20$ and $y = 0$, then $x + 2y = 20$ and $x + y = 20$. However, if $x = 18$ and $y = 1$, then $x + 2y = 20$ and $x + y = 19$; NOT sufficient.

(2)   It is given that the average of $2x$ and $7y$ is 32. Therefore, $\dfrac{2x + 7y}{2} = 32$, or $2x + 7y = 64$. Because the value of $x + y$ is desired, rewrite the last equation as $2(x + y) + 5y = 64$, or $x + y = \dfrac{64 - 5y}{2}$. This shows that the value of $x + y$ can vary. For example, if $x = 32$ and $y = 0$, then $2x + 7y = 64$ and $x + y = 32$. However, if $x = 4$ and $y = 8$, then $2x + 7y = 64$ and $x + y = 12$; NOT sufficient.

Given (1) and (2), it follows that $x + 2y = 20$ and $2x + 7y = 64$. These two equations can be solved simultaneously to obtain the individual values of x and y, which can then be used to determine the average of x and y. From $x + 2y = 20$ it follows that $x = 20 - 2y$. Substituting $20 - 2y$ for x in $2x + 7y = 64$ gives $2(20 - 2y) + 7y = 64$, or $40 - 4y + 7y = 64$, or $3y = 24$, or $y = 8$. Thus, using $x = 20 - 2y$, the value of x is $20 - 2(8) = 4$. Alternatively, it can be seen that unique values for x and y are determined from (1) and (2) by the fact that the equations $x + 2y = 20$ and $2x + 7y = 64$ represent two nonparallel lines in the standard (x,y) coordinate plane, which have a unique point in common.

The correct answer is C; both statements together are sufficient.

13. What is the value of $\frac{r}{2} + \frac{s}{2}$?

(1) $\frac{r+s}{2} = 5$

(2) $r + s = 10$

Arithmetic Operations with rational numbers

Since $\frac{r}{2} + \frac{s}{2} = \frac{r+s}{2} = \frac{1}{2}(r+s)$, the value of $\frac{r}{2} + \frac{s}{2}$ can be determined exactly when either the value of $\frac{r+s}{2}$ can be determined or the value of $r+s$ can be determined.

(1) It is given that $\frac{r+s}{2} = 5$. Therefore, $\frac{r}{2} + \frac{s}{2} = 5$; SUFFICIENT.

(2) It is given that $r + s = 10$. Therefore, $\frac{r}{2} + \frac{s}{2} = \frac{1}{2}(r+s) = \frac{1}{2}(10) = 5$; SUFFICIENT.

The correct answer is D; each statement alone is sufficient

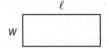

14. If ℓ and w represent the length and width, respectively, of the rectangle above, what is the perimeter?

(1) $2\ell + w = 40$

(2) $\ell + w = 25$

Geometry Perimeter

The perimeter of the rectangle is $2(\ell + w)$, which can be determined exactly when the value of $\ell + w$ can be determined.

(1) It is given that $2\ell + w = 40$. Therefore, $(2\ell + w) - \ell = 40 - \ell$, or $\ell + w = 40 - \ell$. Therefore, different values of $\ell + w$ can be obtained by choosing different values of ℓ. For example, if $\ell = 10$ and $w = 40 - 2\ell = 20$, then $\ell + w = 30$. However, if $\ell = 15$ and $w = 40 - 2\ell = 10$, then $\ell + w = 25$; NOT sufficient.

(2) It is given that $\ell + w = 25$; SUFFICIENT.

The correct answer is B; statement 2 alone is sufficient.

15. For all x, the expression x^* is defined to be $ax + a$, where a is a constant. What is the value of 2^* ?

(1) $3^* = 2$

(2) $5^* = 3$

Algebra Linear equations

Determine the value of $2^* = (a)(2) + a = 3a$, or equivalently, determine the value of a.

(1) Given that $3^* = 2$, it follows that $(a)(3) + a = 2$, or $4a = 2$, or $a = \frac{1}{2}$; SUFFICIENT.

(2) Given that $5^* = 3$, it follows that $(a)(5) + a = 3$, or $6a = 3$, or $a = \frac{1}{2}$; SUFFICIENT.

The correct answer is D; each statement alone is sufficient.

16. Is $k + m < 0$?

    (1) $k < 0$
    (2) $km > 0$

Arithmetic Properties of numbers

(1) Given that k is negative, it is not possible to determine whether $k + m$ is negative. For example, if $k = -2$ and $m = 1$, then $k + m$ is negative. However, if $k = -2$ and $m = 3$, then $k + m$ is not negative; NOT sufficient.

(2) Given that km is positive, it is not possible to determine whether $k + m$ is negative. For example, if $k = -2$ and $m = -1$, then km is positive and $k + m$ is negative. However, if $k = 2$ and $m = 1$, then km is positive and $k + m$ is not negative; NOT sufficient.

Taking (1) and (2) together, k is negative and km is positive, it follows that m is negative. Therefore, both k and m are negative, and hence $k + m$ is negative.

**The correct answer is C;
both statements together are sufficient.**

17. A retailer purchased a television set for x percent less than its list price, and then sold it for y percent less than its list price. What was the list price of the television set?

    (1) $x = 15$
    (2) $x - y = 5$

Arithmetic Percents

(1) This provides information only about the value of x. The list price cannot be determined using x because no dollar value for the purchase price is given; NOT sufficient.

(2) This provides information about the relationship between x and y but does not provide dollar values for either of these variables; NOT sufficient.

The list price cannot be determined without a dollar value for either the retailer's purchase price or the retailer's selling price. Even though the values for x and y are given or can be determined, taking (1) and (2) together provides no dollar value for either.

**The correct answer is E;
both statements together are still not sufficient.**

18. If Ann saves x dollars each week and Beth saves y dollars each week, what is the total amount that they save per week?

    (1) Beth saves $5 more per week than Ann saves per week.
    (2) It takes Ann 6 weeks to save the same amount that Beth saves in 5 weeks.

Algebra Simultaneous equations

Determine the value of $x + y$.

(1) It is given that $y = 5 + x$. Therefore, $x + y = x + (5 + x) = 2x + 5$, which can vary in value. For example, if $x = 5$ and $y = 10$, then $y = 5 + x$ and $x + y = 15$. However, if $x = 10$ and $y = 15$, then $y = 5 + x$ and $x + y = 25$; NOT sufficient.

(2) It is given that $6x = 5y$, or $y = \dfrac{6}{5}x$. Therefore, $x + y = x + \dfrac{6}{5}x = \dfrac{11}{5}x$, which can vary in value. For example, if $x = 5$ and $y = 6$, then $y = \dfrac{6}{5}x$ and $x + y = 11$. However, if $x = 10$ and $y = 12$, then $y = \dfrac{6}{5}x$ and $x + y = 22$; NOT sufficient.

Given (1) and (2), it follows that $y = 5 + x$ and $y = \dfrac{6}{5}x$. These two equations can be solved simultaneously to obtain the individual values of x and y, which can then be used to determine $x + y$. Equating the two expressions for y gives $5 + x = \dfrac{6}{5}x$, or $25 + 5x = 6x$, or $25 = x$. Therefore, $y = 5 + 25 = 30$ and $x + y = 55$.

**The correct answer is C;
both statements together are sufficient.**

19. What is the total number of executives at Company P ?

    (1) The number of male executives is $\frac{3}{5}$ the number of female executives.

    (2) There are 4 more female executives than male executives.

Algebra Simultaneous equations

Let M be the number of male executives at Company P and let F be the number of female executives at Company P. Determine the value of $M + F$.

(1) Given that $M = \frac{3}{5} F$, it is not possible to determine the value of $M + F$. For example, if $M = 3$ and $F = 5$, then $M = \frac{3}{5} F$ and $M + F = 8$. However, if $M = 6$ and $F = 10$, then $M = \frac{3}{5} F$ and $M + F = 16$; NOT sufficient.

(2) Given that $F = M + 4$, it is not possible to determine the value of $M + F$. For example, if $M = 3$ and $F = 7$, then $F = M + 4$ and $M + F = 10$. However, if $M = 4$ and $F = 8$, then $F = M + 4$ and $M + F = 12$; NOT sufficient.

Taking (1) and (2) together, then $F = M + 4$ and $M = \frac{3}{5} F$, so $F = \frac{3}{5} F + 4$. Now solve for F to get $\frac{2}{5} F = 4$ and $F = 10$. Therefore, using $F = 10$ and $F = M + 4$, it follows that $M = 6$, and hence $M + F = 6 + 10 = 16$.

The correct answer is C; both statements together are sufficient.

20. What is the ratio of c to d ?

    (1) The ratio of $3c$ to $3d$ is 3 to 4.

    (2) The ratio of $c + 3$ to $d + 3$ is 4 to 5.

Arithmetic Ratio and proportion

Determine the value of $\frac{c}{d}$.

(1) Given that $\frac{3c}{3d} = \frac{3}{4}$, it follows that $\frac{\cancel{3}c}{\cancel{3}d} = \frac{c}{d} = \frac{3}{4}$; SUFFICIENT.

(2) Given that $\frac{c + 3}{d + 3} = \frac{4}{5}$, then it is not possible to determine the value of $\frac{c}{d}$. For example, if $c = 1$ and $d = 2$, then $\frac{c + 3}{d + 3} = \frac{4}{5}$ and $\frac{c}{d} = \frac{1}{2}$. However, if $c = 5$ and $d = 7$, then $\frac{c + 3}{d + 3} = \frac{8}{10} = \frac{4}{5}$ and $\frac{c}{d} = \frac{5}{7}$; NOT sufficient.

The correct answer is A; statement (1) alone is sufficient.

21. A certain dealership has a number of cars to be sold by its salespeople. How many cars are to be sold?

    (1) If each of the salespeople sells 4 of the cars, 23 cars will remain unsold.

    (2) If each of the salespeople sells 6 of the cars, 5 cars will remain unsold.

Algebra Simultaneous equations

Let T be the total number of cars to be sold and S be the number of salespeople. Determine the value of T.

(1) Given that $T = 4S + 23$, it follows that the positive integer value of T can vary, since the positive integer value of S cannot be determined; NOT sufficient.

(2) Given that $T = 6S + 5$, it follows that the positive integer value of T can vary, since the positive integer value of S cannot be determined; NOT sufficient.

(1) and (2) together give a system of two equations in two unknowns. Equating the two expressions for T gives $4S + 23 = 6S + 5$, or $18 = 2S$, or $S = 9$. From this the value of T can be determined by $4(9) + 23$ or $6(9) + 5$.

The correct answer is C; both statements together are sufficient.

22. Committee member W wants to schedule a one-hour meeting on Thursday for himself and three other committee members, X, Y, and Z. Is there a one-hour period on Thursday that is open for all four members?

    (1) On Thursday W and X have an open period from 9:00 a.m. to 12:00 noon.
    (2) On Thursday Y has an open period from 10:00 a.m. to 1:00 p.m. and Z has an open period from 8:00 a.m. to 11:00 a.m.

Arithmetic Sets

(1) There is no information about Y and Z, only information about W and X; NOT sufficient.

(2) Similarly, there is no information about W and X, only information about Y and Z; NOT sufficient.

Together, (1) and (2) detail information about all four committee members, and it can be determined that on Thursday all four members have an open one-hour period from 10:00 a.m. to 11:00 a.m.

The correct answer is C; both statements together are sufficient.

23. Some computers at a certain company are Brand X and the rest are Brand Y. If the ratio of the number of Brand Y computers to the number of Brand X computers at the company is 5 to 6, how many of the computers are Brand Y?

    (1) There are 80 more Brand X computers than Brand Y computers at the company.
    (2) There is a total of 880 computers at the company.

Algebra Simultaneous equations

Let x and y be the numbers of Brand X computers and Brand Y computers, respectively, at the company. Then $\frac{y}{x} = \frac{5}{6}$, or after cross multiplying, $6y = 5x$. Determine the value of y.

(1) Given that $x = 80 + y$, it follows that $5x = 5(80 + y) = 400 + 5y$. Substituting $6y$ for $5x$ on the left side of the last equation gives $6y = 400 + 5y$, or $y = 400$. Alternatively, it can be seen that unique values for x and y are determined by the fact that $6y = 5x$ and

$x = 80 + y$ represent the equations of two nonparallel lines in the standard (x,y) coordinate plane, which have a unique point in common; SUFFICIENT.

(2) Given that $x + y = 880$, it follows that $5x + 5y = 5(880)$. Substituting $6y$ for $5x$ on the left side of the last equation gives $6y + 5y = 5(880)$, or $11y = 5(880)$, or $y = 5(80) = 400$. Alternatively, it can be seen that unique values for x and y are determined by the fact that $6y = 5x$ and $x + y = 880$ represent the equations of two nonparallel lines in the standard (x,y) coordinate plane, which have a unique point in common; SUFFICIENT.

The correct answer is D; each statement alone is sufficient.

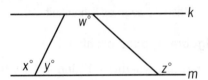

24. In the figure shown, lines k and m are parallel to each other. Is $x = z$?

    (1) $x = w$
    (2) $y = 180 - w$

Geometry Angles

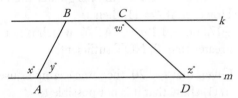

Since lines k and m are parallel, it follows from properties of parallel lines that in the diagram above x is the degree measure of $\angle ABC$ in quadrilateral $ABCD$. Therefore, because $y = 180 - x$, the four interior angles of quadrilateral $ABCD$ have degree measures $(180 - x)$, x, w, and $(180 - z)$.

(1) Given that $x = w$, then because the sum of the degree measures of the angles of the quadrilateral $ABCD$ is 360, it follows that $(180 - x) + x + x + (180 - z) = 360$, or $x - z = 0$, or $x = z$; SUFFICIENT.

(2) Given that $y = 180 - w$, then because $y = 180 - x$, it follows that $180 - w = 180 - x$, or $x = w$. However, it is shown in (1) that $x = w$ is sufficient; SUFFICIENT.

The correct answer is D; each statement alone is sufficient.

25. When the wind speed is 9 miles per hour, the wind-chill factor w is given by

$$w = -17.366 + 1.19t,$$

where t is the temperature in degrees Fahrenheit. If at noon yesterday the wind speed was 9 miles per hour, was the wind-chill factor greater than 0 ?

(1) The temperature at noon yesterday was greater than 10 degrees Fahrenheit.

(2) The temperature at noon yesterday was less than 20 degrees Fahrenheit.

Algebra Applied problems

Determine whether $-17.366 + 1.19t$ is greater than 0.

(1) Given that $t > 10$, it follows that $-17.366 + 1.19t > -17.366 + 1.19(10)$, or $-17.366 + 1.19t > -5.466$. However, it is not possible to determine whether $-17.366 + 1.19t$ is greater than 0. For example, if $t = 19$, then $-17.366 + 1.19t = 5.244$ is greater than 0. However, if $t = 11$, then $-17.366 + 1.19t = -4.276$, which is not greater than 0; NOT sufficient.

(2) Given that $t < 20$, the same examples used in (1) show that it is not possible to determine whether $-17.366 + 1.19t$ is greater than 0; NOT sufficient.

Taking (1) and (2) together is of no more help than either (1) or (2) taken separately because the same examples were used in both (1) and (2).

The correct answer is E; both statements together are still not sufficient.

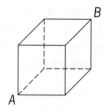

26. What is the volume of the cube above?

(1) The surface area of the cube is 600 square inches.

(2) The length of diagonal AB is $10\sqrt{3}$ inches.

Geometry Volume

This problem can be solved by determining the side length, s, of the cube.

(1) This indicates that $6s^2 = 600$, from which it follows that $s^2 = 100$ and $s = 10$; SUFFICIENT.

(2) To determine diagonal AB, first determine diagonal AN by applying the Pythagorean theorem to $\triangle AMN$: $AN = \sqrt{s^2 + s^2} = \sqrt{2s^2}$. Now determine AB by applying the Pythagorean theorem to $\triangle ANB$: $AB = \sqrt{(AN)^2 + (NB)^2} = \sqrt{2s^2 + s^2} = \sqrt{3s^2} = s\sqrt{3}$. It is given that $AB = 10\sqrt{3}$, and so $s = 10$; SUFFICIENT.

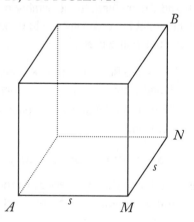

The correct answer is D; each statement alone is sufficient.

27. Of the 230 single-family homes built in City X last year, how many were occupied at the end of the year?

    (1) Of all single-family homes in City X, 90 percent were occupied at the end of last year.
    (2) A total of 7,200 single-family homes in City X were occupied at the end of last year.

Arithmetic Percents

(1) The percentage of the occupied single-family homes that were *built* last year is not given, and so the number occupied cannot be found; NOT sufficient.

(2) Again, there is no information about the occupancy of the single-family homes that were *built* last year; NOT sufficient.

Together (1) and (2) yield only the total number of the single-family homes that were occupied. Neither statement offers the needed information as to how many of the single-family homes *built* last year were occupied at the end of last year.

The correct answer is E;
both statements together are still not sufficient.

28. If *J*, *S*, and *V* are points on the number line, what is the distance between *S* and *V* ?

    (1) The distance between *J* and *S* is 20.
    (2) The distance between *J* and *V* is 25.

Arithmetic Properties of numbers

(1) Since no restriction is placed on the location of *V*, the distance between *S* and *V* could be any positive real number; NOT sufficient.

(2) Since no restriction is placed on the location of *S*, the distance between *S* and *V* could be any positive real number; NOT sufficient.

Given (1) and (2) together, it follows that *JS* = 20 and *JV* = 25. However, *V* could be on the left side of *S* or *V* could be on the right side of *S*. For example, suppose *J* is located at 0 and *S* is located at 20. If *V* were on the left side of *S*, then *V* would be located at −25, and thus *SV* would be 25 + 20 = 45, as shown below.

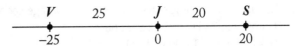

However, if *V* were on the right side of *S*, then *V* would be located at 25, and thus *SV* would be 25 − 20 = 5, as shown below.

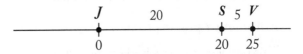

The correct answer is E;
both statements together are still not sufficient.

29. If *x* is a positive integer, what is the value of *x* ?

    (1) $x^2 = \sqrt{x}$
    (2) $\dfrac{n}{x} = n$ and $n \neq 0$.

Algebra Operations with radicals

(1) It is given that *x* is a positive integer. Then,

$$
\begin{aligned}
x^2 &= \sqrt{x} & \text{given} \\
x^4 &= x & \text{square both sides} \\
x^4 - x &= 0 & \text{subtract } x \text{ from both sides} \\
x(x-1)(x^2+x+1) &= 0 & \text{factor left side}
\end{aligned}
$$

Thus, the positive integer value of *x* being sought will be a solution of this equation. One solution of this equation is *x* = 0, which is not a positive integer. Another solution is *x* = 1, which is a positive integer. Also, $x^2 + x + 1$ is a positive integer for all positive integer values of *x*, and so $x^2 + x + 1 = 0$ has no positive integer solutions. Thus, the only possible positive integer value of *x* is 1; SUFFICIENT.

(2) It is given that $n \neq 0$. Then,

$$
\begin{aligned}
\frac{n}{x} &= n & \text{given} \\
n &= nx & \text{multiply both sides by } x \\
1 &= x & \text{divide both sides by } n, \text{ where } n \neq 0
\end{aligned}
$$

Thus, *x* = 1; SUFFICIENT.

The correct answer is D;
each statement alone is sufficient.

30. During a certain bicycle ride, was Sherry's average speed faster than 24 kilometers per hour?
    (1 kilometer = 1,000 meters)

    (1) Sherry's average speed during the bicycle ride was faster than 7 meters per second.
    (2) Sherry's average speed during the bicycle ride was slower than 8 meters per second.

Arithmetic Applied problems

This problem can be solved by converting 24 kilometers per hour into meters per second. First, 24 kilometers is equivalent to 24,000 meters and 1 hour is equivalent to 3,600 seconds. Then, traveling 24 kilometers in 1 hour is equivalent to traveling 24,000 meters in 3,600 seconds, or $\frac{24,000}{3,600} = 6\frac{2}{3}$ meters per second.

(1) This indicates that Sherry's average speed was faster than 7 meters per second, which is faster than $6\frac{2}{3}$ meters per second and, therefore, faster than 24 kilometers per hour; SUFFICIENT.

(2) This indicates that Sherry's average speed was slower than 8 meters per second. Her average speed could have been 7 meters per second (since 7 < 8), in which case her average speed was faster than $6\frac{2}{3}$ meters per second and, therefore, faster than 24 kilometers per hour. Or her average speed could have been 5 meters per second (since 5 < 8), in which case her average speed was not faster than $6\frac{2}{3}$ meters per second and, therefore, not faster than 24 kilometers per hour; NOT sufficient.

**The correct answer is A;
statement 1 alone is sufficient.**

31. If x and y are integers, what is the value of x?

    (1) $xy = 1$
    (2) $x \neq -1$

Arithmetic Properties of integers

Given that x and y are integers, determine the value of x.

(1) If $x = y = -1$, then $xy = 1$, and if $x = y = 1$, then $xy = 1$; NOT sufficient.

(2) Given that $x \neq -1$, the value of x could be any other integer; NOT sufficient.

Taking (1) and (2) together, since the two possibilities for the value of x are $x = -1$ or $x = 1$ by (1), and $x \neq -1$ by (2), then $x = 1$.

**The correct answer is C;
both statements together are sufficient**

32. If p, s, and t are positive, is $|ps - pt| > p(s - t)$?

    (1) $p < s$
    (2) $s < t$

Algebra Absolute value

Since p is positive, it follows that $|p(s - t)| = |p||s - t| = p|s - t|$. Therefore, the task is to determine if $|s - t| > s - t$. Since $|s - t| = s - t$ if and only if $s - t \geq 0$, it follows that $|s - t| > s - t$ if and only if $s - t < 0$.

(1) This indicates that $p < s$ but does not provide information about the relationship between s and t. For example, if $p = 5$, $s = 10$, and $t = 15$, then $p < s$ and $s < t$, but if $p = 5$, $s = 10$, and $t = 3$, then $p < s$ and $s > t$; NOT sufficient.

(2) This indicates that $s < t$, or equivalently, $s - t < 0$; SUFFICIENT.

**The correct answer is B;
statement 2 alone is sufficient.**

33. What were the gross revenues from ticket sales for a certain film during the second week in which it was shown?

    (1) Gross revenues during the second week were $1.5 million less than during the first week.
    (2) Gross revenues during the third week were $2.0 million less than during the first week.

    Arithmetic Arithmetic operations

    (1) Since the amount of gross revenues during the first week is not given, the gross revenues during the second week cannot be determined; NOT sufficient.

    (2) No information is provided, directly or indirectly, about gross revenues during the second week; NOT sufficient.

    With (1) and (2) taken together, additional information, such as the amount of gross revenues during either the first or the third week, is still needed.

    The correct answer is E; both statements together are still not sufficient.

34. The total cost of an office dinner was shared equally by k of the n employees who attended the dinner. What was the total cost of the dinner?

    (1) Each of the k employees who shared the cost of the dinner paid $19.
    (2) If the total cost of the dinner had been shared equally by $k+1$ of the n employees who attended the dinner, each of the $k+1$ employees would have paid $18.

    Algebra Simultaneous equations

    (1) Given that each of the k employees paid $19, it follows that the total cost of the dinner, in dollars, is $19k$. However, since k cannot be determined, the value of $19k$ cannot be determined; NOT sufficient.

    (2) Given that each of $(k+1)$ employees would have paid $18, it follows that the total cost of the dinner, in dollars, is $18(k+1)$. However, since k cannot be determined, the value of $18(k+1)$ cannot be determined; NOT sufficient.

Given (1) and (2) together, it follows that $19k = 18(k+1)$, or $19k = 18k + 18$, or $k = 18$. Therefore, the total cost of the dinner is

$$(\$19)k = (\$19)(18).$$

The correct answer is C; both statements together are sufficient.

35. For a recent play performance, the ticket prices were $25 per adult and $15 per child. A total of 500 tickets were sold for the performance. How many of the tickets sold were for adults?

    (1) Revenue from ticket sales for this performance totaled $10,500.
    (2) The average (arithmetic mean) price per ticket sold was $21.

    Algebra Simultaneous equations

    Let A and C be the numbers of adult and child tickets sold, respectively. Given that $A + C = 500$, or $C = 500 - A$, determine the value of A.

    (1) Given that $25A + 15C = 10,500$, or $5A + 3C = 2,100$, it follows by substituting $500 - A$ for C that $5A + 3(500 - A) = 2,100$, which can be solved to obtain a unique value for A. Alternatively, it can be seen that unique values for A and C are determined by the fact that $A + C = 500$ and $5A + 3C = 2,100$ represent the equations of two nonparallel lines in the standard (x,y) coordinate plane, which have a unique point in common; SUFFICIENT.

    (2) It is given that $\dfrac{25A + 15C}{500} = 21$, or $25A + 15C = (21)(500) = 10,500$, which is the same information given in (1). Therefore, A can be determined, as shown in (1) above; SUFFICIENT.

    The correct answer is D; each statement alone is sufficient.

36. What is the value of x ?

   (1) $x + 1 = 2 - 3x$

   (2) $\dfrac{1}{2x} = 2$

Algebra First- and second-degree equations

   (1)   Transposing terms gives the equivalent equation $4x = 1$, or $x = \dfrac{1}{4}$; SUFFICIENT.

   (2)   Multiplying both sides by $2x$ gives the equivalent equation $1 = 4x$, or $x = \dfrac{1}{4}$; SUFFICIENT.

**The correct answer is D;
each statement alone is sufficient.**

37. If x and y are positive integers, what is the remainder when $10^x + y$ is divided by 3 ?

   (1) $x = 5$

   (2) $y = 2$

Arithmetic Properties of numbers

   (1)   Given that $x = 5$, then $10^x + y = 100,000 + y$. More than one remainder is possible when $100,000 + y$ is divided by 3. For example, by long division, or by using the fact that $100,000 + y = 99,999 + (1 + y)$
$= 3(33,333) + (1 + y)$, the remainder is 2 when $y = 1$ and the remainder is 0 when $y = 2$; NOT sufficient.

   (2)   Given that $y = 2$, then $10^x + y = 10^x + 2$. Since the sum of the digits of $10^x + 2$ is 3, which is divisible by 3, it follows that $10^x + 2$ is divisible by 3, and hence has remainder 0 when divided by 3. This can also be seen by writing $10^x + 2$ as $(10^x - 1 + 1) + 2$
$= (10^x - 1) + 1 + 2 = 999\ldots99,999 + 3$
$= 3(333\ldots33,333 + 1)$, which is divisible by 3; SUFFICIENT.

**The correct answer is B;
statement 2 alone is sufficient.**

38. What was the amount of money donated to a certain charity?

   (1)   Of the amount donated, 40 percent came from corporate donations.

   (2)   Of the amount donated, \$1.5 million came from noncorporate donations.

Arithmetic Percents

The statements suggest considering the amount of money donated to be the total of the corporate donations and the noncorporate donations.

   (1)   From this, only the portion that represented corporate donations is known, with no means of determining the total amount donated; NOT sufficient.

   (2)   From this, only the dollar amount that represented noncorporate donations is known, with no means of determining the portion of the total donations that it represents; NOT sufficient.

Letting x represent the total dollar amount donated, it follows from (1) that the amount donated from corporate sources can be represented as $0.40x$. Combining the information from (1) and (2) yields the equation $0.40x + \$1,500,000 = x$, which can be solved to obtain exactly one solution for x.

**The correct answer is C;
both statements together are sufficient.**

39. What is the value of the positive integer n ?

   (1) $n^4 < 25$

   (2) $n \neq n^2$

Arithmetic Arithmetic operations

   (1)   If n is a positive integer and $n^4 < 25$, then n can be either 1 or 2, since $1^4 = 1 \times 1 \times 1 \times 1 = 1$ and $2^4 = 2 \times 2 \times 2 \times 2 = 16$; NOT sufficient.

   (2)   Since the only positive integer equal to its square is 1, each positive integer that is not equal to 1 satisfies (2); NOT sufficient.

Using (1) and (2) together, it follows from (1) that $n = 1$ or $n = 2$, and it follows from (2) that $n \neq 1$, and hence the value of n must be 2.

**The correct answer is C;
both statements together are sufficient.**

40. If the set S consists of five consecutive positive integers, what is the sum of these five integers?

    (1) The integer 11 is in S, but 10 is not in S.
    (2) The sum of the even integers in S is 26.

Arithmetic Sequences

(1) This indicates that the least integer in S is 11 since S consists of consecutive integers and 11 is in S, but 10 is not in S. Thus, the integers in S are 11, 12, 13, 14, and 15, and their sum can be determined; SUFFICIENT.

(2) This indicates that the sum of the even integers in S is 26. In a set of 5 consecutive integers, either two of the integers or three of the integers are even. If there are three even integers, then the first integer in S must be even. Also, since $\frac{26}{3} = 8\frac{2}{3}$, the three even integers must be around 8. The three even integers could be 6, 8, and 10, but are not because their sum is less than 26; or they could be 8, 10, and 12, but are not because their sum is greater than 26. Therefore, S cannot contain three even integers and must contain only two even integers. Those integers must be 12 and 14 since 12 + 14 = 26. It follows that the integers in S are 11, 12, 13, 14, and 15, and their sum can be determined; SUFFICIENT.

Alternately, if n, $n + 1$, $n + 2$, $n + 3$, and $n + 4$ represent the five consecutive integers and three of them are even, then $n + (n + 2) + (n + 4) = 26$, or $3n = 20$, or $n = \frac{20}{3}$, which is not an integer.

On the other hand, if two of the integers are even, then $(n +1) + (n +3) = 26$, or $2n = 22$, or $n = 11$. It follows that the integers are 11, 12, 13, 14, and 15, and their sum can be determined; SUFFICIENT.

The correct answer is D;
each statement alone is sufficient.

41. A total of 20 amounts are entered on a spreadsheet that has 5 rows and 4 columns; each of the 20 positions in the spreadsheet contains one amount. The average (arithmetic mean) of the amounts in row i is R_i $(1 \le i \le 5)$. The average of the amounts in column j is C_j $(1 \le j \le 4)$. What is the average of all 20 amounts on the spreadsheet?

    (1) $R_1 + R_2 + R_3 + R_4 + R_5 = 550$
    (2) $C_1 + C_2 + C_3 + C_4 = 440$

Arithmetic Statistics

It is given that R_i represents the average of the amounts in row i. Since there are four amounts in each row, $4R_i$ represents the total of the amounts in row i. Likewise, it is given that C_j represents the average of the amounts in column j. Since there are five amounts in each column, $5C_j$ represents the total of the amounts in column j.

(1) It is given that $R_1 + R_2 + R_3 + R_4 + R_5 = 550$, and so $4(R_1 + R_2 + R_3 + R_4 + R_5) = 4R_1 + 4R_2 + 4R_3 + 4R_4 + 4R_5 = 4(550) = 2,200$. Therefore, 2,200 is the sum of all 20 amounts (4 amounts in each of 5 rows), and the average of all 20 amounts is $\frac{2,200}{20} = 110$; SUFFICIENT.

(2) It is given that $C_1 + C_2 + C_3 + C_4 = 440$, and so $5(C_1 + C_2 + C_3 + C_4) = 5C_1 + 5C_2 + 5C_3 + 5C_4 = 5(440) = 2,200$. Therefore, 2,200 is the sum of all 20 amounts (5 amounts in each of 4 columns), and the average of all 20 amounts is $\frac{2,200}{20} = 110$; SUFFICIENT.

The correct answer is D;
each statement alone is sufficient.

42. Was the range of the amounts of money that Company Y budgeted for its projects last year equal to the range of the amounts of money that it budgeted for its projects this year?

    (1) Both last year and this year, Company Y budgeted money for 12 projects and the least amount of money that it budgeted for a project was $400.

    (2) Both last year and this year, the average (arithmetic mean) amount of money that Company Y budgeted per project was $2,000.

Arithmetic Statistics

Let G_1 and L_1 represent the greatest and least amounts, respectively, of money that Company Y budgeted for its projects last year, and let G_2 and L_2 represent the greatest and least amounts, respectively, of money that Company Y budgeted for its projects this year. Determine if the range of the amounts of money Company Y budgeted for its projects last year is equal to the range of amounts budgeted for its projects this year; that is, determine if $G_1 - L_1 = G_2 - L_2$.

    (1) This indicates that $L_1 = L_2 = \$400$, but does not give any information about G_1 or G_2; NOT sufficient.

    (2) This indicates that the average amount Company Y budgeted for its projects both last year and this year was $2,000 per project, but does not give any information about the least and greatest amounts that it budgeted for its projects either year; NOT sufficient.

Taking (1) and (2) together, it is known that $L_1 = L_2 = \$400$ and that the average amount Company Y budgeted for its projects both last year and this year was $2,000 per project, but there is no information about G_1 or G_2. For example, if, for each year, Company Y budgeted $400 for each of 2 projects and $2,320 for each of the 10 others, then (1) and (2) are true and the range for each year was $2,320 − $400 = $1,920. However,

if, last year, Company Y budgeted $400 for each of 2 projects and $2,320 for each of the 10 others, and, this year, budgeted $400 for each of 11 projects and $19,600 for 1 project, then (1) and (2) are true, but the range for last year was $1,920 and the range for this year was $19,600 − $400 = $19,200.

The correct answer is E; both statements together are still not sufficient.

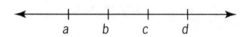

43. If a, b, c, and d are numbers on the number line shown and if the tick marks are equally spaced, what is the value of $a + c$?

    (1) $a + b = -8$
    (2) $a + d = 0$

Algebra Sequences

It is given that the distance between a and b is the same as the distance between b and c, which is the same as the distance between c and d. Letting q represent this distance, then $b = a + q$, $c = a + 2q$, and $d = a + 3q$. The value of $a + c$ can be determined if the value of $a + (a + 2q) = 2a + 2q$ can be determined.

    (1) It is given that $a + b = -8$. Then, $a + (a + q) = 2a + q = -8$. From this, the value of $2a + 2q$ cannot be determined. For example, the values of a and q could be −5 and 2, respectively, or they could be −6 and 4, respectively; NOT sufficient.

    (2) It is given that $a + d = 0$. Then, $a + (a + 3q) = 2a + 3q = 0$. From this, the value of $2a + 2q$ cannot be determined. For example, the values of a and q could be −3 and 2, respectively, or they could be −6 and 4, respectively; NOT sufficient.

Taking (1) and (2) together, adding the equations, $2a + q = -8$ and $2a + 3q = 0$ gives $4a + 4q = -8$ and so $2a + 2q = \dfrac{-8}{2} = -4$.

The correct answer is C; both statements together are sufficient.

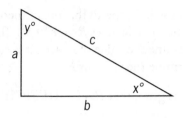

44. In the triangle above, does $a^2 + b^2 = c^2$?

    (1) $x + y = 90$
    (2) $x = y$

Geometry Triangles

The Pythagorean theorem states that $a^2 + b^2 = c^2$ for any right triangle with legs of lengths a and b and hypotenuse of length c. A right triangle is a triangle whose largest angle has measure $90°$. The converse of the Pythagorean theorem also holds: If $a^2 + b^2 = c^2$, then the triangle is a right triangle.

(1)   The sum of the degree measures of the three interior angles of a triangle is $180°$. It is given that $x + y = 90$. Thus, the remaining interior angle (not labeled) has degree measure $180 - 90 = 90$. Therefore, the triangle is a right triangle, and hence it follows from the Pythagorean theorem that $a^2 + b^2 = c^2$; SUFFICIENT.

(2)   Given that $x = y$, the triangle could be a right triangle (for example, $x = y = 45$) or fail to be a right triangle (for example, $x = y = 40$), and hence $a^2 + b^2 = c^2$ can be true (this follows from the Pythagorean theorem) or $a^2 + b^2 = c^2$ can be false (this follows from the converse of the Pythagorean theorem); NOT sufficient.

**The correct answer is A;
statement 1 alone is sufficient.**

45. If $rs \neq 0$, is $\frac{1}{r} + \frac{1}{s} = 4$?

    (1) $r + s = 4rs$
    (2) $r = s$

Algebra First- and second-degree equations

(1)   Dividing each side of the equation $r + s = 4rs$ by rs gives $\frac{r+s}{rs} = \frac{4rs}{rs}$, or $\frac{r}{rs} + \frac{s}{rs} = \frac{4rs}{rs}$, or $\frac{1}{s} + \frac{1}{r} = 4$; SUFFICIENT.

(2)   If $r = s = \frac{1}{2}$, then $\frac{1}{r} + \frac{1}{s} = 4$, but if $r = s = 1$, then $\frac{1}{s} + \frac{1}{r} = 2$; NOT sufficient.

**The correct answer is A;
statement 1 alone is sufficient.**

46. If x, y, and z are three integers, are they consecutive integers?

    (1) $z - x = 2$
    (2) $x < y < z$

Arithmetic Properties of numbers

(1)   Given $z - x = 2$, it is possible to choose y so that x, y, and z are consecutive integers (for example, $x = 1$, $y = 2$, and $z = 3$) and it is possible to choose y so that x, y, and z are not consecutive integers (for example, $x = 1$, $y = 4$, and $z = 3$); NOT sufficient.

(2)   Given that $x < y < z$, the three integers can be consecutive (for example, $x = 1$, $y = 2$, and $z = 3$) and the three integers can fail to be consecutive (for example, $x = 1$, $y = 3$, and $z = 4$); NOT sufficient.

Using (1) and (2) together, it follows that y is the unique integer between x and z and hence the three integers are consecutive.

**The correct answer is C;
both statements together are sufficient.**

47. A collection of 36 cards consists of 4 sets of 9 cards each. The 9 cards in each set are numbered 1 through 9. If one card has been removed from the collection, what is the number on that card?

    (1) The units digit of the sum of the numbers on the remaining 35 cards is 6.
    (2) The sum of the numbers on the remaining 35 cards is 176.

Arithmetic Properties of numbers

The sum $1 + 2 + \ldots + 9$ can be evaluated quickly by several methods. One method is to group the terms as $(1+9)+(2+8)+(3+7)+(4+6)+5$, and therefore the sum is $(4)(10)+5 = 45$. Thus, the sum of the numbers on all 36 cards is $(4)(45) = 180$.

    (1) It is given that the units digit of the sum of the numbers on the remaining 35 cards is 6. Since the sum of the numbers on all 36 cards is 180, the sum of the numbers on the remaining 35 cards must be 179, 178, 177, ..., 171, and of these values, only 176 has a units digit of 6. Therefore, the number on the card removed must be $180 - 176 = 4$; SUFFICIENT.

    (2) It is given that the sum of the numbers on the remaining 35 cards is 176. Since the sum of the numbers on all 36 cards is 180, it follows that the number on the card removed must be $180 - 176 = 4$; SUFFICIENT.

**The correct answer is D;
each statement alone is sufficient.**

48. In the xy-plane, point (r,s) lies on a circle with center at the origin. What is the value of $r^2 + s^2$?

    (1) The circle has radius 2.
    (2) The point $\left(\sqrt{2}, -\sqrt{2}\right)$ lies on the circle.

Geometry Simple coordinate geometry

Let R be the radius of the circle. A right triangle with legs of lengths $|r|$ and $|s|$ can be formed so that the line segment with endpoints (r,s) and $(0,0)$ is the hypotenuse. Since the length of the hypotenuse is R, the Pythagorean theorem for this right triangle gives $R^2 = r^2 + s^2$. Therefore, to determine the value of $r^2 + s^2$, it is sufficient to determine the value of R.

    (1) It is given that $R = 2$; SUFFICIENT.

    (2) It is given that $\left(\sqrt{2}, -\sqrt{2}\right)$ lies on the circle. A right triangle with legs each of length $\sqrt{2}$ can be formed so that the line segment with endpoints $\left(\sqrt{2}, -\sqrt{2}\right)$ and $(0,0)$ is the hypotenuse. Since the length of the hypotenuse is the radius of the circle, which is R, where $R^2 = r^2 + s^2$, the Pythagorean theorem for this right triangle gives $R^2 = \left(\sqrt{2}\right)^2 + \left(\sqrt{2}\right)^2 = 2+2 = 4$. Therefore, $r^2 + s^2 = 4$; SUFFICIENT.

**The correct answer is D;
each statement alone is sufficient.**

49. If r, s, and t are nonzero integers, is $r^5 s^3 t^4$ negative?

    (1) rt is negative.
    (2) s is negative.

Arithmetic Properties of numbers

Since $r^5 s^3 t^4 = (rt)^4 rs^3$ and $(rt)^4$ is positive, $r^5 s^3 t^4$ will be negative if and only if rs^3 is negative, or if and only if r and s have opposite signs.

    (1) It is given that rt is negative, but nothing can be determined about the sign of s. If the sign of s is the opposite of the sign of r, then $r^5 s^3 t^4 = (rt)^4 rs^3$ will be negative. However, if the sign of s is the same as the sign of r, then $r^5 s^3 t^4 = (rt)^4 rs^3$ will be positive; NOT sufficient.

    (2) It is given that s is negative, but nothing can be determined about the sign of r. If r is positive, then $r^5 s^3 t^4 = (rt)^4 rs^3$ will be negative. However, if r is negative, then $r^5 s^3 t^4 = (rt)^4 rs^3$ will be positive; NOT sufficient.

Given (1) and (2), it is still not possible to determine whether r and s have opposite signs. For example, (1) and (2) hold if r is positive, s is negative, and t is negative, and in this case r and s have opposite signs. However, (1) and (2) hold if r is negative, s is negative, and t is positive, and in this case r and s have the same sign.

**The correct answer is E;
both statements together are still not sufficient.**

50. If x and y are integers, what is the value of y ?

    (1) $xy = 27$
    (2) $x = y^2$

Arithmetic Arithmetic operations

(1) Many different pairs of integers have the product 27, for example, $(-3)(-9)$ and $(1)(27)$. There is no way to determine which pair of integers is intended, and there is also no way to determine which member of a pair is x and which member of a pair is y; NOT sufficient.

(2) Given that $x = y^2$, more than one integer value for y is possible. For example, y could be 1 (with the value of x being 1) or y could be 2 (with the value of x being 4); NOT sufficient.

Using both (1) and (2), y^2 can be substituted for the value of x in (1) to give $y^3 = 27$, which has exactly one solution, $y = 3$.

**The correct answer is C;
both statements together are sufficient.**

51. How many newspapers were sold at a certain newsstand today?

    (1) A total of 100 newspapers were sold at the newsstand yesterday, 10 fewer than twice the number sold today.
    (2) The number of newspapers sold at the newsstand yesterday was 45 more than the number sold today.

Algebra First- and second-degree equations

Let t be the number of newspapers sold today.

(1) The given information can be expressed as $100 = 2t - 10$, which can be solved for a unique value of t; SUFFICIENT.

(2) It is given that $45 + t$ newspapers were sold at the newsstand yesterday. Since the number sold yesterday is unknown, t cannot be determined; NOT sufficient.

**The correct answer is A;
statement 1 alone is sufficient.**

52. John took a test that had 60 questions numbered from 1 to 60. How many of the questions did he answer correctly?

    (1) The number of questions he answered correctly in the first half of the test was 7 more than the number he answered correctly in the second half of the test.

    (2) He answered $\frac{5}{6}$ of the odd-numbered questions correctly and $\frac{4}{5}$ of the even-numbered questions correctly.

Arithmetic Fractions

(1) Let f represent the number of questions answered correctly in the first half of the test and let s represent the number of questions answered correctly in the second half of the test. Then the given information can be expressed as $f = 7 + s$, which has several solutions in which f and s are integers between 1 and 60, leading to different values of $f + s$. For example, f could be 10 and s could be 3, which gives $f + s = 13$, or f could be 11 and s could be 4, which gives $f + s = 15$; NOT sufficient.

(2) Since there are 30 odd-numbered questions and 30 even-numbered questions in a 60-question test, from the information given it follows that the number of questions answered correctly was equal to $\frac{5}{6}(30) + \frac{4}{5}(30)$; SUFFICIENT.

**The correct answer is B;
statement 2 alone is sufficient.**

53. If x is a positive integer, is $\sqrt{x}$ an integer?

    (1) $\sqrt{4x}$ is an integer.
    (2) $\sqrt{3x}$ is not an integer.

Algebra Radicals

(1)   It is given that $\sqrt{4x} = n$, or $4x = n^2$, for some positive integer n. Since $4x$ is the square of an integer, it follows that in the prime factorization of $4x$, each distinct prime factor is repeated an even number of times. Therefore, the same must be true for the prime factorization of x, since the prime factorization of x only differs from the prime factorization of $4x$ by two factors of 2, and hence by an even number of factors of 2; SUFFICIENT.

(2)   Given that $\sqrt{3x}$ is not an integer, it is possible for $\sqrt{x}$ to be an integer (for example, $x = 1$) and it is possible for $\sqrt{x}$ to not be an integer (for example, $x = 2$); NOT sufficient.

The correct answer is A; statement 1 alone is sufficient.

54. Is the value of n closer to 50 than to 75 ?

    (1) $75 - n > n - 50$
    (2) $n > 60$

Algebra Inequalities

Begin by considering the value of n when it is at the exact same distance from both 50 and 75. The value of n is equidistant between 50 and 75 when n is the midpoint between 75 and 50, that is, when $n = \dfrac{50 + 75}{2} = 62.5$. Alternatively stated, n is equidistant between 50 and 75 when the distance that n is below 75 is equal to the distance that n is above 50, i.e., when $75 - n = n - 50$, as indicated on the number line below.

$$n - 50 \ = \ 75 - n$$

55. Last year, if Elena spent a total of \$720 on newspapers, magazines, and books, what amount did she spend on newspapers?

    (1)   Last year, the amount that Elena spent on magazines was 80 percent of the amount that she spent on books.
    (2)   Last year, the amount that Elena spent on newspapers was 60 percent of the total amount that she spent on magazines and books.

(1)   Since here $75 - n > n - 50$, it follows that the value of n is closer to 50 than to 75; SUFFICIENT.

(2)   Although n is greater than 60, for all values of n between 60 and 62.5, n is closer to 50, and for all values of n greater than 62.5, n is closer to 75. Without further information, the value of n relative to 50 and 75 cannot be determined; NOT sufficient.

The correct answer is A; statement 1 alone is sufficient.

Arithmetic Percents

Let n, m, and b be the amounts, in dollars, that Elena spent last year on newspapers, magazines, and books, respectively. Given that $n + m + b = 720$, determine the value of n.

(1)   Given that m is 80% of b, or $m = \dfrac{4}{5}b$, it follows from $n + m + b = 720$ that $n + \dfrac{4}{5}b + b = 720$, or $n = -\dfrac{9}{5}b + 720$. Since more than one positive value of b is possible, the value of n cannot be determined; NOT sufficient.

(2)   Given that n is 60% of the sum of m and b, or $n = \dfrac{3}{5}(m + b)$, or $\dfrac{5}{3}n = m + b$, it follows from $n + m + b = 720$ that $n + \dfrac{5}{3}n = 720$, which can be solved to obtain a unique value of n; SUFFICIENT.

The correct answer is B; statement 2 alone is sufficient.

56. If p, q, x, y, and z are different positive integers, which of the five integers is the median?

    (1) $p + x < q$
    (2) $y < z$

Arithmetic **Statistics**

Since there are five different integers, there are two integers greater and two integers less than the median, which is the middle number.

(1) No information is given about the order of y and z with respect to the other three numbers; NOT sufficient.

(2) This statement does not relate y and z to the other three integers; NOT sufficient.

Because (1) and (2) taken together do not relate p, x, and q to y and z, it is impossible to tell which is the median. For example, if $p = 3$, $x = 4$, $q = 8$, $y = 9$, and $z = 10$, then the median is 8, but if $p = 3$, $x = 4$, $q = 8$, $y = 1$, and $z = 2$, then the median is 3.

**The correct answer is E;
both statements together are still not sufficient.**

57. If $w + z = 28$, what is the value of wz?

    (1) w and z are positive integers.
    (2) w and z are consecutive odd integers.

Arithmetic **Arithmetic operations**

(1) The fact that w and z are both positive integers does not allow the values of w and z to be determined because, for example, if $w = 20$ and $z = 8$, then $wz = 160$, and if $w = 10$ and $z = 18$, then $wz = 180$; NOT sufficient.

(2) Since w and z are consecutive odd integers whose sum is 28, it is reasonable to consider the possibilities for the sum of consecutive odd integers: $\ldots, (-5) + (-3) = -8$, $(-3) + (-1) = -4$, $(-1) + 1 = 0$, $1 + 3 = 4, \ldots$, $9 + 11 = 20$, $11 + 13 = 24$, $13 + 15 = 28$, $15 + 17 = 32, \ldots$. From this list it follows that only one pair of consecutive odd integers has 28 for its sum, and hence there is exactly one possible value for wz.

This problem can also be solved algebraically by letting the consecutive odd integers w and z be represented by $2n + 1$ and $2n + 3$, where n can be any integer. Since $28 = w + z$, it follows that

$$28 = (2n + 1) + (2n + 3)$$

$28 = 4n + 4$ \qquad simplify

$24 = 4n$ \qquad subtract 4 from both sides

$6 = n$ \qquad divide both sides by 4

Thus, $w = 2(6) + 1 = 13$, $z = 2(6) + 3 = 15$, and hence exactly one value can be determined for wz; SUFFICIENT.

**The correct answer is B;
statement 2 alone is sufficient.**

58. What is the value of $a - b$?

    (1) $a = b + 4$
    (2) $(a - b)^2 = 16$

Algebra **First- and second-degree equations**

(1) If $a = b + 4$ then, when b is subtracted from both sides, the resultant equation is $a - b = 4$; SUFFICIENT.

(2) Since $(a - b)^2 = 16$, either $a - b = 4$ or $a - b = -4$. There is no further information available to determine a single numerical value of $a - b$; NOT sufficient.

**The correct answer is A;
statement 1 alone is sufficient.**

59. Machine X runs at a constant rate and produces a lot consisting of 100 cans in 2 hours. How much less time would it take to produce the lot of cans if both Machines X and Y were run simultaneously?

    (1) Both Machines X and Y produce the same number of cans per hour.
    (2) It takes Machine X twice as long to produce the lot of cans as it takes Machines X and Y running simultaneously to produce the lot.

Arithmetic Rate problems

The problem states that the job is to produce 100 cans and that Machine X can do the job in 2 hours. Thus, to determine how much less time it would take for both of them running simultaneously to do the job, it is sufficient to know the rate for Machine Y or the time that Machines X and Y together take to complete the job.

(1) This states that the rate for Y is the same as the rate for X, which is given; SUFFICIENT.

(2) Since double the time corresponds to half the rate, the rate for X is $\frac{1}{2}$ the combined rate for X and Y running simultaneously, it can be determined that X and Y together would take $\frac{1}{2}$ the time, or 1 hour, to do the job; SUFFICIENT.

The correct answer is D;
each statement alone is sufficient.

60. Can the positive integer p be expressed as the product of two integers, each of which is greater than 1 ?

   (1) $31 < p < 37$
   (2) p is odd.

Arithmetic Properties of numbers

(1) This statement implies that p can be only among the integers 32, 33, 34, 35, and 36. Because each of these integers can be expressed as the product of two integers, each of which is greater than 1 (e.g., $32 = 4 \times 8, 33 = 3 \times 11$, etc.), the question can be answered even though the specific value of p is not known; SUFFICIENT.

(2) If $p = 3$, then p cannot be expressed as the product of two integers, each of which is greater than 1. However, if $p = 9$, then p can be expressed as the product of two integers, each of which is greater than 1; NOT sufficient.

The correct answer is A;
statement 1 alone is sufficient.

61. Is $x < y$?

   (1) $z < y$
   (2) $z < x$

Algebra Inequalities

(1) This gives no information about x and its relationship to y; NOT sufficient.

(2) This gives no information about y and its relationship to x; NOT sufficient.

From (1) and (2) together, it can be determined only that z is less than both x and y. It is still not possible to determine the relationship of x and y, and x might be greater than, equal to, or less than y.

The correct answer is E;
both statements together are still not sufficient.

62. If $abc \neq 0$, is $\dfrac{\frac{a}{b}}{c} = \dfrac{a}{\frac{b}{c}}$?

   (1) $a = 1$
   (2) $c = 1$

Algebra Fractions

Since $\dfrac{\frac{a}{b}}{c} = \dfrac{a}{b} \div c = \dfrac{a}{b} \times \dfrac{1}{c} = \dfrac{a}{bc}$ and

$\dfrac{a}{\frac{b}{c}} = a \div \dfrac{b}{c} = a \times \dfrac{c}{b} = \dfrac{ac}{b}$, it is to be determined

whether $\dfrac{a}{bc} = \dfrac{ac}{b}$.

(1) Given that $a = 1$, the equation to be investigated, $\dfrac{a}{bc} = \dfrac{ac}{b}$, is $\dfrac{1}{bc} = \dfrac{c}{b}$. This equation can be true for some nonzero values of b and c (for example, $b = c = 1$) and false for other nonzero values of b and c (for example, $b = 1$ and $c = 2$); NOT sufficient.

(2) Given that $c = 1$, the equation to be investigated, $\dfrac{a}{bc} = \dfrac{ac}{b}$, is $\dfrac{a}{b} = \dfrac{a}{b}$. This equation is true for all nonzero values of a and b; SUFFICIENT.

The correct answer is B;
statement 2 alone is sufficient.

63. A certain list consists of 400 different numbers. Is the average (arithmetic mean) of the numbers in the list greater than the median of the numbers in the list?

    (1) Of the numbers in the list, 280 are less than the average.

    (2) Of the numbers in the list, 30 percent are greater than or equal to the average.

Arithmetic Statistics

In a list of 400 numbers, the median will be halfway between the 200th and the 201st numbers in the list when the numbers are ordered from least to greatest.

(1) This indicates that 280 of the 400 numbers in the list are less than the average of the 400 numbers. This means that both the 200th and the 201st numbers, as well as the median, are less than the average and, therefore, that the average is greater than the median; SUFFICIENT.

(2) This indicates that $(0.3)(400) = 120$ of the numbers are greater than or equal to the average. This means that the other $400 - 120 = 280$ numbers are less than the average, which is the same as the information in (1); SUFFICIENT.

The correct answer is D; each statement alone is sufficient.

64. What is the area of rectangular region R?

    (1) Each diagonal of R has length 5.

    (2) The perimeter of R is 14.

Geometry Rectangles

Let L and W be the length and width of the rectangle, respectively. Determine the value of LW.

(1) It is given that a diagonal's length is 5. Thus, by the Pythagorean theorem, it follows that $L^2 + W^2 = 5^2 = 25$. The value of LW cannot be determined, however, because $L = \sqrt{15}$ and $W = \sqrt{10}$ satisfy $L^2 + W^2 = 25$ with $LW = \sqrt{150}$, and $L = \sqrt{5}$ and $W = \sqrt{20}$ satisfy $L^2 + W^2 = 25$ with $LW = \sqrt{100}$; NOT sufficient.

(2) It is given that $2L + 2W = 14$, or $L + W = 7$, or $L = 7 - W$. Therefore, $LW = (7 - W)W$, which can vary in value. For example, if $L = 3$ and $W = 4$, then $L + W = 7$ and $LW = 12$. However, if $L = 2$ and $W = 5$, then $L + W = 7$ and $LW = 10$; NOT sufficient.

Given (1) and (2) together, it follows from (2) that $(L + W)^2 = 7^2 = 49$, or $L^2 + W^2 + 2LW = 49$. Using (1), 25 can be substituted for $L^2 + W^2$ to obtain $25 + 2LW = 49$, or $2LW = 24$, or $LW = 12$. Alternatively, $7 - W$ can be substituted for L in $L^2 + W^2 = 25$ to obtain the quadratic equation $(7 - W)^2 + W^2 = 25$, or $49 - 14W + W^2 + W^2 = 25$, or $2W^2 - 14W + 24 = 0$, or $W^2 - 7W + 12 = 0$. The left side of the last equation can be factored to give $(W - 4)(W - 3) = 0$. Therefore, $W = 4$, which gives $L = 7 - W = 7 - 4 = 3$ and $LW = (3)(4) = 12$, or $W = 3$, which gives $L = 7 - W = 7 - 3 = 4$ and $LW = (4)(3) = 12$. Since $LW = 12$ in either case, a unique value for LW can be determined.

The correct answer is C; both statements together are sufficient.

65. If Q is an integer between 10 and 100, what is the value of Q?

    (1) One of Q's digits is 3 more than the other, and the sum of its digits is 9.

    (2) $Q < 50$

Algebra Properties of numbers

(1) While it is quite possible to guess that the two integers satisfying these stipulations are 36 and 63, these two integers can also be determined algebraically. Letting x and y be the digits of Q, the given information can be expressed as $x = y + 3$ and $x + y = 9$. These equations can be solved simultaneously to obtain the digits 3 and 6, leading to the integers 36 and 63. However, it is unknown which of these two integers is the value of Q; NOT sufficient.

(2) There is more than one integer between 10 and 49; NOT sufficient.

When the information from (1) and (2) is combined, the value of Q can be uniquely determined, because, of the two possible values for Q, only 36 is between 10 and 49.

The correct answer is C; both statements together are sufficient.

66. If p and q are positive integers and $pq = 24$, what is the value of p ?

(1) $\dfrac{q}{6}$ is an integer.

(2) $\dfrac{p}{2}$ is an integer.

Arithmetic Arithmetic operations

There are four pairs of positive integers whose product is 24: 1 and 24, 2 and 12, 3 and 8, and 4 and 6.

(1) The possible values of q are therefore 6, 12, and 24, and for each of these there is a different value of p (4, 2, and 1); NOT sufficient.

(2) The possible values of p are therefore 2, 4, 6, 8, 12, and 24; NOT sufficient.

From (1) and (2) together, the possible values of q can only be narrowed down to 6 or 12, with corresponding values of p being either 4 or 2.

The correct answer is E; both statements together are still not sufficient.

67. What is the value of $x^2 - y^2$?

(1) $x - y = y + 2$

(2) $x - y = \dfrac{1}{x + y}$

Algebra First- and second-degree equations

(1) If $x - y = y + 2$, then $x = 2y + 2$. When this expression for x is substituted in $x^2 - y^2$, the result is $(2y + 2)^2 - y^2$, which can vary in value. For example, if $y = 0$ (and hence, $x = 2$), then $(2y + 2)^2 - y^2 = 4$. However, if $y = 1$ (and hence, $x = 4$), then $(2y + 2)^2 - y^2 = 15$; NOT sufficient.

(2) Since $x - y = \dfrac{1}{x + y}$, $(x - y)(x + y) = 1$, or $x^2 - y^2 = 1$. Thus, the value of $x^2 - y^2$ is 1; SUFFICIENT.

The correct answer is B; statement 2 alone is sufficient.

68. How many integers n are there such that $r < n < s$?

(1) $s - r = 5$

(2) r and s are not integers.

Arithmetic Properties of numbers

(1) The difference between s and r is 5. If r and s are integers (e.g., 7 and 12), the number of integers between them (i.e., n could be 8, 9, 10, or 11) is 4. If r and s are not integers (e.g., 6.5 and 11.5), then the number of integers between them (i.e., n could be 7, 8, 9, 10, or 11) is 5. No information is given that allows a determination of whether s and r are integers; NOT sufficient.

(2) No information is given about the difference between r and s. If $r = 0.4$ and $s = 0.5$, then r and s have no integers between them. However, if $r = 0.4$ and $s = 3.5$, then r and s have 3 integers between them; NOT sufficient.

Using the information from both (1) and (2), it can be determined that, because r and s are not integers, there are 5 integers between them.

The correct answer is C; both statements together are sufficient.

69. If the total price of n equally priced shares of a certain stock was \$12,000, what was the price per share of the stock?

    (1) If the price per share of the stock had been \$1 more, the total price of the n shares would have been \$300 more.
    (2) If the price per share of the stock had been \$2 less, the total price of the n shares would have been 5 percent less.

Arithmetic Arithmetic operations; Percents

Since the price per share of the stock can be expressed as $\dfrac{\$12,000}{n}$, determining the value of n is sufficient to answer this question.

(1) A per-share increase of \$1 and a total increase of \$300 for n shares of stock mean together that $n(\$1) = \$300$. It follows that $n = 300$; SUFFICIENT.

(2) If the price of each of the n shares had been reduced by \$2, the total reduction in price would have been 5 percent less or $0.05(\$12,000)$. The equation $2n = 0.05(\$12,000)$ expresses this relationship. The value of n can be determined to be 300 from this equation; SUFFICIENT.

**The correct answer is D;
each statement alone is sufficient.**

70. If n is positive, is $\sqrt{n} > 100$?

    (1) $\sqrt{n-1} > 99$
    (2) $\sqrt{n+1} > 101$

Algebra Radicals

Determine if $\sqrt{n} > 100$, or equivalently, if $n > (100)(100) = 10,000$.

(1) Given that $\sqrt{n-1} > 99$, or equivalently, $n - 1 > (99)(99)$, it follows from

$$(99)(99) = 99(100 - 1)$$
$$= 9,900 - 99$$
$$= 9,801$$

that $\sqrt{n-1} > 99$ is equivalent to $n - 1 > 9,801$, or $n > 9,802$. Since $n > 9,802$ allows for values of n that are greater than 10,000 and $n > 9,802$ allows for values of n that are not greater than 10,000, it cannot be determined if $n > 10,000$; NOT sufficient.

(2) Given that $\sqrt{n+1} > 101$, or equivalently, $n + 1 > (101)(101)$, it follows from

$$(101)(101) = 101(100 + 1)$$
$$= 10,100 + 101$$
$$= 10,201$$

that $\sqrt{n+1} > 101$ is equivalent to $n + 1 > 10,201$, or $n > 10,200$. Since $10,200 > 10,000$, it can be determined that $n > 10,000$; SUFFICIENT.

**The correct answer is B;
statement 2 alone is sufficient.**

71. Is $xy > 5$?

    (1) $1 \leq x \leq 3$ and $2 \leq y \leq 4$.
    (2) $x + y = 5$

Algebra Inequalities

(1) While it is known that $1 \leq x \leq 3$ and $2 \leq y \leq 4$, xy could be $(3)(4) = 12$, which is greater than 5, or xy could be $(1)(2) = 2$, which is not greater than 5; NOT sufficient.

(2) Given that $x + y = 5$, xy could be 6 (when $x = 2$ and $y = 3$), which is greater than 5, and xy could be 4 (when $x = 1$ and $y = 4$), which is not greater than 5; NOT sufficient.

Both (1) and (2) together are not sufficient since the two examples given in (2) are consistent with both statements.

**The correct answer is E;
both statements together are still not sufficient.**

72. In Year X, 8.7 percent of the men in the labor force were unemployed in June compared with 8.4 percent in May. If the number of men in the labor force was the same for both months, how many men were unemployed in June of that year?

    (1) In May of Year X, the number of unemployed men in the labor force was 3.36 million.
    (2) In Year X, 120,000 more men in the labor force were unemployed in June than in May.

Arithmetic Percents

Since 8.7 percent of the men in the labor force were unemployed in June, the number of unemployed men could be calculated if the total number of men in the labor force was known. Let t represent the total number of men in the labor force.

(1) This implies that for May $(8.4\%)t = 3,360,000$, from which the value of t can be determined; SUFFICIENT.

(2) This implies that $(8.7\% - 8.4\%)t = 120,000$ or $(0.3\%)t = 120,000$. This equation can be solved for t; SUFFICIENT.

**The correct answer is D;
each statement alone is sufficient.**

73. If $x \neq 0$, what is the value of $\left(\dfrac{x^p}{x^q}\right)^4$?

    (1) $p = q$
    (2) $x = 3$

**Arithmetic; Algebra Arithmetic operations;
Simplifying expressions**

(1) Since $p = q$, it follows that
$\left(\dfrac{x^p}{x^q}\right)^4 = \left(\dfrac{x^p}{x^p}\right)^4 = (1)^4$; SUFFICIENT.

(2) Since $x = 3$ (and, therefore, $x \neq 1$) and the values of p or q are unknown, the value of the expression $\left(\dfrac{x^p}{x^q}\right)^4$ cannot be determined; NOT sufficient.

**The correct answer is A;
statement 1 alone is sufficient.**

74. On Monday morning a certain machine ran continuously at a uniform rate to fill a production order. At what time did it completely fill the order that morning?

    (1) The machine began filling the order at 9:30 a.m.
    (2) The machine had filled $\dfrac{1}{2}$ of the order by 10:30 a.m. and $\dfrac{5}{6}$ of the order by 11:10 a.m.

Arithmetic Arithmetic operations

(1) This merely states what time the machine began filling the order; NOT sufficient.

(2) In the 40 minutes between 10:30 a.m. and 11:10 a.m., $\dfrac{5}{6} - \dfrac{1}{2} = \dfrac{1}{3}$ of the order was filled. Therefore, the entire order was completely filled in $3 \times 40 = 120$ minutes, or 2 hours. Since half the order took 1 hour and was filled by 10:30 a.m., the second half of the order, and thus the entire order, was filled by 11:30 a.m.; SUFFICIENT.

**The correct answer is B;
statement 2 alone is sufficient.**

75. If $kmn \neq 0$, is $\dfrac{x}{m}(m^2 + n^2 + k^2) = xm + yn + zk$?

    (1) $\dfrac{z}{k} = \dfrac{x}{m}$
    (2) $\dfrac{x}{m} = \dfrac{y}{n}$

Algebra First- and second-degree equations

The equation $\dfrac{x}{m}(m^2 + n^2 + k^2) = xm + yn + zk$ can be manipulated to obtain the following equivalent equations:

$$x(m^2 + n^2 + k^2) = m(xm + yn + zk) \quad \text{multiply both sides by } m$$

$$xm^2 + xn^2 + xk^2 = m^2x + myn + mzk \quad \text{remove parentheses}$$

$$xn^2 + xk^2 = myn + mzk \quad \text{subtract } xm^2$$

(1) When cross multiplied, $\dfrac{z}{k} = \dfrac{x}{m}$ becomes $xk = mz$, or $xk^2 = mzk$ when both sides are then multiplied by k. Thus, the equation $xn^2 + xk^2 = myn + mzk$ is equivalent to the equation $xn^2 = myn$, and hence equivalent to

the equation $xn = my$, which can be true or false, depending on the values of x, n, m, and y; NOT sufficient.

(2)   When cross multiplied, $\dfrac{x}{m} = \dfrac{y}{n}$ becomes $xn = my$, or $xn^2 = myn$ when both sides are then multiplied by n. Thus, the equation $xn^2 + xk^2 = myn + mzk$ is equivalent to the equation $xk^2 = mzk$, and hence equivalent to the equation $xk = mz$, which can be true or false, depending on the values of x, k, m, and z; NOT sufficient.

Combining the information in both (1) and (2), it follows from (1) that $xn^2 + xk^2 = myn + mzk$ is equivalent to $xn = my$, which is true by (2).

The correct answer is C;
both statements together are sufficient.

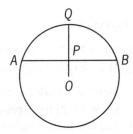

76.   What is the radius of the circle above with center O ?

(1)   The ratio of OP to PQ is 1 to 2.
(2) P is the midpoint of chord AB.

Geometry Circles

(1)   It can be concluded only that the radius is 3 times the length of OP, which is unknown; NOT sufficient.

(2)   It can be concluded only that $AP = PB$, and the chord is irrelevant to the radius; NOT sufficient.

Together, (1) and (2) do not give the length of any line segment shown in the circle. In fact, if the circle and all the line segments were uniformly expanded by a factor of, say, 5, the resulting circle and line segments would still satisfy both (1) and (2). Therefore, the radius of the circle cannot be determined from (1) and (2) together.

The correct answer is E;
both statements together are still not sufficient.

77.   What is the number of 360-degree rotations that a bicycle wheel made while rolling 100 meters in a straight line without slipping?

(1)   The diameter of the bicycle wheel, including the tire, was 0.5 meter.
(2)   The wheel made twenty 360-degree rotations per minute.

Geometry Circles

For each 360-degree rotation, the wheel has traveled a distance equal to its circumference. Given either the circumference of the wheel or the means to calculate its circumference, it is thus possible to determine the number of times the circumference of the wheel was laid out along the straight-line path of 100 meters.

(1)   The circumference of the bicycle wheel can be determined from the given diameter using the equation $C = \pi d$, where d = the diameter; SUFFICIENT.

(2)   The speed of the rotations is irrelevant, and no dimensions of the wheel are given; NOT sufficient.

The correct answer is A;
statement 1 alone is sufficient.

78.   If $2x(5n) = t$, what is the value of t ?

(1) $x = n + 3$
(2) $2x = 32$

Algebra First- and second-degree equations

Because $t = 10xn$, the value of t can be determined exactly when the value of xn can be determined.

(1)   Given that $x = n + 3$, more than one value of xn is possible. For example, xn could be 0 (if $x = 3$ and $n = 0$) and xn could be 4 (if $x = 4$ and $n = 1$); NOT sufficient.

(2) Given that $2x = 32$, or $x = 16$, more than one value of xn is possible, since $xn = 16n$, which will vary in value when n varies in value; NOT sufficient.

The value of x determined from equation (2) can be substituted in equation (1) to obtain $16 = n + 3$, or $n = 13$. Therefore, $xn = (16)(13)$.

**The correct answer is C;
both statements together are sufficient.**

79. In the equation $x^2 + bx + 12 = 0$, x is a variable and b is a constant. What is the value of b?

    (1) $x - 3$ is a factor of $x^2 + bx + 12$.
    (2) 4 is a root of the equation $x^2 + bx + 12 = 0$.

Algebra First- and second-degree equations

(1) Method 1: If $x - 3$ is a factor, then
$x^2 + bx + 12 = (x - 3)(x + c)$ for some

constant c. Equating the constant terms (or substituting $x = 0$), it follows that $12 = -3c$, or $c = -4$. Therefore, the quadratic polynomial is $(x - 3)(x - 4)$, which is equal to $x^2 - 7x + 12$, and hence $b = -7$.

Method 2: If $x - 3$ is a factor of $x^2 + bx + 12$, then 3 is a root of $x^2 + bx + 12 = 0$. Therefore, $3^2 + 3b + 12 = 0$, which can be solved to get $b = -7$.

Method 3: The value of b can be found by long division:

$$\begin{array}{r} x + (b + 3) \\ x - 3 \overline{\smash{)}\, x^2 + bx + 12} \\ \underline{x^2 - 3x} \\ (b + 3)x + 12 \\ \underline{(b + 3)x - 3b - 9} \\ 3b + 21 \end{array}$$

These calculations show that the remainder is $3b + 21$. Since the remainder must be 0, it follows that $3b + 21 = 0$, or $b = -7$; SUFFICIENT.

(2) If 4 is a root of the equation, then 4 can be substituted for x in the equation $x^2 + bx + 12 = 0$, yielding $4^2 + 4b + 12 = 0$. This last equation can be solved to obtain a unique value for b; SUFFICIENT.

**The correct answer is D;
each statement alone is sufficient.**

80. A Town T has 20,000 residents, 60 percent of whom are female. What percent of the residents were born in Town T?

    (1) The number of female residents who were born in Town T is twice the number of male residents who were <u>not</u> born in Town T.
    (2) The number of female residents who were <u>not</u> born in Town T is twice the number of female residents who were born in Town T.

Arithmetic Percents

Since 60 percent of the residents are female, there are $0.6(20,000) = 12,000$ female residents. The remaining residents are male, so there are $20,000 - 12,000 = 8,000$ male residents. Let N be the number of residents who were born in Town T. The percent of the residents who were born in Town T is $\dfrac{N}{20,000}$, which can be determined exactly when N can be determined.

This information is displayed in the following table:

Table 1			
	Male	Female	Total
Born in Town T			N
Not Born in Town T			
Total	8,000	12,000	20,000

(1) Let x represent the number of male residents who were not born in Town T. Then the number of female residents who were born in Town T is $2x$. Adding this information to Table 1 gives

Table 2			
	Male	Female	Total
Born in Town T		$2x$	N
Not Born in Town T	x		
Total	8,000	12,000	20,000

Other cells in the table can then be filled in as shown below.

Table 3			
	Male	Female	Total
Born in Town T	$8,000 - x$	$2x$	N
Not Born in Town T	x	$12,000 - 2x$	$12,000 - x$
Total	$8,000$	$12,000$	$20,000$

Then, it can be seen from Table 3 that $N = (8,000 - x) + 2x = 8,000 + x$ and also that $N = 20,000 - (12,000 - x) = 8,000 + x$. However, without a value for x, the value of N cannot be determined; NOT sufficient.

(2) Let y represent the number of female residents who were born in Town T. Then the number of female residents who were not born in Town T is $2y$. Adding this information to Table 1 gives

Table 4			
	Male	Female	Total
Born in Town T		y	N
Not Born in Town T		$2y$	
Total	$8,000$	$12,000$	$20,000$

From Table 4 it can be seen that $y + 2y = 12,000$, so $3y = 12,000$ and $y = 4,000$. With this value, the table can be expanded to

Table 5			
	Male	Female	Total
Born in Town T		$4,000$	N
Not Born in Town T		$8,000$	
Total	$8,000$	$12,000$	$20,000$

However, there is not enough information to determine the value of N; NOT sufficient.

Given (1) and (2) together, the information from Table 3, which uses the information given in (1), can be combined with Table 5, which uses the information given in (2), to obtain $2x = 4,000$. Therefore, $x = 2,000$ and thus $N = 8,000 + 2,000 = 10,000$.

The correct answer is C;
both statements together are sufficient.

81. In $\triangle XYZ$, what is the length of YZ?

(1) The length of XY is 3.
(2) The length of XZ is 5.

Geometry Triangles

Given the length of one side of a triangle, it is known that the sum of the lengths of the other two sides is greater than that given length. The length of either of the other two sides, however, can be any positive number.

(1) Only the length of one side, XY, is given, and that is not enough to determine the length of YZ; NOT sufficient.

(2) Again, only the length of one side, XZ, is given and that is not enough to determine the length of YZ; NOT sufficient.

Even by using the triangle inequality stated above, only a range of values for YZ can be determined from (1) and (2). If the length of side YZ is represented by k, then it is known both that $3 + 5 > k$ and that $3 + k > 5$, or $k > 2$. Combining these inequalities to determine the length of k yields only that $8 > k > 2$.

The correct answer is E;
both statements together are still not sufficient.

82. If the average (arithmetic mean) of n consecutive odd integers is 10, what is the least of the integers?

(1) The range of the n integers is 14.
(2) The greatest of the n integers is 17.

Arithmetic Statistics

Let k be the least of the n consecutive odd integers. Then the n consecutive odd integers are $k, k + 2, k + 4, ..., k + 2(n - 1)$, where $k + 2(n - 1)$ is the greatest of the n consecutive odd integers and $[k + 2(n - 1)] - k = 2(n - 1)$ is the range of the n consecutive odd integers. Determine the value of k.

(1) Given that the range of the odd integers is 14, it follows that $2(n - 1) = 14$, or $n - 1 = 7$, or $n = 8$. It is also given that the average of the 8 consecutive odd integers is 10, and so $$\frac{k + (k + 2) + (k + 4) + ... + (k + 14)}{8} = 10, \text{ from}$$

which a unique value for k can be determined; SUFFICIENT.

(2) Given that the greatest of the odd integers is 17, it follows that the n consecutive odd integers can be expressed as $17, 17-2$, $17-4, ..., 17-2(n-1)$. Since the average of the n consecutive odd integers is 10, then

$$\frac{17+(17-2)+(17-4)+...+[17-2(n-1)]}{n}=10,$$

or

$$17+(17-2)+(17-4)+...+[17-2(n-1)]=10n \text{ (i)}$$

The n consecutive odd integers can also be expressed as $k, k+2, k+4, ..., k+2(n-1)$. Since the average of the n consecutive odd integers is 10, then

$$\frac{k+(k+2)+(k+4)+...+[k+2(n-1)]}{n}=10,$$

or

$$k+(k+2)+(k+4)+...+[k+2(n-1)]=10n \text{ (ii)}$$

Adding equations (i) and (ii) gives

$$(17+k)+(17+k)+(17+k)+...+(17+k)=20n$$

$$n(17+k)=20n$$

$$17+k=20$$

$$k=3$$

Alternatively, because the numbers are consecutive odd integers, they form a data set that is symmetric about its average, and so the average of the numbers is the average of the least and greatest numbers. Therefore, $10=\frac{k+17}{2}$, from which a unique value for k can be determined; SUFFICIENT.

The correct answer is D; each statement alone is sufficient.

83. What was the ratio of the number of cars to the number of trucks produced by Company X last year?

(1) Last year, if the number of cars produced by Company X had been 8 percent greater, the number of cars produced would have been 150 percent of the number of trucks produced by Company X.

(2) Last year Company X produced 565,000 cars and 406,800 trucks.

Arithmetic Ratio; Percents

Let c equal the number of cars and t the number of trucks produced by Company X last year. The ratio of cars to trucks produced last year can be expressed as $\frac{c}{t}$.

(1) An 8 percent increase in the number of cars produced can be expressed as 108 percent of c, or $1.08c$. Similarly, 150 percent of the number of trucks produced can be expressed as $1.5t$. The relationship between the two can be expressed in the equation $1.08c = 1.5t$. From this:

$$\frac{1.08c}{t}=1.5 \qquad \text{divide both sides by } t$$

$$\frac{c}{t}=\frac{1.5}{1.08} \qquad \text{divide both sides by 1.08}$$

Thus the ratio of cars to trucks produced last year can be determined; SUFFICIENT.

(2) The values of c and t are given; so the ratio $\frac{c}{t}$ can be determined; SUFFICIENT.

The correct answer is D; each statement alone is sufficient.

84. If x, y, and z are positive numbers, is $x > y > z$?

(1) $xz > yz$

(2) $yx > yz$

Algebra Inequalities

(1) Dividing both sides of the inequality by z yields $x > y$. However, there is no information relating z to either x or y; NOT sufficient.

(2) Dividing both sides of the inequality by y yields only that $x > z$, with no further information relating y to either x or z; NOT sufficient.

From (1) and (2) it can be determined that x is greater than both y and z. Since it still cannot be determined which of y or z is the least, the correct ordering of the three numbers also cannot be determined.

The correct answer is E; both statements together are still not sufficient.

85. K is a set of numbers such that

    (i)   if x is in K, then $-x$ is in K, and

    (ii)   if each of x and y is in K, then xy is in K.

    Is 12 in K ?

    (1)   2 is in K.
    (2)   3 is in K.

Arithmetic Properties of numbers

(1) Given that 2 is in K, it follows that K could be the set of all real numbers, which contains 12. However, if K is the set $\{..., -16, -8, -4, -2, 2, 4, 8, 16, ...\}$, then K contains 2 and K satisfies both (i) and (ii), but K does not contain 12. To see that K satisfies (ii), note that K can be written as $\{..., -2^4, -2^3, -2^2, -2^1, 2^1, 2^2, 2^3, 2^4, ...\}$, and thus a verification of (ii) can reduce to verifying that the sum of two positive integer exponents is a positive integer exponent; NOT sufficient.

(2) Given that 3 is in K, it follows that K could be the set of all real numbers, which contains 12. However, if K is the set $\{..., -81, -27, -9, -3, 3, 9, 27, 81, ...\}$, then K contains 3 and K satisfies both (i) and (ii), but K does not contain 12. To see that K satisfies (ii), note that K can be written as $\{..., -3^4, -3^3, -3^2, -3^1, 3^1, 3^2, 3^3, 3^4, ...\}$, and thus a verification of (ii) can reduce to verifying that the sum of two positive integer exponents is a positive integer exponent; NOT sufficient.

Given (1) and (2), it follows that both 2 and 3 are in K. Thus, by (ii), $(2)(3) = 6$ is in K. Therefore, by (ii), $(2)(6) = 12$ is in K.

The correct answer is C; both statements together are sufficient.

86. If $x^2 + y^2 = 29$, what is the value of $(x - y)^2$?

    (1) $xy = 10$
    (2) $x = 5$

Algebra Simplifying algebraic expressions

Since $(x - y)^2 = (x^2 + y^2) - 2xy$ and it is given that $x^2 + y^2 = 29$, it follows that $(x - y)^2 = 29 - 2xy$.

Therefore, the value of $(x - y)^2$ can be determined if and only if the value of xy can be determined.

(1) Since the value of xy is given, the value of $(x - y)^2$ can be determined; SUFFICIENT.

(2) Given only that $x = 5$, it is not possible to determine the value of xy. Therefore, the value of $(x - y)^2$ cannot be determined; NOT sufficient.

The correct answer is A; statement 1 alone is sufficient.

87. If x, y, and z are numbers, is $z = 18$?

    (1)   The average (arithmetic mean) of x, y, and z is 6.
    (2) $x = -y$

Arithmetic Statistics

(1) From this, it is known that $\dfrac{x + y + z}{3} = 6$ or, when both sides are multiplied by 3, $x + y + z = 18$.

   Since nothing is known about the value of $x + y$, no conclusion can be drawn about the value of z; NOT sufficient.

(2) This implies that $x + y = 0$ but gives no further information about the values of x, y, and z; NOT sufficient.

Taking (1) and (2) together is sufficient since 0 can be substituted for $x + y$ in the equation $x + y + z = 18$ to yield $z = 18$.

The correct answer is C; both statements together are sufficient.

88. After winning 50 percent of the first 20 games it played, Team A won all of the remaining games it played. What was the total number of games that Team A won?

    (1) Team A played 25 games altogether.
    (2) Team A won 60 percent of all the games it played.

Arithmetic Percents

Let r be the number of the remaining games played, all of which the team won. Since the team won $(50\%)(20) = 10$ of the first 20 games and the r remaining games, the total number of games the team won is $10 + r$. Also, the total number of games the team played is $20 + r$. Determine the value of r.

    (1) Given that the total number of games played is 25, it follows that $20 + r = 25$, or $r = 5$; SUFFICIENT.

    (2) It is given that the total number of games won is $(60\%)(20 + r)$, which can be expanded as $12 + 0.6r$. Since it is also known that the number of games won is $10 + r$, it follows that $12 + 0.6r = 10 + r$. Solving this equation gives $12 - 10 = r - 0.6r$, or $2 = 0.4r$, or $r = 5$; SUFFICIENT.

**The correct answer is D;
each statement alone is sufficient.**

89. Is x between 0 and 1 ?

    (1) x^2 is less than x.
    (2) x^3 is positive.

Arithmetic Arithmetic operations

    (1) Since x^2 is always positive, it follows that here x must also be positive, that is, greater than 0. Furthermore, if x is greater than 1, then x^2 is greater than x. If $x = 0$ or 1, then $x^2 = x$. Therefore, x must be between 0 and 1; SUFFICIENT.

    (2) If x^3 is positive, then x is positive, but x can be any positive number; NOT sufficient.

**The correct answer is A;
statement 1 alone is sufficient.**

90. Is p^2 an odd integer?

    (1) p is an odd integer.
    (2) $\sqrt{p}$ is an odd integer.

Arithmetic Properties of numbers

The product of two or more odd integers is always odd.

    (1) Since p is an odd integer, $p \times p = p^2$ is an odd integer; SUFFICIENT.

    (2) If $\sqrt{p}$ is an odd integer, then $\sqrt{p} \times \sqrt{p} = p$ is an odd integer. Therefore, $p \times p = p^2$ is also an odd integer; SUFFICIENT.

**The correct answer is D;
each statement alone is sufficient.**

91. If m and n are nonzero integers, is m^n an integer?

    (1) n^m is positive.
    (2) n^m is an integer.

Arithmetic Properties of numbers

It is useful to note that if $m > 1$ and $n < 0$, then $0 < m^n < 1$, and therefore m^n will not be an integer. For example, if $m = 3$ and $n = -2$, then $m^n = 3^{-2} = \dfrac{1}{3^2} = \dfrac{1}{9}$.

    (1) Although it is given that n^m is positive, m^n can be an integer or m^n can fail to be an integer. For example, if $m = 2$ and $n = 2$, then $n^m = 2^2 = 4$ is positive and $m^n = 2^2 = 4$ is an integer. However, if $m = 2$ and $n = -2$, then $n^m = (-2)^2 = 4$ is positive and $m^n = 2^{-2} = \dfrac{1}{2^2} = \dfrac{1}{4}$ is not an integer; NOT sufficient.

    (2) Although it is given that n^m is an integer, m^n can be an integer or m^n can fail to be an integer. For example, if $m = 2$ and $n = 2$, then $n^m = 2^2 = 4$ is an integer and $m^n = 2^2 = 4$ is an integer. However, if $m = 2$ and $n = -2$, then $n^m = (-2)^2 = 4$ is an integer and $m^n = 2^{-2} = \dfrac{1}{2^2} = \dfrac{1}{4}$ is not an integer; NOT sufficient.

Taking (1) and (2) together, it is still not possible to determine if m^n is an integer, since the same examples are used in both (1) and (2) above.

The correct answer is E;
both statements together are still not sufficient.

92. What is the value of xy ?

(1) $x + y = 10$
(2) $x - y = 6$

Algebra First- and second-degree equations; Simultaneous equations

(1) Given $x + y = 10$, or $y = 10 - x$, it follows that $xy = x(10 - x)$, which does not have a unique value. For example, if $x = 0$, then $xy = (0)(10) = 0$, but if $x = 1$, then $xy = (1)(9) = 9$; NOT sufficient.

(2) Given $x - y = 6$, or $y = x - 6$, it follows that $xy = x(x - 6)$, which does not have a unique value. For example, if $x = 0$, then $xy = (0)(-6) = 0$, but if $x = 1$, then $xy = (1)(-5) = -5$; NOT sufficient.

Using (1) and (2) together, the two equations can be solved simultaneously for x and y. One way to do this is by adding the two equations, $x + y = 10$ and $x - y = 6$, to get $2x = 16$, or $x = 8$. Then substitute $x = 8$ into either of the equations to obtain an equation that can be solved to get $y = 2$. Thus, xy can be determined to have the value $(8)(2) = 16$. Alternatively, the two equations correspond to a pair of nonparallel lines in the (x,y) coordinate plane, which have a unique point in common.

The correct answer is C;
both statements together are sufficient.

93. Is x^2 greater than x ?

(1) x^2 is greater than 1.
(2) x is greater than -1.

Arithmetic; Algebra Exponents; Inequalities

(1) Given $x^2 > 1$, it follows that either $x > 1$ or $x < -1$. If $x > 1$, then multiplying both sides of the inequality by the positive number x gives $x^2 > x$. On the other hand, if $x < -1$, then x is negative and x^2 is positive (because $x^2 > 1$), which also gives $x^2 > x$; SUFFICIENT.

(2) Given $x > -1$, x^2 can be greater than x (for example, $x = 2$) and x^2 can fail to be greater than x (for example, $x = 0$); NOT sufficient.

The correct answer is A;
statement 1 alone is sufficient.

94. Michael arranged all his books in a bookcase with 10 books on each shelf and no books left over. After Michael acquired 10 additional books, he arranged all his books in a new bookcase with 12 books on each shelf and no books left over. How many books did Michael have before he acquired the 10 additional books?

(1) Before Michael acquired the 10 additional books, he had fewer than 96 books.

(2) Before Michael acquired the 10 additional books, he had more than 24 books.

Arithmetic Properties of numbers

If x is the number of books Michael had before he acquired the 10 additional books, then x is a multiple of 10. After Michael acquired the 10 additional books, he had $x + 10$ books and $x + 10$ is a multiple of 12.

(1) If $x < 96$, where x is a multiple of 10, then $x = 10, 20, 30, 40, 50, 60, 70, 80,$ or 90 and $x + 10 = 20, 30, 40, 50, 60, 70, 80, 90,$ or 100. Since $x + 10$ is a multiple of 12, then $x + 10 = 60$ and $x = 50$; SUFFICIENT.

(2) If $x > 24$, where x is a multiple of 10, then x must be one of the numbers 30, 40, 50, 60, 70, 80, 90, 100, 110, ..., and $x + 10$ must be one of the numbers 40, 50, 60, 70, 80, 90, 100, 110, 120, ... Since there is more than one multiple of 12 among these numbers (for example, 60 and 120), the value of $x + 10$, and therefore the value of x, cannot be determined; NOT sufficient.

The correct answer is A;
statement 1 alone is sufficient.

95. If $xy > 0$, does $(x-1)(y-1) = 1$?

    (1) $x + y = xy$
    (2) $x = y$

    Algebra First- and second-degree equations

    By expanding the product $(x-1)(y-1)$, the question is equivalent to whether $xy - y - x + 1 = 1$, or $xy - y - x = 0$, when $xy > 0$.

    (1)   If $x + y = xy$, then $xy - y - x = 0$, and hence by the remarks above, $(x-1)(y-1) = 1$; SUFFICIENT.

    (2)   If $x = y$, then $(x-1)(y-1) = 1$ can be true $(x = y = 2)$ and $(x-1)(y-1) = 1$ can be false $(x = y = 1)$; NOT sufficient.

    **The correct answer is A;
    statement 1 alone is sufficient.**

96. Last year in a group of 30 businesses, 21 reported a net profit and 15 had investments in foreign markets. How many of the businesses did not report a net profit nor invest in foreign markets last year?

    (1)   Last year 12 of the 30 businesses reported a net profit and had investments in foreign markets.
    (2)   Last year 24 of the 30 businesses reported a net profit or invested in foreign markets, or both.

    Arithmetic Concepts of sets

    Consider the Venn diagram below in which x represents the number of businesses that reported a net profit and had investments in foreign markets. Since 21 businesses reported a net profit, $21 - x$ businesses reported a net profit only. Since 15 businesses had investments in foreign markets, $15 - x$ businesses had investments in foreign markets only. Finally, since there is a total of 30 businesses, the number of businesses that did not report a net profit and did not invest in foreign markets is $30 - (21 - x + x + 15 - x) = x - 6$. Determine the value of $x - 6$, or equivalently, the value of x.

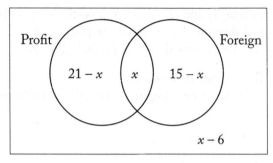

(1)   It is given that $12 = x$; SUFFICIENT.

(2)   It is given that $24 = (21 - x) + x + (15 - x)$. Therefore, $24 = 36 - x$, or $x = 12$.

      Alternatively, the information given is exactly the number of businesses that are not among those to be counted in answering the question posed in the problem, and therefore the number of businesses that are to be counted is $30 - 24 = 6$; SUFFICIENT.

**The correct answer is D;
each statement alone is sufficient.**

97. If k and n are integers, is n divisible by 7 ?

    (1) $n - 3 = 2k$
    (2) $2k - 4$ is divisible by 7.

    Arithmetic Properties of numbers

    (1)   This is equivalent to the equation $n = 2k + 3$. By picking various integers to be the value of k, it can be shown that for some values of k (e.g., $k = 2$), $2k + 3$ is divisible by 7, and for some other values of k (e.g., $k = 1$), $2k + 3$ is not divisible by 7; NOT sufficient.

    (2)   While $2k - 4$ is divisible by 7, this imposes no constraints on the integer n, and therefore n could be divisible by 7 (e.g., $n = 7$) and n could be not divisible by 7 (e.g., $n = 8$); NOT sufficient.

    Applying both (1) and (2), it is possible to answer the question. From (1), it follows that $n - 3$ can be substituted for $2k$. Carrying this out in (2), it follows that $(n - 3) - 4$, or $n - 7$, is divisible by 7. This means that $n - 7 = 7q$ for some integer q. It follows that $n = 7q + 7 = 7(q + 1)$, and so n is divisible by 7.

    **The correct answer is C;
    both statements together are sufficient.**

98. Is the perimeter of square S greater than the perimeter of equilateral triangle T ?

    (1) The ratio of the length of a side of S to the length of a side of T is 4:5.
    (2) The sum of the lengths of a side of S and a side of T is 18.

    Geometry Perimeter

    Letting s and t be the side lengths of square S and triangle T, respectively, the task is to determine if $4s > 3t$, which is equivalent (divide both sides by $4t$) to determining if $\frac{s}{t} > \frac{3}{4}$.

    (1) It is given that $\frac{s}{t} = \frac{4}{5}$. Since $\frac{4}{5} > \frac{3}{4}$, it follows that $\frac{s}{t} > \frac{3}{4}$; SUFFICIENT.

    (2) Many possible pairs of numbers have the sum of 18. For some of these (s,t) pairs it is the case that $\frac{s}{t} > \frac{3}{4}$ (for example, $s = t = 9$), and for others of these pairs it is not the case that $\frac{s}{t} > \frac{3}{4}$ (for example, $s = 1$ and $t = 17$); NOT sufficient.

    The correct answer is A; statement 1 alone is sufficient.

99. If $x + y + z > 0$, is $z > 1$?

    (1) $z > x + y + 1$
    (2) $x + y + 1 < 0$

    Algebra Inequalities

    (1) The inequality $x + y + z > 0$ gives $z > -x - y$. Adding this last inequality to the given inequality, $z > x + y + 1$, gives $2z > 1$, or $z > \frac{1}{2}$, which suggests that (1) is not sufficient. Indeed, z could be 2 ($x = y = 0$ and $z = 2$ satisfy both $x + y + z > 0$ and $z > x + y + 1$), which is greater than 1, and z could be $\frac{3}{4}$ ($x = y = -\frac{1}{4}$ and $z = \frac{3}{4}$ satisfy both $x + y + z > 0$ and $z > x + y + 1$), which is not greater than 1; NOT sufficient.

    (2) It follows from the inequality $x + y + z > 0$ that $z > -(x + y)$. It is given that $x + y + 1 < 0$, or $(x + y) < -1$, or $-(x + y) > 1$. Therefore,

$z > -(x + y)$ and $-(x + y) > 1$, from which it follows that $z > 1$; SUFFICIENT.

The correct answer is B; statement 2 alone is sufficient.

100. Can the positive integer n be written as the sum of two different positive prime numbers?

    (1) n is greater than 3.
    (2) n is odd.

    Arithmetic Properties of numbers

    The prime numbers are 2, 3, 5, 7, 11, 13, 17, 19, etc., that is, those integers $p > 1$ whose only positive factors are 1 and p.

    (1) If $n = 5$, then n can be written as the sum of two different primes $(5 = 2 + 3)$. If $n = 4$, however, then n cannot be written as the sum of two different primes. (Note that while $4 = 1 + 3 = 2 + 2$, neither of these sums satisfies both requirements of the question.) This value of n does not allow an answer to be determined; NOT sufficient.

    (2) While some odd integers can be written as the sum of two different primes (e.g., $5 = 2 + 3$), others cannot (e.g., 11). This value of n does not allow an answer to be determined; NOT sufficient.

Since the sum of two odd integers is always even, for an odd integer greater than 3 to be the sum of two prime numbers, one of those prime numbers must be an even number. The only even prime number is 2. Thus, the only odd integers that can be expressed as the sum of two different prime numbers are those for which $n - 2$ is an odd prime number. Using the example of 11 (an odd integer greater than 3), $11 - 2 = 9$, which is not a prime number. Statements (1) and (2) together do not define n well enough to determine the answer.

The correct answer is E; both statements together are still not sufficient.

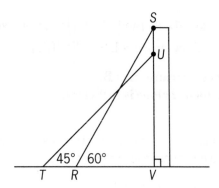

101. In the figure above, segments *RS* and *TU* represent two positions of the same ladder leaning against the side *SV* of a wall. The length of *TV* is how much greater than the length of *RV* ?

    (1)   The length of *TU* is 10 meters.

    (2)   The length of *RV* is 5 meters.

Geometry Triangles

The Pythagorean theorem $\left(a^2 + b^2 = c^2\right)$ can be applied here. Since the triangle *TUV* is a $45° - 45° - 90°$ triangle, the lengths of the sides are in the ratio $1:1:\sqrt{2}$; so the length of any one side determines the length of the other two sides. Similarly, the triangle *RSV* is a $30° - 60° - 90°$ triangle with the lengths of the sides in the ratio $1:\sqrt{3}:2$; so the length of any one side determines the length of the other two sides. Also, the length of the hypotenuse is the same in both triangles, because it is the length of the ladder. Hence, the length of any one side of either triangle determines the lengths of all sides of both triangles.

    (1)   Since the length of one side of triangle *TUV* is given, the length of any side of either triangle can be found. Therefore, the difference between *TV* and *RV* can also be found; SUFFICIENT.

    (2)   Since the length of one side of triangle *RSV* is given, the length of any side of either triangle can be found. Therefore, the difference between *TV* and *RV* can also be found; SUFFICIENT.

The correct answer is D;
both statements alone are sufficient.

Cancellation Fees	
Days Prior to Departure	Percent of Package Price
46 or more	10%
45–31	35%
30–16	50%
15–5	65%
4 or fewer	100%

102. The table above shows the cancellation fee schedule that a travel agency uses to determine the fee charged to a tourist who cancels a trip prior to departure. If a tourist canceled a trip with a package price of $1,700 and a departure date of September 4, on what day was the trip canceled?

    (1)   The cancellation fee was $595.

    (2)   If the trip had been canceled one day later, the cancellation fee would have been $255 more.

Arithmetic Percents

    (1)   The cancellation fee given is $\frac{\$595}{\$1,700} = 35\%$ of the package price, which is the percent charged for cancellation 45–31 days prior to the departure date of September 4. However, there is no further information to determine exactly when within this interval the trip was cancelled; NOT sufficient.

    (2)   This implies that the increase in the cancellation fee for canceling one day later would have been $\frac{\$255}{\$1,700} = 15\%$ of the package price. The cancellation could thus have occurred either 31 days or 16 days prior to the departure date of September 4 because the cancellation fee would have increased by that percentage either 30 days before departure or 15 days before departure. However, there is no further information to establish whether the interval before departure was 31 days or 16 days; NOT sufficient.

Taking (1) and (2) together establishes that the trip was canceled 31 days prior to September 4.

The correct answer is C;
both statements together are sufficient.

103. If P and Q are each circular regions, what is the radius of the larger of these regions?

    (1)   The area of P plus the area of Q is equal to 90π.
    (2)   The larger circular region has a radius that is 3 times the radius of the smaller circular region.

Geometry Circles

The area of a circle with a radius of r is equal to πr^2. For this problem, let r represent the radius of the smaller circular region, and let R represent the radius of the larger circular region.

    (1)   This can be expressed as $\pi r^2 + \pi R^2 = 90\pi$. Dividing both sides of the equation by π gives $r^2 + R^2 = 90$, but this is not nough information to determine R; NOT sufficient.

    (2)   This can be expressed as $R = 3r$, which by itself is not enough to determine R; NOT sufficient.

Using (1) and (2), the value of R, or the radius of the larger circular region, can be determined. In (2), $R = 3r$, and thus $r = \dfrac{R}{3}$. Therefore, $\dfrac{R}{3}$ can be substituted for r in the equation $\pi r^2 + \pi R^2 = 90\pi$ from (1). The result is the equation $\pi \left(\dfrac{R}{3}\right)^2 + \pi R^2 = 90\pi$ that can be solved for a unique value of R^2, and thus for a unique positive value of R. Remember that it is only necessary to establish the sufficiency of the data; there is no need to actually find the value of R.

The correct answer is C; both statements together are sufficient.

104. For all z, $\lceil z \rceil$ denotes the least integer greater than or equal to z. Is $\lceil x \rceil = 0$?

    (1) $-1 < x < -0.1$
    (2) $\lceil x + 0.5 \rceil = 1$

Algebra Operations with real numbers

Determining if $\lceil x \rceil = 0$ is equivalent to determining if $-1 < x \le 0$. This can be inferred by examining a few representative examples, such as $\lceil -1.1 \rceil = -1, \lceil -1 \rceil = -1, \lceil -0.9 \rceil = 0, \lceil -0.1 \rceil = 0, \lceil 0 \rceil = 0$, and $\lceil 0.1 \rceil = 1$.

    (1)   Given $-1 < x < -0.1$, it follows that $-1 < x \le 0$, since $-1 < x \le 0$ represents all numbers x that satisfy $-1 < x < -0.1$ along with all numbers x that satisfy $-0.1 \le x \le 0$; SUFFICIENT.

    (2)   Given $\lceil x + 0.5 \rceil = 1$, it follows from the same reasoning used just before (1) above that this equality is equivalent to $0 < x + 0.5 \le 1$, which in turn is equivalent to $-0.5 < x \le 0.5$. Since from among these values of x it is possible for $-1 < x \le 0$ to be true (for example, $x = -0.1$) and it is possible for $-1 < x \le 0$ to be false (for example, $x = 0.1$), it cannot be determined if $\lceil x \rceil = 0$; NOT sufficient.

The correct answer is A; statement 1 alone is sufficient.

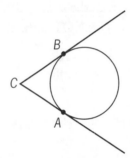

105. The circular base of an above-ground swimming pool lies in a level yard and just touches two straight sides of a fence at points A and B, as shown in the figure above. Point C is on the ground where the two sides of the fence meet. How far from the center of the pool's base is point A?

    (1)   The base has area 250 square feet.
    (2)   The center of the base is 20 feet from point C.

Geometry Circles

Let Q be the center of the pool's base and r be the distance from Q to A, as shown in the figure below.

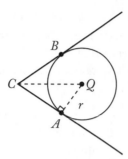

Since A is a point on the circular base, QA is a radius (r) of the base.

(1) Since the formula for the area of a circle is area $= \pi r^2$, this information can be stated as $250 = \pi r^2$ or $\sqrt{\dfrac{250}{\pi}} = r$; SUFFICIENT.

(2) Since $\overline{CA}$ is tangent to the base, ΔQAC is a right triangle. It is given that $QC = 20$, but there is not enough information to use the Pythagorean theorem to determine the length of QA; NOT sufficient.

**The correct answer is A;
statement 1 alone is sufficient.**

106. If $xy = -6$, what is the value of $xy(x+y)$?

(1) $x - y = 5$
(2) $xy^2 = 18$

Algebra First- and second-degree equations

By substituting -6 as the value of xy, the question can be simplified to "What is the value of $-6(x+y)$?"

(1) Adding y to both sides of $x - y = 5$ gives $x = y + 5$. When $y + 5$ is substituted for x in the equation $xy = -6$, the equation yields $(y + 5)y = -6$, or $y^2 + 5y + 6 = 0$. Factoring the left side of this equation gives $(y + 2)(y + 3) = 0$. Thus, y may have a value of -2 or -3. Since a unique value of y is not determined, neither the value of x nor the value of xy can be determined; NOT sufficient.

(2) Since $xy^2 = (xy)y$ and $xy^2 = 18$, it follows that $(xy)y = 18$. When -6 is substituted for xy, this equation yields $-6y = 18$, and hence $y = -3$. Since $y = -3$ and $xy = -6$, it follows that $-3x = -6$, or $x = 2$. Therefore, the value of $x + y$, and hence the value of $xy(x + y) = -6(x + y)$ can be determined; SUFFICIENT.

**The correct answer is B;
statement 2 alone is sufficient.**

107. If the average (arithmetic mean) of 4 numbers is 50, how many of the numbers are greater than 50 ?

(1) None of the four numbers is equal to 50.
(2) Two of the numbers are equal to 25.

Arithmetic Statistics

Let w, x, y, and z be the four numbers. The average of these 4 numbers can be represented by the following equation: $\dfrac{w + x + y + z}{4} = 50$.

(1) The only information about the 4 numbers is that none of the numbers is equal to 50. The 4 numbers could be 25, 25, 26, and 124, which have an average of 50, and only 1 of the numbers would be greater than 50. The 4 numbers could also be 25, 25, 75, and 75, which have an average of 50, and 2 of the numbers would be greater than 50; NOT sufficient.

(2) Each of the examples in (1) has exactly 2 numbers equal to 25; NOT sufficient.

Taking (1) and (2) together, the examples in (1) also illustrate the insufficiency of (2). Thus, there is more than one possibility for how many numbers are greater than 50.

**The correct answer is E;
both statements together are still not sufficient.**

108. [y] denotes the greatest integer less than or equal to y. Is $d < 1$?

    (1) $d = y - [y]$
    (2) $[d] = 0$

    Algebra Operations with real numbers

    (1) It is given $d = y - [y]$. If y is an integer, then $y = [y]$, and thus $y - [y] = 0$, which is less than 1. If y is not an integer, then y lies between two consecutive integers, the smaller of which is equal to [y]. Since each of these two consecutive integers is at a distance of less than 1 from y, it follows that [y] is at a distance of less than 1 from y, or $y - [y] < 1$. Thus, regardless of whether y is an integer or y is not an integer, it can be determined that $d < 1$; SUFFICIENT.

    (2) It is given that $[d] = 0$, which is equivalent to $0 \le d < 1$. This can be inferred by examining a few representative examples, such as $[-0.1] = -1, [0] = 0, [0.1] = 0, [0.9] = 0,$ and $[1.1] = 1$. From $0 \le d < 1$, it follows that $d < 1$; SUFFICIENT.

    The correct answer is D;
    each statement alone is sufficient.

109. If m is a positive integer, then m^3 has how many digits?

    (1) m has 3 digits.
    (2) m^2 has 5 digits.

    Arithmetic Properties of numbers

    (1) Given that m has 3 digits, then m could be 100 and $m^3 = 1,000,000$ would have 7 digits, or m could be 300 and $m^3 = 27,000,000$ would have 8 digits; NOT sufficient.

    (2) Given that m^2 has 5 digits, then m could be 100 (because $100^2 = 10,000$ has 5 digits) or m could be 300 (because $300^2 = 90,000$ has 5 digits). In the former case, $m^3 = 1,000,000$ has 7 digits and in the latter case, $m^3 = 27,000,000$ has 8 digits; NOT sufficient.

Given (1) and (2), it is still possible for m to be 100 or for m to be 300, and thus m^3 could have 7 digits or m^3 could have 8 digits.

The correct answer is E;
both statements together are still not sufficient.

110. For each landscaping job that takes more than 4 hours, a certain contractor charges a total of r dollars for the first 4 hours plus 0.2r dollars for each additional hour or fraction of an hour, where $r > 100$. Did a particular landscaping job take more than 10 hours?

    (1) The contractor charged a total of $288 for the job.
    (2) The contractor charged a total of 2.4r dollars for the job.

    Algebra Applied problems

    If y represents the total number of hours the particular landscaping job took, determine if $y > 10$.

    (1) This indicates that the total charge for the job was $288, which means that $r + 0.2r(y - 4) = 288$. From this it cannot be determined if $y > 10$. For example, if $r = 120$ and $y = 11$, then $120 + 0.2(120)(7) = 288$, and the job took more than 10 hours. However, if $r = 160$ and $y = 8$, then $160 + 0.2(160)(4) = 288$, and the job took less than 10 hours; NOT sufficient.

    (2) This indicates that $r + 0.2r(y - 4) = 2.4r$, from which it follows that

$r + 0.2ry - 0.8r = 2.4r$	use distributive property
$0.2ry = 2.2r$	subtract $(r - 0.8r)$ from both sides
$y = 11$	divide both sides by 0.2r

    Therefore, the job took more than 10 hours; SUFFICIENT.

    The correct answer is B;
    statement 2 alone is sufficient.

111. The sequence s_1, s_2, s_3, ..., s_n, ... is such that

$s_n = \dfrac{1}{n} - \dfrac{1}{n+1}$ for all integers $n \geq 1$. If k is a positive

integer, is the sum of the first k terms of the sequence

greater than $\dfrac{9}{10}$?

  (1) $k > 10$

  (2) $k < 19$

Arithmetic Sequences

The sum of the first k terms can be written as

$\left(\dfrac{1}{1} - \dfrac{1}{2}\right) + \left(\dfrac{1}{2} - \dfrac{1}{3}\right) + \dots + \left(\dfrac{1}{k-1} - \dfrac{1}{k}\right) + \left(\dfrac{1}{k} - \dfrac{1}{k+1}\right)$

$= 1 + \left(-\dfrac{1}{2} + \dfrac{1}{2}\right) + \left(-\dfrac{1}{3} + \dfrac{1}{3}\right) + \dots + \left(-\dfrac{1}{k} + \dfrac{1}{k}\right) - \dfrac{1}{k+1}$

$= 1 - \dfrac{1}{k+1}$.

Therefore, the sum of the first k terms is greater

than $\dfrac{9}{10}$ if and only if $1 - \dfrac{1}{k+1} > \dfrac{9}{10}$, or

$1 - \dfrac{9}{10} > \dfrac{1}{k+1}$, or $\dfrac{1}{10} > \dfrac{1}{k+1}$. Multiplying both

sides of the last inequality by $10(k+1)$ gives the

equivalent condition $k+1 > 10$, or $k > 9$.

  (1) Given that $k > 10$, then it follows that $k > 9$; SUFFICIENT.

  (2) Given that $k < 19$, it is possible to have $k > 9$ (for example, $k = 15$) and it is possible to not have $k > 9$ (for example, $k = 5$); NOT sufficient.

The correct answer is A;
statement 1 alone is sufficient.

112. If x and y are nonzero integers, is $x^y < y^x$?

  (1) $x = y^2$

  (2) $y > 2$

Arithmetic; Algebra Arithmetic operations;
    Inequalities

It is helpful to note that $\left(x^r\right)^s = x^{rs}$.

  (1) Given $x = y^2$, then $x^y = \left(y^2\right)^y = y^{2y}$ and $y^x = y^{y^2}$. Compare x^y to y^x by comparing y^{2y} to y^{y^2} or, when the base y is greater than 1,

by comparing the exponents $2y$ and y^2. If $y = 3$, then $2y = 6$ is less than $y^2 = 9$, and hence x^y would be less than y^x. However, if $y = 2$, then $2y = 4$ is not less than $y^2 = 4$, and hence x^y would not be less than y^x; NOT sufficient.

  (2) It is known that $y > 2$, but no information about x is given. For example, let $y = 3$. If $x = 1$, then $x^y = 1^3 = 1$ is less than $y^x = 3^1 = 3$, but if $x = 3$, then $x^y = 3^3$ is not less than $y^x = 3^3$; NOT sufficient.

If both (1) and (2) are taken together, then from (1) $2y$ is compared to y^2 and from (2) it is known that $y > 2$. Since $2y < y^2$ when $y > 2$, it follows that $x^y < y^x$.

The correct answer is C;
both statements together are sufficient.

113. In the sequence S of numbers, each term after the first two terms is the sum of the two immediately preceding terms. What is the 5th term of S ?

  (1) The 6th term of S minus the 4th term equals 5.

  (2) The 6th term of S plus the 7th term equals 21.

Arithmetic Sequences

If the first two terms of sequence S are a and b, then the remaining terms of sequence S can be expressed in terms of a and b as follows.

n	nth term of sequence S
1	a
2	b
3	$a + b$
4	$a + 2b$
5	$2a + 3b$
6	$3a + 5b$
7	$5a + 8b$

For example, the 6th term of sequence S is $3a + 5b$ because $(a + 2b) + (2a + 3b) = 3a + 5b$. Determine the value of the 5th term of sequence S, that is, the value of $2a + 3b$.

(1) Given that the 6th term of S minus the 4th term of S is 5, it follows that $(3a + 5b) - (a + 2b) = 5$. Combining like terms, this equation can be rewritten as $2a + 3b = 5$, and thus the 5th term of sequence S is 5; SUFFICIENT.

(2) Given that the 6th term of S plus the 7th term of S is 21, it follows that $(3a + 5b) + (5a + 8b) = 21$. Combining like terms, this equation can be rewritten as $8a + 13b = 21$. Letting e represent the 5th term of sequence S, this last equation is equivalent to $4(2a + 3b) + b = 21$, or $4e + b = 21$, which gives a direct correspondence between the 5th term of sequence S and the 2nd term of sequence S. Therefore, the 5th term of sequence S can be determined if and only if the 2nd term of sequence S can be determined. Since the 2nd term of sequence S cannot be determined, the 5th term of sequence S cannot be determined. For example, if $a = 1$ and $b = 1$, then $8a + 13b = 8(1) + 13(1) = 21$ and the 5th term of sequence S is $2a + 3b = 2(1) + 3(1) = 5$. However, if $a = 0$ and $b = \frac{21}{13}$, then $8a + 13b = 8(0) + 13\left(\frac{21}{13}\right) = 21$ and the 5th term of sequence S is $2a + 3b = 2(0) + 3\left(\frac{21}{13}\right) = \frac{63}{13}$; NOT sufficient.

The correct answer is A; statement 1 alone is sufficient.

114. If d is a positive integer, is $\sqrt{d}$ an integer ?

(1) d is the square of an integer.
(2) $\sqrt{d}$ is the square of an integer.

Arithmetic Properties of numbers

The square of an integer must also be an integer.

(1) This can be expressed as $d = x^2$, where x is a nonzero integer. Then, $\sqrt{d} = \sqrt{x^2}$ which in turn equals x or $-x$, depending on whether x is a positive integer or a negative integer, respectively. In either case, $\sqrt{d}$ is also an integer; SUFFICIENT.

(2) This can be expressed as $\sqrt{d} = x^2$, where x is a nonzero integer. The square of an integer (x^2) must always be an integer; therefore, $\sqrt{d}$ must also be an integer; SUFFICIENT.

The correct answer is D; each statement alone is sufficient.

115. Is the positive integer n a multiple of 24 ?

(1) n is a multiple of 4.
(2) n is a multiple of 6.

Arithmetic Properties of numbers

(1) This says only that n is a multiple of 4 (i.e., n could be 8 or 24), some of which would be multiples of 24 and some would not; NOT sufficient.

(2) This says only that n is a multiple of 6 (i.e., n could be 12 or 48), some of which would be multiples of 24 and some would not; NOT sufficient.

Both statements together imply only that n is a multiple of the least common multiple of 4 and 6. The smallest integer that is divisible by both 4 and 6 is 12. Some of the multiples of 12 (e.g., n could be 48 or 36) are also multiples of 24, but some are not.

The correct answer is E; both statements together are still not sufficient.

116. If 75 percent of the guests at a certain banquet ordered dessert, what percent of the guests ordered coffee?

    (1) 60 percent of the guests who ordered dessert also ordered coffee.
    (2) 90 percent of the guests who ordered coffee also ordered dessert.

Arithmetic Concepts of sets; Percents

Consider the Venn diagram below that displays the various percentages of 4 groups of the guests. Thus, x percent of the guests ordered both dessert and coffee and y percent of the guests ordered coffee only. Since 75 percent of the guests ordered dessert, $(75 - x)\%$ of the guests ordered dessert only. Also, because the 4 percentages represented in the Venn diagram have a total sum of 100 percent, the percentage of guests who did not order either dessert or coffee is $100 - \left[(75 - x) + x + y\right] = 25 - y$. Determine the percentage of guests who ordered coffee, or equivalently, the value of $x + y$.

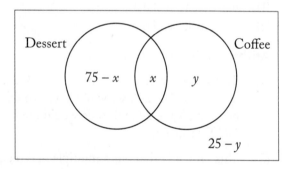

    (1) Given that x is equal to 60 percent of 75, or 45, the value of $x + y$ cannot be determined; NOT sufficient.

    (2) Given that 90 percent of $x + y$ is equal to x, it follows that $0.9(x + y) = x$, or $9(x + y) = 10x$. Therefore, $9x + 9y = 10x$, or $9y = x$. From this the value of $x + y$ cannot be determined. For example, if $x = 9$ and $y = 1$, then all 4 percentages in the Venn diagram are between 0 and 100, $9y = x$, and $x + y = 10$. However, if $x = 18$ and $y = 2$, then all 4 percentages in the Venn diagram are between 0 and 100, $9y = x$, and $x + y = 20$; NOT sufficient.

Given both (1) and (2), it follows that $x = 45$ and $9y = x$. Therefore, $9y = 45$, or $y = 5$, and hence $x + y = 45 + 5 = 50$.

The correct answer is C; both statements together are sufficient.

117. A tank containing water started to leak. Did the tank contain more than 30 gallons of water when it started to leak? (Note: 1 gallon = 128 ounces)

    (1) The water leaked from the tank at a constant rate of 6.4 ounces per minute.
    (2) The tank became empty less than 12 hours after it started to leak.

Arithmetic Rate problems

    (1) Given that the water leaked from the tank at a constant rate of 6.4 ounces per minute, it is not possible to determine if the tank leaked more than 30 gallons of water. In fact, any nonzero amount of water leaking from the tank is consistent with a leakage rate of 6.4 ounces per minute, since nothing can be determined about the amount of time the water was leaking from the tank; NOT sufficient.

    (2) Given that the tank became empty in less than 12 hours, it is not possible to determine if the tank leaked more than 30 gallons of water because the rate at which water leaked from the tank is unknown. For example, the tank could have originally contained 1 gallon of water that emptied in exactly 10 hours or the tank could have originally contained 31 gallons of water that emptied in exactly 10 hours; NOT sufficient.

Given (1) and (2) together, the tank emptied at a constant rate of

$$\left(6.4\frac{\text{oz}}{\text{min}}\right)\left(60\frac{\text{min}}{\text{hr}}\right)\left(\frac{1}{128}\frac{\text{gal}}{\text{oz}}\right) = \frac{(64)(6)}{128}\frac{\text{gal}}{\text{hr}} =$$

$$\frac{(64)(6)}{(64)(2)}\frac{\text{gal}}{\text{hr}} = 3\frac{\text{gal}}{\text{hr}}$$ for less than 12 hours.

If t is the total number of hours the water leaked from the tank, then the total amount of water emptied from the tank, in gallons, is $3t$, which is therefore less than $(3)(12) = 36$. From this it is not possible to determine if the tank originally contained more than 30 gallons of water. For example, if the tank leaked water for a total of 11 hours, then the tank originally contained $(3)(11)$ gallons of water, which is more than 30 gallons of water. However, if the tank leaked water for a total of 2 hours, then the tank originally contained $(3)(2)$ gallons of water, which is not more than 30 gallons of water.

**The correct answer is E;
both statements together are still not sufficient.**

118. If x is an integer, is y an integer?

    (1) The average (arithmetic mean) of x, y, and $y - 2$ is x.
    (2) The average (arithmetic mean) of x and y is <u>not</u> an integer.

    Arithmetic Statistics; Properties of numbers

    (1) From this, it is known that

    $$\frac{x + y + (y - 2)}{3} = x, \text{ or:}$$

    $$x + y + y - 2 = 3x \quad \text{multiply both sides by 3}$$

    $$2y - 2 = 2x \quad \text{combine like terms;}$$
    $$\text{subtract } x \text{ from both sides}$$

    $$y - 1 = x \quad \text{divide both sides by 2}$$

    This simplifies to $y = x + 1$. Since x is an integer, this equation shows that x and y are consecutive integers; SUFFICIENT.

    (2) According to this, y might be an integer (e.g., $x = 5$ and $y = 6$, with an average of 5.5), or y might not be an integer (e.g., $x = 5$ and $y = 6.2$, with an average of 5.6); NOT sufficient.

    **The correct answer is A;
    statement 1 alone is sufficient.**

119. If 2 different representatives are to be selected at random from a group of 10 employees and if p is the probability that both representatives selected will be women, is $p > \frac{1}{2}$?

    (1) More than $\frac{1}{2}$ of the 10 employees are women.

    (2) The probability that both representatives selected will be men is less than $\frac{1}{10}$.

    Arithmetic Probability

    Let m and w be the numbers of men and women in the group, respectively. Then $m + w = 10$ and the probability that both representatives selected will be a woman is $p =$

    $$\left(\frac{\text{\# of women}}{\text{\# of people}}\right)\left(\frac{\text{\# of women after 1 woman is removed}}{\text{\# of people after 1 woman is removed}}\right)$$

    $$= \left(\frac{w}{10}\right)\left(\frac{w - 1}{9}\right). \text{ Therefore, determining if } p > \frac{1}{2}$$

    is equivalent to determining if $\left(\frac{w}{10}\right)\left(\frac{w - 1}{9}\right) > \frac{1}{2}$.

    Multiplying both sides by $(10)(9)(2)$ gives the equivalent condition $2w(w - 1) > 90$, or $w(w - 1) > 45$. By considering the values of $(2)(1)$, $(3)(2), ..., (10)(9)$, it follows that $p > \frac{1}{2}$ if and only if w is equal to 8, 9, or 10.

    (1) Given that $w > 5$, it is possible that w is equal to 8, 9, or 10 (for example, $w = 8$) and it is possible that w is not equal to 8, 9, or 10 (for example, $w = 7$); NOT sufficient.

    (2) Given the probability that both selections will be men is less than $\frac{1}{10}$, it follows that $\left(\frac{m}{10}\right)\left(\frac{m - 1}{9}\right) < \frac{1}{10}$. Multiplying both sides by $(9)(10)$ gives $m(m - 1) < 9$. Thus, by numerical evaluation, the only possibilities for m are 0, 1, 2, and 3. Therefore, the only possibilities for w are 10, 9, 8, or 7. However, it is still possible that w is equal to 8, 9, or 10 (for example, $w = 8$) and it is still possible that w is not equal to 8, 9, or 10 (for example, $w = 7$); NOT sufficient.

Given (1) and (2), it is not possible to determine if w is equal to 8, 9, or 10. For example, if $w = 8$, then both (1) and (2) are true and w is equal to 8, 9, or 10. However, if $w = 7$, then both (1) and (2) are true and w is not equal to 8, 9, or 10.

The correct answer is E; both statements together are still not sufficient.

120. In the xy-plane, lines k and ℓ intersect at the point (1,1). Is the y-intercept of k greater than the y-intercept of ℓ ?

    (1) The slope of k is less than the slope of ℓ.
    (2) The slope of ℓ is positive.

Algebra Coordinate geometry

Let m_1 and m_2 represent the slopes of lines k and ℓ, respectively. Then, using the point-slope form for the equation of a line, an equation of line k can be determined: $y - 1 = m_1(x - 1)$, or $y = m_1x + (1 - m_1)$. Similarly, an equation for line ℓ is $y = m_2x + (1 - m_2)$. Determine if $(1 - m_1) > (1 - m_2)$, or equivalently if $m_1 < m_2$.

    (1) This indicates that $m_1 < m_2$; SUFFICIENT.
    (2) This indicates that $m_2 > 0$. If $m_1 = -1$, for example, then $m_1 < m_2$, but if $m_2 = 4$ and $m_1 = 5$, then $m_1 > m_2$; NOT sufficient.

The correct answer is A; statement 1 alone is sufficient.

121. Each of the 45 books on a shelf is written either in English or in Spanish, and each of the books is either a hardcover book or a paperback. If a book is to be selected at random from the books on the shelf, is the probability less than $\frac{1}{2}$ that the book selected will be a paperback written in Spanish?

    (1) Of the books on the shelf, 30 are paperbacks.
    (2) Of the books on the shelf, 15 are written in Spanish.

Arithmetic Probability

    (1) This indicates that 30 of the 45 books are paperbacks. Of the 30 paperbacks, 25 could be written in Spanish. In this case, the probability of randomly selecting a paperback book written in Spanish is $\frac{25}{45} > \frac{1}{2}$. On the other hand, it is possible that only 5 of the paperback books are written in Spanish. In this case, the probability of randomly selecting a paperback book written in Spanish is $\frac{5}{45} < \frac{1}{2}$; NOT sufficient.

    (2) This indicates that 15 of the books are written in Spanish. Then, at most 15 of the 45 books on the shelf are paperbacks written in Spanish, and the probability of randomly selecting a paperback book written in Spanish is at most $\frac{15}{45} < \frac{1}{2}$; SUFFICIENT.

The correct answer is B; statement 2 alone is sufficient.

122. If S is a set of four numbers w, x, y, and z, is the range of the numbers in S greater than 2 ?

    (1) $w - z > 2$
    (2) z is the least number in S.

Arithmetic Statistics

The range of the numbers w, x, y, and z is equal to the greatest of those numbers minus the least of those numbers.

    (1) This reveals that the difference between two of the numbers in the set is greater than 2, which means that the range of the four numbers must also be greater than 2; SUFFICIENT.

    (2) The information that z is the least number gives no information regarding the other numbers or their range; NOT sufficient.

The correct answer is A; statement 1 alone is sufficient.

123. Stations X and Y are connected by two separate, straight, parallel rail lines that are 250 miles long. Train P and train Q simultaneously left Station X and Station Y, respectively, and each train traveled to the other's point of departure. The two trains passed each other after traveling for 2 hours. When the two trains passed, which train was nearer to its destination?

    (1) At the time when the two trains passed, train P had averaged a speed of 70 miles per hour.

    (2) Train Q averaged a speed of 55 miles per hour for the entire trip.

    Arithmetic Applied problem; rates

    (1) This indicates that Train P had traveled $2(70) = 140$ miles when it passed Train Q. It follows that Train P was $250 - 140 = 110$ miles from its destination and Train Q was 140 miles from its destination, which means that Train P was nearer to its destination when the trains passed each other; SUFFICIENT.

    (2) This indicates that Train Q averaged a speed of 55 miles per hour for the entire trip, but no information is given about the speed of Train P. If Train Q traveled for 2 hours at an average speed of 55 miles per hour and Train P traveled for 2 hours at an average speed of 70 miles per hour, then Train P was nearer to its destination when the trains passed. However, if Train Q traveled for 2 hours at an average speed of 65 miles per hour and Train P traveled for 2 hours at an average speed of 60 miles per hour, then Train Q was nearer to its destination when the trains passed. Note that if Train Q traveled at $\dfrac{(120)(55)}{140} = 47\dfrac{1}{7}$ miles per hour for the remainder of the trip, then its average speed for the whole trip was 55 miles per hour; NOT sufficient.

    The correct answer is A; statement 1 alone is sufficient.

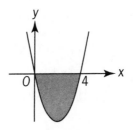

124. In the xy-plane shown, the shaded region consists of all points that lie above the graph of $y = x^2 - 4x$ and below the x-axis. Does the point (a,b) (not shown) lie in the shaded region if $b < 0$?

    (1) $0 < a < 4$

    (2) $a^2 - 4a < b$

    Algebra Coordinate geometry

    In order for (a,b) to lie in the shaded region, it must lie above the graph of $y = x^2 - 4x$ and below the x-axis. Since $b < 0$, the point (a,b) lies below the x-axis. In order for (a,b) to lie above the graph of $y = x^2 - 4x$, it must be true that $b > a^2 - 4a$.

    (1) This indicates that $0 < a < 4$. If $a = 2$, then $a^2 - 4a = 2^2 - 4(2) = -4$, so if $b = -1$, then $b > a^2 - 4a$ and (a,b) is in the shaded region. But if $b = -5$, then $b < a^2 - 4a$ and (a,b) is not in the shaded region; NOT sufficient.

    (2) This indicates that $b > a^2 - 4a$, and thus, (a,b) is in the shaded region; SUFFICIENT.

    The correct answer is B; statement 2 alone is sufficient.

Appendix A   Answer Sheets

Problem Solving Answer Sheet

1.	37.	73.	109.	145.
2.	38.	74.	110.	146.
3.	39.	75.	111.	147.
4.	40.	76.	112.	148.
5.	41.	77.	113.	149.
6.	42.	78.	114.	150.
7.	43.	79.	115.	151.
8.	44.	80.	116.	152.
9.	45.	81.	117.	153.
10.	46.	82.	118.	154.
11.	47.	83.	119.	155.
12.	48.	84.	120.	156.
13.	49.	85.	121.	157.
14.	50.	86.	122.	158.
15.	51.	87.	123.	159.
16.	52.	88.	124.	160.
17.	53.	89.	125.	161.
18.	54.	90.	126.	162.
19.	55.	91.	127.	163.
20.	56.	92.	128.	164.
21.	57.	93.	129.	165.
22.	58.	94.	130.	166.
23.	59.	95.	131.	167.
24.	60.	96.	132.	168.
25.	61.	97.	133.	169.
26.	62.	98.	134.	170.
27.	63.	99.	135.	171.
28.	64.	100.	136.	172.
29.	65.	101.	137.	173.
30.	66.	102.	138.	174.
31.	67.	103.	139.	175.
32.	68.	104.	140.	176.
33.	69.	105.	141.	
34.	70.	106.	142.	
35.	71.	107.	143.	
36.	72.	108.	144.	

Data Sufficiency Answer Sheet

1.	32.	63.	94.
2.	33.	64.	95.
3.	34.	65.	96.
4.	35.	66.	97.
5.	36.	67.	98.
6.	37.	68.	99.
7.	38.	69.	100.
8.	39.	70.	101.
9.	40.	71.	102.
10.	41.	72.	103.
11.	42.	73.	104.
12.	43.	74.	105.
13.	44.	75.	106.
14.	45.	76.	107.
15.	46.	77.	108.
16.	47.	78.	109.
17.	48.	79.	110.
18.	49.	80.	111.
19.	50.	81.	112.
20.	51.	82.	113.
21.	52.	83.	114.
22.	53.	84.	115.
23.	54.	85.	116.
24.	55.	86.	117.
25.	56.	87.	118.
26.	57.	88.	119.
27.	58.	89.	120.
28.	59.	90.	121.
29.	60.	91.	122.
30.	61.	92.	123.
31.	62.	93.	124.

PRACTICE MORE FOR THE GMAT® EXAM

More official questions, more answers, and more explanations from GMAC, the creators of the test.

Improve your level of preparation with **official** books, software, paper tests, and practice exams.

Available at
mba.com/store

MAKERS OF THE GMAT® EXAM

GRADUATE MANAGEMENT
ADMISSION COUNCIL